AUDIONARRATOLOGY

THEORY AND INTERPRETATION OF NARRATIVE
James Phelan, Katra Byram, and Faye Halpern, Series Editors

AUDIONARRATOLOGY

LESSONS FROM RADIO DRAMA

Edited by Lars Bernaerts
and Jarmila Mildorf

THE OHIO STATE UNIVERSITY PRESS
COLUMBUS

Copyright © 2021 by The Ohio State University.
All rights reserved.

Library of Congress Cataloging-in-Publication Data
Names: Bernaerts, Lars, 1980– editor. | Mildorf, Jarmila, editor.
Title: Audionarratology : lessons from radio drama / edited by Lars Bernaerts, Jarmila Mildorf.
Other titles: Theory and interpretation of narrative series.
Description: Columbus : The Ohio State University Press, [2021] | Series: Theory and interpretation of narrative | Includes bibliographical references and index. | Summary: "Explores how radio dramas such as *I Love a Mystery* and *The Hitchhiker's Guide to the Galaxy* construct narrative through sound, music, language, and voice"—Provided by publisher.
Identifiers: LCCN 2020058460 | ISBN 9780814214725 (cloth) | ISBN 081421472X (cloth) | ISBN 9780814281307 (ebook) | ISBN 0814281303 (ebook)
Subjects: LCSH: Radio plays—History and criticism. | Narration (Rhetoric)
Classification: LCC PN1991.65 .A93 2021 | DDC 809.2/22—dc23
LC record available at https://lccn.loc.gov/2020058460

Other identifiers: ISBN 9780814257968 (paper)

Cover design by Derek Thornton
Text design by Juliet Williams
Type set in Adobe Minion Pro

CONTENTS

INTRODUCTION When Sounds Make Stories: Lessons for Narrative Theory from the Study of Radio Drama
LARS BERNAERTS AND JARMILA MILDORF 1

PART I NARRATOLOGICAL CHALLENGES IN THEORY AND PRACTICE

CHAPTER 1 The Audio Dramatist's Critical Vocabulary in Great Britain
TIM CROOK 17

CHAPTER 2 "Stage" Directions in the Radio Script: A Transgeneric Narratological Approach
JANINE HAUTHAL 41

CHAPTER 3 Narrative Mediation and the Case of Audio Drama
LARS BERNAERTS 63

CHAPTER 4 Earwitnessing: Focalization in Radio Drama
SIEBE BLUIJS 82

CHAPTER 5 Simultaneity and the Soundscapes of Audio Fiction
CAROLINE A. KITA 101

PART II NARRATIVE GENRES AND NARRATIVE EXPERIMENTS IN AUDIO DRAMA

CHAPTER 6 "There ain't no sense to nothin'": Serial Storytelling, Radio Consciousness, and the Gothic of Audition
HARRY HEUSER 121

CHAPTER 7	Auricularization and Narrative-Epistemic Stance in Louis Nowra's *Echo Point*	
	JARMILA MILDORF	144
CHAPTER 8	"Arthur Lolled": Audiophony and Humor in *The Hitchhiker's Guide to the Galaxy*	
	OLIVIER COUDER	164
CHAPTER 9	Gargantuan Adaptations: Narrative and Non-Narrative Soundscapes in English and German Radio Plays and Radio Operas Based on François Rabelais and Johann Fischart	
	TILL KINZEL	182
CHAPTER 10	Music, Voice, and (De)Narrativization in Samuel Beckett's Radio Play *Cascando*	
	PIM VERHULST	196
CODA	Radio Drama between Mimetic and Diegetic Presentation	
	MARIE-LAURE RYAN	215
Appendix	List of Radio Plays	225
Contributors		227
Index		231

INTRODUCTION

When Sounds Make Stories

Lessons for Narrative Theory from the Study of Radio Drama

LARS BERNAERTS AND JARMILA MILDORF

THE CRYSTAL-CLEAR SOUND of water being poured into a glass. Someone whistling on his or her fingers. Then, a voice, asking a question: "Can you recover from a scare like that?" Someone answers: "They buttoned up my jacket and pulled it down over my shoulders, so I couldn't move my arms anymore" (Handke 1991: 197). The experimental radio play *Hörspiel* (1968) by the Austrian playwright Peter Handke showcases and at the same time undermines the way the audiophonic, dramatized narratives we call "radio play" or "audio drama"[1] can conjure up a setting, characters, actions, and events. The display already starts in the self-conscious title "Hörspiel" ("radio play") and is continued in the use of sound, voice, and dialogue in the opening lines. Still, the picture painted by these auditive signs is not coherent: Is the person whistling also the one who pours the water? Is the whistle associated with fear, as the subsequent question intimates? The male character testifies about a violent cross-examination, which forms the central narrative anchor point in the piece. Although the listener is eager to learn why this man is interrogated and tortured (with language being one of the weapons used), the radio play offers little explanation. It strings together seemingly random familiar sounds, frag-

---

1. The term "radio play" is closely linked to the medium of radio. However, since radio plays are nowadays also broadcast via the internet and in the form of podcasts, it is more accurate to talk about "audio drama." Throughout this book, the two terms will be used interchangeably.

ments of music, voices of interrogators, and the answers by the interrogated man. We hear the sound of a toy trumpet, breaking glass, someone biting an apple, and a variety of musical instruments without a direct connection to the cross-examination, which itself is already fragmented. Still, all these sounds have a narrative potential, as they suggest actions, events, objects, agents, and affects in a story world.

This radio play emphatically demonstrates the narrativity of audio drama. The metanarrative reflection starts with the title and its link to the central narrative situation: The "Hörspiel" (radio play) contains a "Verhör" (interrogation) and requires a "Hörer" (listener). Although there is no extradiegetic voice, the aural mediation of the narrative can be understood as ironic, since it deploys the typical armamentarium of a radio play without the narrative coherence one would expect. In the script, the irony surfaces in the frequent use of "*Hörspiel*" in the stage directions describing the sounds: "*audio-dramatic sound for water,*" "*audio-dramatic sound for distant wind*" (Handke 1970: 87), "*audio-dramatic children's crying*" ("*Hörspielkindergeschrei*"; 91), and so on. The English translation by Robert Goss (Handke 1991) spells out the nature of these sounds in the initial stage directions: "*All sorts of radio-drama sound effects used briefly and abruptly—they are never complete*" and "*sound effects are always used musically rather than realistically—to surprise, not to explain*" (197). Indeed, listening to the piece, one forms the impression that these sounds are artificial and stereotypical for the genre. We are alerted to the fact that the curiosity, suspense, and surprise that are part and parcel of narrativity (Sternberg 1992), the tensions in the narrative discourse and the instabilities in the character relations (Phelan 2007), and the gappy, fragmented "unnatural" narration (Richardson 2006) all emerge from audiophonic choices. As this example suggests, narrative theory is well placed to provide basic tools that allow us to investigate the form and functioning of dramatized audiophonic narratives. One could of course raise the question: Why not use drama-analytical tools instead since radio drama, as the name suggests, is a form of drama? It is true that radio drama, especially in its early days, adopted stage drama and followed many of its conventions (see the following). However, in the course of its development, radio drama has also borrowed conventions from film and literary narrative and has brought forth its own media-specific affordances. It can therefore be considered under the aspect of remediation (Bernaerts 2019). Narrative as a feature pervading all these media and genres thus constitutes a perfect conceptual framework within which to analyze radio drama. While this is certainly true, the present volume reminds the reader, first, that this has rarely been done (Huwiler 2005b and some other German studies are notable exceptions). Narrative theory has a long tradition of describing and analyzing verbal, visual, and audiovisual narratives, but audiophonic fiction has been mostly ignored. Second, the volume also argues that audio drama requires more media-specific or "media-conscious" (Ryan and Thon 2014) narratological concepts and reconsiderations of familiar ideas. In short, paying attention to narrative meaning-making in audiophonic fiction is what not just Handke's piece but also this volume and its contributions call for. In the remainder of the introduction, we sketch out the context of the project and introduce the main ideas and structure of the book. We will introduce the chapters as we discuss the main questions broached in this book rather than listing them in the order in which they appear.

Toward a Narrative Study of Audio Drama: Mixed-Method Approaches

In recent decades, a lot of groundwork has been done in transmedial narratology and sound studies. The works of Marie-Laure Ryan (2004) and Jan-Noël Thon (2016), to name only a few prominent scholars, have covered a lot of ground in the study of narrative across media, reflecting upon the diverse and similar ways in which media shape characters, plots, settings, and narrational strategies. In the flourishing area of sound studies (Sterne 2012), scholars and sound artists have developed a framework from which the narrative role of sound in a broad sense (including music, voice, white noise, and silence) clearly emerges. Sound affects our narrativization of experiences and is thus a distinct dimension of storytelling in all media, even the silent ones, where it is evoked, suggested, and imagined by readers or viewers. Our memories of significant moments in our lives are often linked to certain sounds or music, and everyday storytelling thrives on voice quality and prosody as well as words to achieve its effectiveness.

More recently, the study of narrative across media has joined forces with the study of sound, voice, silence, and music in the project of audionarratology. The collections of essays in *Audionarratology: Interfaces of Sound and Narrative* (Mildorf and Kinzel 2016a), *Narrating Sounds* (a forum in *Partial Answers*; Mildorf and Kinzel 2017), and *Aural Worldmaking* (a forum in *CounterText*; Mildorf 2019) dealt with diverse instances in which a sonic dimension supports (or cuts across) the narrative or in which narrative meaning-making is a fundamentally aural matter: audiobooks, audio guides, computer games, radio plays, poetry performance, and sound art. The current volume builds on this work and starts from a genre that deserves to be placed center stage in the development of audionarratology, but that has hardly received any attention within narratology more generally: audio drama (also known as *radio plays* or *radio drama*, covering dramatized audiophonic narratives in their various forms and channels of dissemination).

Literary studies have largely neglected audio drama or have given it a secondary position (see, however, Döhl 1988; Drakakis 1981; Frank 1981). As introductions to the history of the genre point out, radio play production in the early days relied heavily on the adaptation of theater plays to the new medium, and the radio play counted as a *literary* genre (Hand and Traynor 2011; Huwiler 2005a). Even though original radio plays began to be commissioned as early as 1924,[2] it was only in the late 1960s and '70s that the radio play came to be regarded as an artistic form in its own right, and radio play artists working in the wake of the New Radio Play (Neues Hörspiel), such as Handke in his *Hörspiel*, experimented with the specific audiophonic means the radio afforded them and thus also paved the way for a new aesthetic of the radio play (Huwiler 2005a: 100–2). In theater studies or radio studies, its position has been equally marginal. As Tim Crook, the head of Radio at Goldsmiths College and himself a radio practitioner, writes in the opening of his book *Radio Drama: Theory and Practice* (1999): "Radio drama has been one of the most unappreciated and understated literary forms of the twentieth century" (3). Note that he also still classifies radio drama as a subcategory of literature rather than giving it the independent status that, for example, film has long been granted. And yet, as Ian Rodger (1982) argues, radio drama—rather than being a "second-hand form of theater for the mass audience" (25)—in fact influenced fiction writing, film, and television in ways that deserve further investigation. Rodger already points to the kinds of transmedial crossovers that are nowadays discussed under the buzzword "media convergence" (see also Thon 2016); audio drama, however, is still often left out of the picture.

Media studies approaches foreground the technical-technological intricacies of audio drama and frequently overlook its specifically narrative dimension, or they use other theoretical frameworks such as semiotics (Schmedes 2002). Some authors take narrative dimensions into consideration but do not adopt a narratological approach per se. Frédéric Antoine (2012), for example, aims to create a typology of radiophonic narrativity, in which the radio play is

---

2. Richard Hughes's *A Comedy of Danger* is often credited with being the first original radio play, that is, one that was specifically written for the radio, but, as Huwiler (2005a: 91) points out, the Dutch radio play *Nieuwjaars-wensch van de Amateurs Thomasvaer en Pieternel* by Willem Vogt was broadcast even a few days before Hughes's radio play (see Bulte 1984: 55). The earliest radiophonic fiction in France is said to have been broadcast even earlier, in 1922 (Antoine 2012: 14).

only one narrative form among many others (reportage, bulletin, commercial, etc.) characterized by its fictionality. Anne Dunn (2005), building on Crisell (1994), highlights the genre's specificity by looking into its "flexibility in the handling of time and space" (195) and the creation of perspective. In many respects, the exceptions to the rule once again show that the narratology of the radio play has not received due attention. John V. Pavlik's recent book *Masterful Stories: Lessons from Golden Age Radio* (2017) is another case in point. In order to be a masterful story, Pavlik argues, "a narrative must engage the audience to a high degree, either intellectually or emotionally (or both)" and "the narrative must also engage the audience by transcending the human condition, by connecting the specifics of an individual story across time, place, or culture" (19). More specifically, Pavlik analyzes the following elements to assess what contributes to masterful storytelling in his selected plays: writing, acting, research, dramatic structure, perspective, adaptation, acoustical environments, music, narration, social meaning, surprise, venue and vividness, and authenticity. Although many of these elements are also key to narratological inquiry, Pavlik's discussion of the actual radio plays remains disappointingly flat in this regard. And yet, it is precisely on the level of radio drama's narrative design that indeed lessons can be learned. Thus, the subtitle to our volume, which incidentally echoes the subtitle of Pavlik's book, is doubly programmatic: The contributions attest to the richness of narrative creativity to be found in radio drama while at the same time reflecting on what can be gleaned for the study of narrative more generally.

After all, many radio plays squarely fall into what some narratologists call "mimetic-narrative" genres (Schmid 2014). Like theater plays, audio drama usually emphasizes showing over telling. Like movies, audio drama employs the affective qualities of sounds, voices, and music to create drama. Unlike those two artistic media, audio drama relies solely on the auditory channel for its effects, offering special "audio positions" (Verma 2012) to audiences and using specific audiophonic means to achieve narrativity. How exactly sound and narrative support and dovetail one another in audio drama is the key question to be answered by the contributions to this volume. They revisit key narrative concepts (e.g., focalization, mediation, voice) and encourage reconsiderations of ideas circulating in recent narrative approaches (cognitive, transmedial, transgeneric, and rhetorical) from the viewpoint of audio drama. Moreover, the book argues that the aural makeup of audiophonic narratives stimulates and even necessitates reconsiderations in narrative theory. Given the predominantly auditory nature of this art form (for a critical assessment of this claim, see Hauthal in this volume), the question of how audio drama organizes narrative features and structural elements becomes particularly relevant in the context of media-conscious and transmedial postclassical narratologies. What media-specific (i.e., audiophonic) affordances does audio drama offer to create story-world existents such as characters, spaces, and time(s), as well as discourse-level features such as emplotment, discourse time, and viewpoint? The volume explores how sound, music, language, and voice work together or contradict each other to convey narrative information such as spatial configurations, temporal shifts, narratorial unreliability, humor in characterization, and so on.

Narrative voices, focalization, and narrative embedding are only a few cases in point that show how desirable and necessary a more media-sensitive audio drama narratology has become. For example, Genette's (1972: 219–74) category of voice (*voix*) has little to do with actual voice qualities but instead determines the narrator's positioning and his or her relationship to the narrated world (see also Blödorn, Langer, and Scheffel 2006; Mildorf 2017). In audio drama, by contrast, actualized voices add layers of meaning to the presented story because their timbre, volume, intonation patterns, and overall modulation also convey narrative-relevant information (Pinto 2012). Genette's (1972) term "focalization," which refers to the perspective that orients a narrative (194–200), seems to be ill suited to the auditory medium of radio because of its underlying visual metaphor (see Bluijs's discussion in this volume). In the context of film, Jost (1987) suggested the usage of the term "auricularization" instead. Just as in film, the question arises of who or what assumes the task of perspectivization in a radio play narrative. One could argue, as does Lutostański (2016), that the microphone becomes the focal point through which the presented action is positioned for the listener. Thus, sounds' and voices' closeness to or distance from the microphone and the technique of stereophony may give us a sense of spatial depth, of characters' presence or absence in a given scene. However, with new recording technologies, such effects are becoming increasingly complex and may lead to ever more refined possibilities for achieving auricularization. Indeed, this may also have ramifications for the receiving end. As Dann (2014) argues, the manifold ways in which audio drama can nowadays be streamed (e.g., online and downloadable) and consumed by listeners may even blur the boundaries between the real and the fictive.

Through the Lens of Postclassical Narratologies

The latter point suggests that audio drama may indeed be of interest to narratologists with diverse theoretical backgrounds. Not only transmedial narratology may gain new insights from a stronger focus on the aural art form, but so may, for example, fictionality studies. After all, radio drama has brought forth mixed genres such as dramatized *reportages,* which report fictive events, and the radio *feature,* which can be considered a "mixtum compositum" (Fischer 1964: 85) because it embellishes dramatized radio narratives with documentary material and gives that material a poetic quality. The radio feature originated in Anglo-American broadcasting traditions, and it is there that the feature's boundaries to radio plays have also often been blurred. One could argue, as Rodger (1982, 38) does, that because radio had to reach a large and heterogenous audience, greater narrative intervention became necessary to contextualize stories better and to thus make them more accessible. Moreover, the narrative form has supported the instructional character of much of radio broadcasting from its inception to this day.

Feminist narratology may find the gendering of voices or gendered perspectives in audio drama a fruitful new terrain, and because of its reliance on dialogue (Bernaerts 2017), audio drama also holds many areas of interest for rhetorical approaches to narrative. Moreover, the metaphors of the "inner stage" ("innere Bühne") (Wickert 1954) or the "theater of the mind" (Verma 2012) that are used time and again in radio play studies allude to the imaginative work that listeners must accomplish when tuning in to audio drama broadcasts. Listeners' imagination may also turn the reception of a radio play into a multisensory experience that both is and is not like reading fiction (see Mildorf and Kinzel 2016b). As in reading fiction or listening to audiobooks (Kuzmičova 2016), listening to audio drama also activates mental imagery; however, the latter is arguably different because it actualizes one presented sense perception: audioception. What happens on the way from the ear to the mind? In that sense, audio drama may also prove relevant for cognitive narratology.

This book also explores how some of these postclassical narratologies may fruitfully contribute to a specific audio drama narratology. The volume opens with a contribution that takes a "practical" approach to narrative in that it looks at how radio drama practitioners throughout the history of the art form have conceptualized radio plays and their own work. Tim Crook offers useful insights into the production side and audio drama producers' self-reflexive stances. The contributions by Harry Heuser, Jarmila Mildorf, Olivier Couder, and Till Kinzel all raise questions regarding audiodramatic subgenres and their respective conventions, as well as listeners' expectations. Heuser's discussion of the radio serial *I Love a Mystery* explores the conventions of gothic and detective genres. Mildorf's question whether Australian author Louis Nowra's radio play *Echo Point* is a ghost story or a story about mental delusions also touches on the conventions and aesthetic effects of these and related genres such as the gothic. Couder analyzes the science fiction comedy *The Hitchhiker's Guide to the Galaxy* and looks at how it creates humor. In Kinzel's examples of how the work of Rabelais is audiophonically transposed, the genre of the radio opera is exploited to convey the linguistic and narrative experimentation that is characteristic of *Gargantua and Pantagruel*.

Janine Hauthal asks questions about genre by taking a transgeneric approach. She compares audio drama and theatrical drama and argues that in both cases, the scripted versions of plays must not be ignored because scripts may offer us other kinds of information than their performed versions and may therefore lead to different interpretations. Her case studies, Ursula Krechel's *Wenn man ein gleichschenkliges Dreieck auf den Kopf stellt* (*When One Turns an Isosceles Triangle Upside Down*; 2012), Samuel Beckett's *Cascando* (1963), and Harold Pinter's *A Slight Ache* (1959), nicely illustrate the tensions that can arise between radio play scripts and performances.

Pim Verhulst's contribution on Beckett's *Cascando* focuses more strongly on the text's genesis and compares its English and French versions regarding their uses of language and music. It thus assumes a text-genetic approach to narrative, that is, an approach that takes a work's origins and editorial history into account (Bernaerts and Van Hulle 2013). The contribution also shows the role that an author's intervention in a radio production of his or her works may play. After all, a radio play is no longer merely the product of one author's imagination, but an interpretation arrived at by an entire production team. In this regard, questions of mediation become important, and this point is addressed more fully by Lars Bernaerts, who reflects on how a story is mediated in audio drama in comparison to, say, fiction. A similar approach is taken by Siebe Bluijs, who explores the concept of focalization in various Dutch radio plays. As his examples show, audio drama can afford complex instances of (mixed) focalization that surpass mere aurality, which is why he opts for maintaining Genette's traditional narratological term. Both Bernaerts's and Bluijs's contributions can be situated in the framework of transmedial narratology. Bernaerts's discussion furthermore takes a cognitive-narratological approach as it posits mediation not only as a conglomeration of audiophonic-"textual" means or strategies but as effects created in, or indeed co-created with, the listener. The cognitive approach is also shared by Couder and, implicitly, by many other of the contributions as the question of what effects certain audiophonic elements may have on listening audiences is of vital importance. The question of effects can also be raised from a more "text"-centered or rhetorical position that searches for "intended" meanings, which can be found in Mildorf's contribution as she resorts to some of the key questions raised by narratologists in connection with literary texts, namely about unreliability and ambiguity. Finally, all contributions are more or less informed by audionarratology, which explores the interfaces between sounds, voices, noises, music, and narrative in auditory art forms and which seeks to foreground the significance of these sonic elements as *narrative* means in such art forms.

As our overview shows, a range of narratological approaches is applied and advanced in the chapters of this volume. Cognitive, rhetorical, text-genetic, transmedial, and transgeneric perspectives allow the contributors to broach core issues in the study of audio drama. Also, as mentioned above, they revisit key narratological concepts in the context of audio drama. Verhulst puts the complex issue of musical narrativity into an interesting perspective. He argues that *Cascando* destabilizes the conventional relationship between language and music, "countering it with one of denarrativization." Several chapters look into how characters, settings, and events emerge from aural signs. Couder's chapter, for example, discusses how voice quality, intonation, and sound effects contribute to the characterization of the depressed android Marvin and the concomitant humor. Kinzel demonstrates how narrativity is challenged through sound in the adaptation of Rabelais's poetics of enumeration. Caroline Kita examines how the soundscapes of audio drama—which she reads as *audiotopias*—can conjure up several places and temporal frames at once. In the cases she analyzes, Heinrich Böll's *Tapping Signals* and Jan Rys's *Border Crossers,* the boundaries between past and present, here and there, are blurred by audiophonic techniques such as acoustic motifs and audiopositioning. Moving on to the level of discourse and narration, several chapters offer insight into the affordances and constraints of the radio play. The chapters by Bernaerts and Bluijs offer detailed discussions of narrative mediation and focalization, respectively. Couder specifies how radio plays can create humor through voice, music, and sound, and Mildorf analyzes how the semiotic modes of audio drama create the kind of narrative ambiguity that is related to unreliability. In order to test the broad applicability of narrative theory and to establish the richness of the field of audio drama, the case studies and examples in this volume are deliberately diverse. They include classics from the radio play repertoire such as *The War of the Worlds, The Hitchhiker's Guide to the Galaxy,* and Beckett's *Cascando* as well as experimental and lesser-known examples, such as Nowra's *Echo Point,* from the entire history of the radio play and from a variety of countries. Some of the pieces discussed in this volume, such as *Max Havelaar* or the cases discussed by Kinzel, are based on prose fiction, whereas others, such as Pinter's *A Slight Ache,* show more affinity with stage drama.

The volume consists of two sections: Two larger analytical sections, parts I and II, which are preceded by this introduction. Crook then offers an overview of radio drama practitioners' reflections throughout the history of this art form. In that opening chapter, Crook documents the history of thinking about writing for audio drama. He compares various aesthetic views of the radio play: For some, the radio play offers a creative opportunity or is understood as "theater of the mind"; others merely see it as an equivalent of stage drama. By homing in on the practitioners, Crook also offers an inside view of the performance history of audio drama. Together with the introduction, Crook's chapter provides some vital context to the narratological expeditions in the other chapters. Adopting the vantage point of radio studies and practitioners, it sheds light on the practical narratology of making radiophonic pieces. The advice for scriptwriters, from the early days until the present, is clearly divided along aesthetic lines (e.g., conventional vs. experimental) and is shown to have undergone a development. In the form of handbooks, this kind of advice has actually affected how radiophonic narratives are built and how aural means are deployed to convey narrative structures. This is something the chapter meticulously shows, thereby offering a historical perspective on narratological practices. At the same time, Crook introduces a contemporary approach to this history by framing it in current concerns about the domination of a white, male, and Western view.

Part I of the book is devoted to core concepts in narrative theory and postclassical narrative approaches, which are applied to the radio play and revisited through the lens of the radio play. These chapters demonstrate how analyses of the radio play can reinvigorate or broaden discussions in narrative theory. Part II further pursues these goals in a series of case studies that also address narratological as well as genre-theoretical questions. The concluding remarks by Marie-Laure Ryan revisit the core issue of mimetic versus diegetic presentation in radio drama that is addressed in several chapters. Together, the two parts offer a context for understanding the narratological importance of the genre as well as case studies and detailed reflections upon narrative concepts in the study of audio drama. Just as Handke's piece, with which we started our introduction, offers an emphatic and estranging showcase of the radio play's semiotic resources, this volume itself foregrounds the medium-specificity of the radio play. The chapters in this book demonstrate the powerful means of storytelling characteristic of the medium, which *Hörspiel* puts into practice by challenging the foundations of narrativity. Similarly, we hope that this volume may entice narrative scholars to *listen* more closely and to acknowledge the narrative complexity of audio drama.

As we suggested throughout the introduction, the narrative study of radio drama developed in this volume is not just integral to the project of audionarratology but can also improve our general narratological sensibility and precision in three respects. First, a thorough engagement with radio drama improves our knowledge of auditory meaning-making and the narrativity of aural semiotic systems, as our initial example of Handke already suggested. Second, it alerts us to the vital role of sound (including but not limited to music) across narrative media. If the radio play exploits this potential to the fullest, the study of radio plays can yield insights that apply to sound in cinema, theater, and video games as well. For example, the omnidirectionality of sound prompts us to differentiate more clearly between field of vision and auditory field in the analysis of focalization. Third, the study of radio plays makes us more aware of the aural dimension that inheres in textual and visual narratives as well. In novels, voice quality also contributes to characterization, and soundscapes are a meaningful part of settings and focalization. Music and sound effects are visually evoked in graphic narratives to create tension or emotional climax and so on. To advance our narratological sensibility in all these respects, the following chapters offer us some valuable lessons from radio drama.

Works Cited

Antoine, Frédéric. 2012. "Éléments pour une typologisation de la narration radiophonique." *Recherches en communication* 37: 11–22.

Bernaerts, Lars. 2017. "Dialogue in Audiophonic Fiction: The Case of Audio Drama." In *Dialogue across Media*, edited by Jarmila Mildorf and Bronwen Thomas, 205–23. Amsterdam: John Benjamins.

———. 2019. "The Multimodal Evocation of Minds in Audio Drama." *CounterText* 5, no. 3: 312–31.

Bernaerts, Lars, and Dirk Van Hulle. 2013. "Narrative across Versions: Narratology Meets Genetic Criticism." *Poetics Today* 34, no. 3: 281–326.

Blödorn, Andreas, Daniela Langer, and Michael Scheffel, eds. 2006. *Stimme(n) im Text: Narratologische Positionsbestimmungen*. Berlin: De Gruyter.

Bulte, Ineke. 1984. *Het Nederlandse hoorspel. Aspecten van de bepaling van een tekstsoort*. Utrecht: H&S.

Crisell, Andrew. 1994. *Understanding Radio*. 2nd ed. London: Routledge.

Crook, Timothy. 1999. *Radio Drama: Theory and Practice*. London: Routledge.

Dann, Lance. 2014. "Only Half the Story: Radio Drama, Online Audio and Transmedia Storytelling." *Radio Journal: International Studies in Broadcast & Audio Media* 12, no. 1–2: 141–54.

———. 1988. *Das Neue Hörspiel: Geschichte und Typologie des Hörspiels*. Darmstadt: Wissenschaftliche Buchgesellschaft.

Drakakis, John, ed. 1981. *British Radio Drama*. Cambridge: Cambridge University Press.

Dunn, Anne. 2005. "Structures of Radio Drama." In *Narrative and Media*, edited by Helen Fulton, Rosemary Huisman, Julian Murphet, and Anne Dunn, 191–202. Cambridge: Cambridge University Press.

Fischer, Eugen Kurt. 1964. *Das Hörspiel: Form und Funktion*. Stuttgart: Alfred Kröner Verlag.

Frank, Armin Paul. 1981. *Das englische und amerikanische Hörspiel*. München: Fink.

Genette, Gérard. 1972. *Discours du récit*. Paris: Seuil.

Hand, Richard J., and Mary Traynor. 2011. *Radio Drama Handbook*. London: Continuum.

Handke, Peter. 1970. "Hörspiel." In *Wind und Meer. Vier Hörspiele*, 85–128. Frankfurt am Main: Suhrkamp Verlag.

———. 1991. "Radio Play" (No. 1). Translated by Robert Goss. In *German Radio Plays*, edited by Everett Frost and Margaret Herzfeld-Sander, 195–218. New York: Continuum.

Huwiler, Elke. 2005a. "80 Jahre Hörspiel. Die Entwicklung des Genres zu einer eigenständigen Kunstform." *Neophilologus* 89: 89–114.

———. 2005b. *Erzähl-Ströme im Hörspiel: Zur Narratologie der elektroakustischen Kunst*. Paderborn: Mentis.

Jost, François. 1987. *L'Œil-caméra. Entre film et roman*. Lyon: Presses Universitaires de Lyon.

Kuzmičová, Anežka. 2016. "Audiobooks and Print Narrative: Similarities in Text Experience." In *Audionarratology: Interfaces of Sound and Narrative*, edited by Jarmila Mildorf and Till Kinzel, 217–37. Berlin: De Gruyter.

Lutostański, Bartosz. 2016. "A Narratology of Radio Drama: Voice, Perspective, Space." In *Audionarratology: Interfaces of Sound and Narrative*, edited by Jarmila Mildorf and Till Kinzel, 117–32. Berlin: De Gruyter.

Mildorf, Jarmila. 2017. "Sounding Postmodernity: Radio Adaptation of Alasdair Gray's *Lanark*." *Partial Answers* 15, no. 1: 167–88.

———, ed. 2019. *Aural Worldmaking*. Forum in *CounterText* 5, no. 3.

Mildorf, Jarmila, and Till Kinzel, eds. 2016a. *Audionarratology: Interfaces of Sound and Narrative*. Berlin: De Gruyter.

———. 2016b. "Multisensory Imaginings: An Audionarratological Analysis of Philip Roth's Novel *Indignation* and Its German Radio Play Adaptation *Empörung*." *CounterText* 2, no. 3: 307–21.

———, eds. 2017. *Narrating Sounds*. Forum in *Partial Answers* 15, no. 1.

Pavlik, John V. 2017. *Masterful Stories: Lessons from Golden Age Radio*. New York: Routledge.

Phelan, James. 2007. *Experiencing Fiction: Judgments, Progressions, and the Rhetorical Theory of Narrative*. Columbus: The Ohio State University Press.

Pinto, Vito. 2012. *Stimmen auf der Spur: Zur technischen Realisierung der Stimme in Theater, Hörspiel und Film*. Bielefeld: Transcript.

Richardson, Brian. 2006. *Unnatural Voices: Extreme Narration in Modern and Contemporary Fiction*. Columbus: The Ohio State University Press.

Rodger, Ian. 1982. *Radio Drama*. London: Macmillan.

Ryan, Marie-Laure, ed. 2004. *Narrative across Media: The Languages of Storytelling*. Lincoln: University of Nebraska Press.

Ryan, Marie-Laure, and Jan-Noël Thon. 2014. "Storyworlds across Media: Introduction." In *Storyworlds across Media: Toward a Media-Conscious Narratology*, edited by Marie-Laure Ryan and Jan-Noël Thon, 1–21. Lincoln: University of Nebraska Press.

Schmedes, Götz. 2002. *Medientext Hörspiel: Ansätze einer Hörspielsemiotik am Beispiel der Radioarbeiten von Alfred Behrens*. Münster: Waxmann Verlag.

Schmid, Wolf. 2014. *Elemente der Narratologie*. 3rd ed. Berlin: De Gruyter.

Sternberg, Meir. 1992. "Telling in Time (II): Chronology, Teleology, Narrativity." *Poetics Today* 13, no. 3: 463–541.

Sterne, Jonathan, ed. 2012. *The Sound Studies Reader*. New York: Routledge.

Thon, Jan-Noël. 2016. *Transmedial Narratology and Contemporary Media Culture*. Lincoln: University of Nebraska Press.

Verma, Neil. 2012. *Theater of the Mind: Imagination, Aesthetics, and American Radio Drama*. Chicago: Chicago University Press.

Wickert, Erwin. 1954. "Die innere Bühne." *Akzente* 1: 505–14.

PART I

NARRATOLOGICAL CHALLENGES IN THEORY AND PRACTICE

1

The Audio Dramatist's Critical Vocabulary in Great Britain

TIM CROOK

THIS CHAPTER INVESTIGATES how British audio dramatists and producers developed the notion and theory of practical sonic production narratology. They relied on and interrogated the traditions of theatrical and novelistic storytelling. Authors and auteurs such as Gordon Lea, Lance Sieveking, Tyrone Guthrie, Val Gielgud, Felix Felton, Donald McWhinnie, and William Ash offered little evidence that they fully engaged the theory of Mikhail Bakhtin, Julia Kristeva, Roland Barthes, Vladimir Propp, Gérard Genette, Tzvetan Todorov, Mieke Bal, Claude Bremond, and Franz Karl Stanzel. These auteurs had confident ideas of what would constitute variously described successful sound, microphone, and broadcast and audio plays and dramas. The analysis explores how these authors developed their opinions on techniques and concepts that have given sound drama its unique literary as well as dramatic identity.

Future Directions of Narratological Reflection

It is axiomatic that in the beginning, before academics began to discourse on narratology, practitioners of sound drama discussed and produced their own theory about this genre of storytelling. An analysis of the British tradition alone offers its own narrative of how they understood and valued any unique aspects of their practice. The stability of BBC Radio funding through sound broadcasting monopoly and from 1927 public corporation license fee taxation meant that audio drama had excellent conditions in which to develop content and build audiences during the twentieth century. In the result, it would appear radio drama was first published as dramatic literature in Britain in 1925. This is the case with Reginald Berkeley's full-length play *The White Chateau*, written and produced for Armistice night of that year and politically interrogating the Great War of 1914–1918 and advocating for peace. The script indicates a modernist use of music, and the characterization of the White Chateau building as a central metaphor for the play could arguably be intrinsically radiophonic. It is also the case that Berkeley's play was written and produced for radio first, with its stage and television drama versions following afterward and informing later, longer radio productions of the play. This is hardly the dynamic of what Val Gielgud dismissed as the Cinderella medium. This cultural case history emphasizes that sound drama developed and thrived before sound film and television drama.

Gordon Lea's *Radio Drama and How to Write It* of 1926 immediately sought to define sound drama's unique properties as a narratological medium. He began the journey of past practice and critical analysis that has engendered passionate and important debates about form, style, and the very nature of sound drama as an art form as well as a social and cultural phenomenon. Guthrie, Gielgud, Sieveking, Felton, McWinnie, and Ash continued to recognize and take positions on some of the enduring oscillations in understanding audio dramaturgy and the listening experience. The narrator and self-contained methods were adopted, mixed, and attenuated in order to serve the purpose of successful listening. Similarly, Gielgud and Sieveking's argument over whether technology must be operated or played has often been resolved by the pressure and demand to connect with and be appreciated by the greatest number of listeners. Assertions about sound drama constituting a theater of the mind or imagined cinemascope have been balanced with poetic and intellectual explanations of a more complex embodiment of perception where feeling, emotion, and conscious participation extends well beyond the limited notion of mere imagination.

Words, music, silence, sound effects, soundscapes, voices, and spatiality orchestrated to play upon the consciousness of the individual listener have certainly been identified as the essential tools and devices that constitute the elements of the greater whole in audio storytelling. This history is also marked by an enduring tension between experimentalists of the sound medium seeking to discover and explore a sonic intrinsic narratology that is powerfully creative and poetic, and production entertainers wishing to deploy storytelling strategies for the sound medium that give satisfaction for the greatest number of listeners.

The BBC in Britain was able to host a media institutional accommodation of the experimentalists and entertainers after the Second World War with the national networks branded as the Home Service (later BBC Radio 4) and the Light Programme (later Radio 2), which served the exigencies of entertaining growing popular audiences, and the Third Programme (later BBC Radio 3), which satisfied the need to culturally and artistically impress, and indeed, accentuate a separate literary tradition of radio drama.

The academic interventions in this volume have the potential to expand the creative and aesthetic boundaries of criticizing and understanding audio dramaturgy and narratology, and there is no doubt that the practitioner's critical vocabulary faces some transformative changes and inspiration in the years to come. The following chapters certainly serve to demonstrate whether the British practitioner's praxis was theoretically and philosophically limited and more intuitive than consciously deliberated. Did the how-to writers have the ability to communicate an equivalent skill set of enabling the cognitive, rhetorical, text-genetic, transmedial, and transgeneric dimensions of radio drama? There is no shortage of evidence that Lea, Guthrie, Gielgud, Sieveking, Felton, McWhinnie, and Ash believed that the writer and producer could intend meaning by exploiting the unique tools sound drama provided. But on the axis of the diegetic and nondiegetic interplay of narrative streams of performance, how could they be sure of the construction of meaning and the experience of dramatic and cultural irony?

It might be argued that the sound dramatic medium in performing for hearing consciousness certainly made it easier for writers and producers to transcend time, place, space, and focalization. An individual identity could be dramatized with multiple perspectives, personalities, and positions, sometimes with no specifically signposted and rooted human voice at all. The listener could be given a greater intensity of imaginative participation. The changing technological context magnified, expanded, and extended the range and depth of that participation. Early radio drama was of the moment, incapable of being recorded and played back. Later radio drama became stereophonic and then surround sound. The *microphone play* was first mainly listened to through headphones, then via valve-powered speakers. The marketization of audio books via cassette, CD, computer, smartphone, and online sound meant the sound play could be paused, rewound, and reheard over and over again and with much more sophisticated experiences of sonic immersion conjured for the listener's imagination.

The purpose in starting with an analysis and elucidation of the practitioner's theory in one country where sound drama has been culturally significant, strong, and enduring—indeed is now said to be experiencing a revolution in fictional podcasting production and listening—is that it is a starting point for the academician. It provides a foundation to criticize, analyze, and discourse narratological strengths, lacks, and perhaps some aesthetic and intellectual epiphanies that can provide feedback to the storytellers themselves and their listeners who constitute such a powerful participation in the determination of meaning.

Founding British Radio Drama Narratology

The British how-to writers of sound drama explored key subjects specific to the sound medium such as the point of listening, telling, and showing; characterization; deployment of linking and performative voices; interior and exterior perspectives; spatiality; and sound symbolism and metaphor. These practitioners revealed their awareness of the creative process and their understanding of the techniques that they decided achieved more effective connection with their listening audience.

Some caution is needed in any discourse that relies on texts that operate as monuments or ornaments of oracle by men and for men in what was a patriarchal, imperialist society with entrenched racist and sexist attitudes. When radio drama began to be broadcast by the BBC, there was not an equal franchise for women in general elections, women were subject to humiliating and exclusionary discrimination in many aspects of their participation in society, and the prevailing media consensus represented the view that the United Kingdom was entitled to subjugate nonwhite peoples as a form of civilizing enlightenment. Anything considered worthy in alternative cultures was "Orientalized," to apply the key word in the theory of the late professor Edward Said. In our twenty-first-century analysis, the integrity of our academic analysis must pay heed to consideration of historicism and the historiographical context. Much is to be gained by identifying audio drama production that may have been hidden in plain sight, and rendered invisible by canonization and those who wielded the power and control of publication and broadcasting.

The first book on British radio drama and how to write it was authored by a BBC producer called Gordon Lea in 1926. Lea began with the prophesy: "We shall find, I think, a new sphere of art, achievement in which will react upon literature to its permanent enrichment" (Lea 1926: 23). He talked about a new literary form "which is full of possibilities," observing that "here is the new clay for moulding" (91), and he invited the potters to come forward to take radio drama from its cradle and pioneer and experiment. Lea's text is significant because it was endorsed with a foreword by the first director of drama productions, R. E. Jeffrey, and the BBC's first managing director and later director-general, John Reith, instructed that a copy would be sent to all the BBC stations and centers of production throughout the country. This means the book was a potential and likely reference point and guide for anyone producing and directing radio drama from the time of its publication.

Lea immediately grasped the importance of the role of the listener by means of headphones or loudspeakers: "Objectively, they see nothing, but subjectively they can see everything. This is what the radio dramatist has to bear in mind" (38). Lea regarded the significance and participation of the listener as so crucial he devoted an entire chapter to it, titled "The Listener's Part." There is certainly a case for arguing that Lea may well have been one of the first radio drama philosophers or poets. This is because his pedagogy and criticism were philosophical and poetic in style. His language throughout emphasized the intrinsic over the instrumental: "All art is an expression of imagination—the radio-scene is beyond art. It is reality itself, not an isolated expression of imagination, but imagination itself" (40). He realized that radio drama offered the dramatist "a more spacious structure, whose architecture is more artistic and nearer truth" (33).

Gordon Lea exhorted the idea that radio drama liberates the imagination by scattering the problem of perspective and opening up a new world to the dreamer of dreams: "Anything that is conceivable in the imagination of the dramatist is capable of complete expression and interpretation to the imagination of the playwright's world. If they wish to set their play in the heart of the buttercup, the imagination of the hearer will provide the setting" (41).

He recognized the special intimacy of radio work: "The listener is in direct touch with the player—there is no intervening convention—no barrier. Soul speaks to soul" (69). Lea's text is a celebration of sound drama as an intense political, social, and cultural conjunction of human voice and word, the dialogic fusion of the spoken and written word, of everyday chatter and enduring literature. His understanding of the poetic aesthetic was beautifully expressed when he talked about the voices of the player in radio drama coming out of silence: "They were . . . like jewels against the background of black velvet" (72).

Lea thereby opened the debate about how best to write radio drama through finding a dramatic regulation of performed consciousness. For the auteur, or producing collaboration of playwright, producer/director, and performer, he connected the necessary bridges between orchestration of sound through the audio-dramatic score and its representation of reality and human consciousness through performance and production. When he wrote about the importance and value of music, it was in poetic rather than utilitarian terms: "From out this darkness grew green music, coloring the mind and pointing the emotions to their destined end" (21). He granted a cultural and artistic importance for the writer in radio drama: "The one real essential is something behind the text—the idea or dramatic purpose of the author" (32), and connected this with the importance of appealing to the individual listener: "The radio drama does not make its appeal to a crowd but to an individual . . . for what will appeal to a crowd will almost certainly appeal to the individual, but it is by no means certain that what will appeal to the individual will appeal to the crowd" (37). He recognized the significance of voice as the agency of characterization where an actor's shape and physical characteristics are irrelevant: "What is written in the text will be given pure and untrammeled to the mind of the listener" (39). He realized that through what became a convention of interior voice and listener's point of hearing, radio drama was the ideal medium for the aside and soliloquy: "In stage-work the 'Aside' and the 'Soliloquy' were incapable of sincere use. In radio-work they can be used with every appearance of sincerity and truth" (39).

Lea (1926) emphasized that in radio drama, the unstageable does not need a scene break or transition: "Illusion once created need never be broken in the radio-play. The dramatist can be as extensive as he likes, since the whole world or any part of it can be his setting" (42). The suspension of disbelief and art of illusion in sound drama is, therefore, much more fluid and not so much confined by the physical boundaries of the physical stage set or filmic location. The dramatist has direct access to the listener on the emotions of the play and the radio listening audience is, therefore, immune when "the house is made to 'rock with mirth.' In the quietude of your own room, you can react truly and naturally and so be sincere. All this makes for truth and reality" (42). He directed new practitioners of the craft to the need to adopt a professional attitude rooted in the sound medium. The radio dramatist need not write to communicate a crowd psychology: "In conversation with a friend you can use a direct method, an intimate method, which would not be suitable for an orator's platform. The radio-play gains just this intimacy which a stage-play can never hope to have" (43).

Even as early as 1926, with the technological limits of sound production at that time being on the cusp between mechanical and electrical recording, he advised against an over-immersive indulgence of sound for sound's sake. While "the horizon of the dramatist's dreams is widened beyond all knowledge, some restraint needs to be exercised in respect of sound-effects . . . these should be used sparingly. An ounce of suggestion is worth a ton of irritation" (43).

Lea set the course of debate on the ideal dramatic structure of storytelling in audio drama, and it has not changed much since 1926. He recognized and discussed the merits of the narrator method and the self-contained method. This is the binary of telling and showing. He accepted that using a narrative voice offers the chance to characterize an interesting angle and develop sympathy and tension in the way of Shakespearean drama. The narrator can create *mind pictures* and bridge dramatic action. Narrative voice is a good and convenient method of dramatizing prose and novel writing (44–53).

Lea made it clear that he preferred *the self-contained method,* as do most contemporary writers and directors. He said while the narrator method can knit together and make coherent long stage plays, "as a form for original radio drama, it is not good" (53). By removing the narrator, the writer creates a total mental vision so that the listener can effectively overhear the drama: "It can be made as startling and realistic as if the listener were overhearing something in the next room through a half-open door—with the advantage that the people in the next room obligingly let the eavesdropper know all about it" (54).

Lea (1926) advanced that in the self-contained method, the scenery and setting is indicated by the characters themselves and what they say: "This can be done quite naturally and effectively. The characters should be made to see everything objectively and to think of what they are doing objectively, so that this will appear in their speech . . . [and] produce an illusion of naturalness" (55). He advised writers to avoid making their characters give crude word pictures of where they are when the language is not natural to their personalities. The word picture needs to emerge gradually. Exposition needs to be subtle: "This illusion of appearance and costume is necessary . . . [and] should be done by means of the dialogue in a manner to stimulate the listener's imagination" (56–57).

He argued that dramatic action is better than witty dialogue: "I started out with the theory that plays which depended mainly on witty dialogue and very little on action would be more intelligible to the listener and so be more successful. Imagine my surprise when I discovered that the contrary was the case" (57).

It could be argued that Lea had an holistic multisensory recommendation for playwrights conjuring the color, smell, touch, and texture of their characters' experiences. He was enthusiastic about establishing speed and distance through movement—known as kinesics (speed) and proxemics (distance) in drama (62–64). It might also be argued that Lea was rather postmodernist during a modernist time by articulating the radio drama experience as an embodiment of the relationship between performance and listening participation. There is something phenomenological about his observation that "by the very fact that the listener is called upon to give so much of his own personality to the radio-play is his enjoyment and appreciation of it intensified . . . and he gains through the medium of the human voice a mental pageantry of color and delight which no artist in the world can emulate" (71).

When discussing the technique of radio actors, Lea recognized that voice acting requires absolute control of the voice, and actors need to concentrate their thinking behind the voice enunciation and expression. Lea emphasized that in radio acting, the performer needs to concentrate on "his thinking and the regulation of his consciousness . . . his aim must be to radiate personality—the personality of his particular part—to convey atmosphere by cooperation with other radiating personalities and to do all this through the medium of the voice" (75–79).

Phonographic Context and Erasing the Role of Innovation by Women Writers

Lea's book was strong on rhetoric but very short on successful examples of sound play that demonstrated how to write and produce for the new medium. It ignored the decades of successful sound montage and word-based drama developed by the phonograph industry through short descriptive sketches. Productions of *The Departure of a Troopship* (from 1902) and *The Battle of the Marne* (1914) by Russell Hunting, and Major A. E. Rees's *On Active Service* series for Columbia (1917) had pioneered sound-led dramatic exposition through self-contained montage and, indeed, in the case of *On Active Service*, an origination of the sound drama serial across six episodes.

The book failed to recognize that it was a woman writer, Phyliss M. Twigg, who had inaugurated and authored "the first specially written wireless play, *The Truth about Father Christmas*" (Burrows 1924: 74), which was performed live in the London studio of the BBC's London radio station 2LO at 5 p.m. on Christmas Eve 1922. Her script has not survived and there was certainly no sound of the production ever archived. However, the script of the first full studio production of a modern and original stage play from a BBC studio has survived. This was the achievement of another woman writer, Gertrude E. Jennings. *Five Birds in a Cage* may have been the first play to be broadcast from a BBC studio that was not Shakespeare, on November 29, 1923, but more importantly, it is clear from its previous provenance and content why it should have been discussed as writing that engaged so effectively with the listener's imagination. This one-act farce featuring five people trapped in a London Underground lift was later described as "brilliant" by the *Radio Times* in 1934: "possibly the best ever written by the best-known writer of one-act plays of modern times. It sparkles with wit and draws character with a deft hand" (Jennings 1934: 46). Lea utterly failed to recognize why a play originally produced at the London Haymarket Theatre for a special matinée in 1915 continued there in the evening bill for a further 285 consecutive performances and became one of the BBC's most popular radio plays.

Later histories on BBC Radio Drama and BBC History, all written by men, would perpetuate the trope that a male dramatist, Richard Hughes, originated the first successful play specially written for radio (Gielgud 1957: 20). Intriguingly, his script, *Danger,* seemed inspired by Gertrude Jennings's exploration of the comedy of trapping characters in a claustrophobic situation—in his case, it was a coal mine. *Danger* would subsequently have its canonization further confirmed by a production of the Columbia Radio Workshop live on CBS in the US in 1936.

Advice for Radio Dramatists—Experts 1926 to 1934

In 1931, Tyrone Guthrie engaged thoughts about the microphone play with an introduction to the publication of three of his works written specifically for the medium. *Squirrel's Cage, Matrimonial News,* and *Flowers Are Not For You to Pick* were intended to be experimental, and he hoped "that they may have something to say" (Guthrie 1931: 8). He wrote that though the radio broadcast play is denied "all these sensual sops to Cerberus . . . the mind of the listener is the more free to create its own illusion" (8). Guthrie echoed Lea when he wrote:

> Because its pictures are solely of the mind, they are less substantial but more real than the cardboard grottoes, the calico rosebuds, the dusty grandeur of the stage; less substantial and vivid, because not apprehended visually, more real because the impression is partly created by the listener himself. From the author's clues the listener collects his materials, and embodies them in a picture of his own creation. It is therefore an expression of his own experience—whether physical or psychological—and therefore more real to him than the ready-made picture of the stage designer. (9)

Guthrie appreciated as a writer that the listener's impressions of the microphone play were more intimate and more subtle when received privately at home and "not coarsened by being flung into an auditorium, where individuals are fused together into one mass, which becomes a single crowd personality, easily swayed to laughter or tears, but incapable of the minute pulsations of feeling, the delicate gradations of thought which each member of the crowd experiences when alone" (Guthrie 1931: 10). The deployment of the developing multiple-studio technique in *Squirrel's Cage*—one for the actors, one for the chorus, one for the "noises," and one for the orchestra, all balanced by a mixing control panel—would bring to the sound play the effect of superimposed photography in films and endures in present-day technology through digital multitracking.

In 1933, the second BBC director of productions, Val Gielgud, like Guthrie, offered a triple bill of his own plays, but his introduction was rather apologetic and defensive. He described the radio play as the Cinderella of drama and an "infant in arms" (Gielgud 1933: 11) compared to stage theater. In the *How to Write Broadcast Plays* introduction, he devoted many paragraphs to emphasizing that his own plays included were not "artistic masterpieces" and were interesting more for "their shortcomings than for their merits" (Gielgud 1933: 13).

In contrast, Lance Sieveking's 1934 *The Stuff of Radio* was an explosion of creativity. He positively raged against Tyrone Guthrie's tendency to interpolate his reflections on the status of radio drama with an expression of stage theater's lack as an art form. As for his BBC colleague Val Gielgud's book *How to Write Broadcast Plays,* he found "a great many things with which I disagree violently. But that is only natural, for in life I disagree with him on almost every subject, even about the desirability of being alive at all" (Sieveking 1934: 57). Sieveking picked apart and debunked practically every aspect of Gielgud's guide to writing radio drama, but the essence of their cultural divide can be best explained in their respective attitudes to the role of the mixing desk, introduced to the BBC in the late 1920s, which was somewhat grandiloquently named "The Dramatic Control-Panel." Sieveking growled: "He thinks the instrument should be 'operated,' I think that it should be 'played'" (58).

Sieveking was an evangelist for sound drama in the context of modernism to break out of any prescribed literate straitjacket. Gielgud and other authors advising on a utilitarian approach to writing audio drama discouraged any scripting of the radiophonic or audiogenic—those aspects of sound-based drama that are artistically special and expressive of the sound medium. Sieveking (1934) conjured a new lexicon for writing the sound drama creatively and effectively: The Realistic, Confirmatory Effect; The Realistic, Evocative Effect; The Symbolic, Evocative Effect; The Conventionalized Effect; The Impressionistic Effect; and Music as an Effect (66). Sieveking argued that "It is axiomatic that every Sound Effect, to whatever category it belongs, *must* register in the listener's mind instantaneously. That is one of the primary considerations which should weigh with authors and producers continually" (66). Sieveking makes sound effects and music as much the artistic responsibility of the radio playwright as the director, producer, or sound designer, should any production have the luxury of all these additional roles.

Sieveking (1934) developed Gordon Lea's discussion when he led with the assertion at the beginning of his chapter 8, "Writing for the Microphone": "The art of writing plays for the wireless medium is an art, the practice of which may be treated in the same general terms as any other art, since it is subject to the same aesthetic and emotional laws as any other art" (74). Sieveking tore up the terms and conditions approach of writing radio plays:

> To begin at the beginning: the radio dramatist must ask himself, what are all the things that people see subconsciously? In his play, what are the things which, not seeing, they will desire to see? What are the things which, desiring to see, they *will*, in some form, see? Helped and prompted by him, to what degree? And the degree of his mastery of the technique by means of which those problems can be solved, may be estimated by the degree in which not only he but his audience is unaware of its presence. (74)

Sieveking explained that the radio dramatist is more like the composer of music rather than a novelist or stage playwright: "He *hears* what he writes, conceives and works out his play before his mind's ear. He is more like the composer than the theater playwright in this respect, for whereas the theater playwright has to see his play as it goes along and hear it also, the radio dramatist and the musician are dealing only with things to be heard" (74). Sieveking excitedly enthused that the radio dramatist has by far the greater orchestra to write for since the field of expression is not only the tone, pitch, volume, timbre, and general character of musical instrumentation but words and "every sound in the world which may be taken in its original form, or imitated; which may be used realistically or in some abstract way" (75). In short, Sieveking's grand principle of audio drama writing was that the world is your audience and orchestra, and this is an open-ended phenomenon.

The Missing Links: Modernist Innovation, Science Fiction, and Political Drama

If Lea's text can be criticized for being suffused with a surfeit of loose philosophical and poetic optimism, Gielgud, Guthrie, and Sieveking can be accused of excessive egotism and artifice. They all decided that the art of radio drama writing was best exemplified by referencing their own work, though in Gielgud's case with a disappointing mood of inferiority. Sieveking was somewhat preoccupied with impressive sonic frolicking with modernist artifice in mainly art for art's sake indulgences that tried the patience and understanding of listeners and colleagues. His most visceral and innovative writing never got to air and has largely gone unnoticed as a significant work of audio drama. This was his collaboration with the art photographer Francis Bruguière, published in book form as *Beyond This Point* in 1929, and may have been one of the first sound art installations presented in a London art gallery. Sieveking produced some of his text for phonograph playing in the exhibition, but the records he made have not survived.

His exploration of the nihilistic despair and consciousness of a man blowing his brains out with a revolver would have outraged and provoked the sensibility of BBC censors and listeners, but the challenge was never engaged. Lea, Gielgud, Guthrie, Sieveking, and all the how-to writers after them ignored the innovative and political radio drama landmarks created by Reginald Berkeley in his plays *The White Château* (1925), *The Quest of Elisabeth* (1926), and *Machines* (1927). Perhaps the origination fused with political agitation was too hot to handle, with the last being the most brilliant and significant play to challenge the failures of capitalism and the machine age. *Machines* was favorably compared with Fritz Lang's expressionist science fiction film *Metropolis*. Berkeley made sure it was published, like his two previous BBC plays, for the microphone, as radio drama literature. Sadly, though produced for a few performances in a London theater club in 1931, *Machines* was censored by the BBC and Britain's then theatrical state system of blue penciling known as the Lord Chamberlain.

Successful science fiction in the audio drama format was pioneered and experimented with at the BBC during the 1920s, and this has been neglected by scholars and writers on British radio drama as well as being ignored by the how-to authors. The first director of drama productions, R. E. Jeffrey, somebody largely criticized and dismissed by radio drama scholars as failing to develop the potential of radio drama during the 1920s, appears to have been the pioneer writer and innovator in this genre. Unlike Gielgud and others, he never got around to boastfully publishing his radio playwriting as models of experimentation and accomplishment. And because of the awkwardness at the BBC about producer/directors being auteurs as well, it may well be the case that he was responsible for two important science fiction plays originally written for radio that have designated authorship, continuing his ritual of using a pseudonym.

Jeffrey wrote *Speed* under the name Charles Croker; it was broadcast April 2, 1928, and described as "A Tragi-Comic Fantasy of Gods and Mortals" and conjured "specially for radio transmission" (Croker 1928: 12). The play was scheduled in the *Radio Times* with the modernist ritual of fast racing car, aeroplane, and speedboat illustration. Jeffrey self-consciously implored the audience to be in their listening chairs and plaintively hoped: "If the author has been successful, this fantasy of the gods on high Olympus and the speed-mad, self-destructive mortals below will tell its own story in its own way" (Croker 1928: 12). It is likely Jeffrey commissioned *The Greater Power* by the writer Francis J. Mott. It was broadcast September 18, 1928, and was about "a mad inventor of a death-ray such as science has only dreamed of, who from the island where he lives surrounded with strange apparatus and tended by a hunchback henchman threatens destruction to the civilized world" (Mott 1928: 26). Jeffrey may have additonally written *X* under the pseudonym George Crayton, broadcast October 29, 1928, where "X" is the name given to an unknown radio station broadcasting the same program every night until the one occasion when it was interrupted by a desperate cry for help. The underlying theme of the play is "that unknown quality—that dangerous, incalculable 'X'—that lurks in the machinery made by men" (Crayton 1928: 18). This is a significant pioneering canon of full-length science fiction modernist original writing specially for the radio drama medium hitherto unnoticed by radio scholars. The scripts of *Speed* and *X* have survived. Certainly, they bear testament to Jeffrey's innovation in radio drama science fiction.

Advice for Radio Dramatists—Experts 1949 to 1959

Felix Felton's *The Radio Play* (1949) and Donald McWhinnie's *The Art of Radio* (1959) presented radio drama as an artistic opportunity. The abiding departure and advance they both made was in presenting radio playwriting as a multiplicity of human participation on the part of writers, producer/directors, performers, and listeners and embracing it as an experience. The limitations of the rhetoric of "Theater of the Mind" and "The Mind as a Stage" was that the play, which is certainly *the thing*, becomes confined or trapped in a notion of the mind rather than liberated as an experience that transcends human consciousness.

Felton was a producer, composer, teacher, and actor in the art form. His insight explained to writers what the form could aesthetically achieve by the experience of everyone involved in it. So when he observed that the "actor speaks to that microphone as if it were the ear of his listener" (Felton 1949: 10), we are inspired to reflect upon the question that actors who participate in the production are listening, too, in the radio drama studio or on location should the play be produced like film in situ. Felton used metaphor and symbol to explain an artistic and, in modern philosophical terms, phenomenological experience. The journey from microphone to loudspeaker was a conversion of sound waves, with the speaker "like a microphone in reverse." The waves have become "the exact replica of those which entered the microphone in the studio" (10). This metaphor can be extended to appreciate the idea of words and writing as waves and rhythm participating with the consciousness of the listener.

In Felton's text, "the mechanics of production" were given a dramatic purpose, whereas in Gielgud's 1948 handbook on discouragement, the writer was offered a chapter actually labelled "A Glimpse of the Machine"—that which Gielgud believes was only what the writer should be given and allowed to see. Felton (1949) enthusiastically explained in a broadcast of *Blithe Spirit*: "I gave Elvira's voice a ghostly quality by getting her to work on a microphone of her own placed inside an opened grand piano, with the sustaining pedal pressed down, so that her voice picked up a faint aeolian rustle from the strings" (2).

It is significant that in 1949 Felton made it perfectly clear to writers that "it is also possible to record certain scenes out-of-doors or in other buildings" (Felton 1949: 2). He liberated the imprisonment of sound drama as an art form in the studio. Unlike television drama's migration to film location and a specially constructed set, radio drama production has been largely confined to the studio, and this is true of most present-day BBC practice. There are some inspiring and elegant exceptions. The work of John Dryden at Goldhawk Productions and Roger Elsgood for Art and Adventure has been aesthetically emancipating by taking performance, production, and listener to authentic locations in recent years.

Felton (1949) described Tyrone Guthrie's more positive and much quoted observations that listeners provide their own moonshine and make their own décor as the art of serving a writer's radiophonic or audiogenic intention. He explained:

> There was a beautiful example of this in John Cheatle's production of a radio-play by Robert Kemp, called "The Country Mouse goes to Town". The mouse, and his wife, find themselves in a vast metropolitan pantry, where the holes in the Gruyère cheese are as big as railway tunnels. The problem was to make the listener see the scene through a mouse's eyes. It was swiftly done. One mouse said: "It's so quiet in here you could hear a pin drop," and

immediately a large iron crowbar was sent crashing down upon a slab of concrete. (43)

In his chapter on "The Use of Music," Felton urged that engaging its power for dramatic purpose must also respect the discipline of its artistic integrity. He quoted the composer Arthur Bliss, who before a meeting of radio producers advised: "If, then, they wished to quote a piece of musical prose, they would surely treat its grammar and syntax, that is to say, its phrasing, with similar courtesy" (120). In Felton's text, the working playwright discovers that the art of music can inform the very rhythm and overall structure of the sonic prose script. In the chapter on documentary, he described how he adopted the musical *Rondo Form* for a feature about the journey of a postcard to the Orkneys: "This consists of a Principal tune 'A,' followed by another tune 'B.' 'A' is then repeated; then comes a third tune 'C'; then 'A' again; then a fourth tune 'D,' and so on" (105).

In "The Interpretation of the Script," Felton's experience as a radio actor and director richly informed an explanation of the necessary art of interpreting the playwright's score, the very words upon the page: "He must broadcast, not with his voice, but with his mind. If the microphone is a lens focused on the voice, the voice is another lens focused on the speaker's brain" (Felton 1949: 123). In the process, Felton's interrogative checklist for the actor's necessary imagining provides the writer with a cross-section of understanding: (a) the mental state, (b) the emotional state in which his character is involved at the time of the surprise, (c) the nature of the surprise, and, therefore, (d) the degree of mental and emotional shock likely to be produced. Also, if he is wise, (e) he thinks backwards and forwards in continuity to help "place" his acting in proper sequence and size and shape (133). In understanding the creative art of radio acting, the radio writer better practices the art of writing.

Donald McWhinnie began by giving his 1959 volume the right title: *The Art of Radio*. He then approached the subject with broad approaches for analysis: "The Nature of the Medium," "The Participants," and finally, "The Art As It Exists." All three sections were connected by analyzing the art form of radio drama as an experience and an art form that can be considered existential. He selected examples to show and play rather than tell and operate. In the process, sound storytelling becomes a narrative intertextuality. He quotes from play scripts and authors who are timeless with their artistic achievement and what can be defined as a specific literature in radio drama. The radio plays of Giles Cooper or Samuel Beckett, whom McWhinnie produced, have certainly been academically analyzed and criticized in Britain as significant literature and dramatic literature.

McWhinnie (1959) understood the synthesis of realism and surrealism in audio drama, a medium that has the potential to communicate "subtle and varied patterns, emotions and ideas" (93). He explained:

> To achieve the radio "integrity" they must be blended into an artistic unity. There are no immutable rules governing this transformation, and I should not envy the new-world Aristotle who tried to extract rules from current practice. There is one simple and vital fact governing radio form, which I have already indicated: the radio act comes out of silence, vibrates in the void and in the mind, and returns to silence, like music. (93)

McWhinnie articulates a vital principle for the writer: "There is no limit to the aural magic" (108), but "the quicksand of radio lies between its need for absolute clarity and its fascinating capacity for complexity" (108). The very use of its communication means that it is not blind, but at the same time it is not solely an experience of imaginative spectacle. McWhinnie talks about the writer and creator of sound storytelling giving a "blind" medium a guiding hand so that any listener in the dark has illuminated signs put up to help him find his way, and he properly advises that the most vivid signposts will be those that simultaneously inform on character and plot without awkward superimposition (109). His quotation from Giles Cooper's *Without the Grail* offered up an example of radio drama as significant and high-quality aural literature:

> (*Fade in Car running: It slows and stops.*)
> (*Pause.*)
> INNES: What's the matter?
> INDIAN DRIVER: Stop to cool engine.
> INNES: Okay, you're the driver (*Pause.*) So this is the jungle.
> DRIVER: Yes, all jungle here.
> INNES: H'm. . . . Very dusty looking.
> DRIVER: The road is making it dusty. Inside is green.
> (*Pause.*)
> INNES: There's a railway line over there. Where does it go?
> DRIVER: No place into the jungle, stop.
> INNES: Eh? . . . Why?
> DRIVER: Military reasons. Now abandoned.
> INNES: Wartime?
> DRIVER: Yes, wartime. In Assam there were armies all the time. Now in the jungle here live all things.

INNES: Er—animals, you mean?
DRIVER: No, *things*. Wheels and chains gone rusting. Old guns and tanks not moving. In one place were fifty thousand teeth-brush, abandoned. All Abandoned.
(*Pause.*)
(*Car starts and moves off. Fade out.*) (McWhinnie 1959: 52)

McWhinnie offered this extract as an opportunity to demonstrate how writing pared to the bone when performed can be so rich in overtones. In a very short period of time, heat and exhaustion permeates the world of anyone experiencing the play as a listener. We are in the location. There is insight into the leading character and there is diversion of humor and suspense in the dialogue. By the way, what do fifty thousand abandoned toothbrushes in the jungle look like? The answer is the kind of aural magic that every listener can conjure. McWhinnie explained throughout his book that the answer also lay in the experience of the radio play's happening, its very existence as an art form: "The art of radio cannot be reproduced on the page except as a pale shadow: it is as uncapturable as a half-forgotten song" (151).

Despite the large, almost industrial scale and extent of BBC production of radio plays then, and in the contemporary age, now accompanied by the online distributed podcast or *audio fiction,* McWhinnie advocated intrinsic confidence in pursuing artistic ambition for the art form rather than complacently sustaining some form of managerial and institutional survival: "For me, any radio performance which does not compel attention and belief, inevitably and irresistibly, is so much wasted effort. And better a thousand failures which try to explore new recesses of the medium than a dozen supremely competent reproductions" (182).

The BBC's Arrogant Silo—Audio Drama Nationalism and Imperialism

The how-to texts covering this period render invisible the contribution and significance of origination, audio drama authoring, and production by women. There are no reference points to the work of Mabel Constanduros, who founded the sitcom in British radio with her live short story multivoiced performances of *The Buggins Family* through the late 1920s, '30s, '40s, and '50s, until her death in 1957. She was a prolific dramatist and dramatizer. Her friend Ursula Bloom was also a significant original writer of radio drama through the 1940s, '50s, and early '60s. They worked closely with accomplished, experimental, and originating producer/directors such as Mary Hope Allen, Barbara Burnham, Nester Paine, Betty Davies, and Audrey Cameron. The significance and performance of political radio drama is another silence, despite the pioneering drama-documentary and feature output of the BBC Manchester School under the editorship of E. A. "Archie" Harding, who included the brilliant modernist verse playwright D. G. Bridson and the impactful social producer-writer team of Joan Littlewood and Olive Shapley.

I would argue that the how-to books reflect a cultural silo of arrogance. Too many of the practitioners and proponents of British radio drama were nationalistic in their creative mindset and conceived British radio drama as being a superior, almost imperialist source of authority and practice—something to be exported and taught. In the result, British audio drama writing was not fully informed or inspired by American sound dramatists such as Lucille Fletcher, whose *Hitchhiker* (1941) and *Sorry Wrong Number* (1943) were acknowledged and in one case actually reproduced as models of innovative and successful radio scriptwriting in US how-to books (Mackey 1951: 271, 378).

African and Asian writers were excluded from commissioning and production because of racism. A variety program, *The Kentucky Minstrels,* replicated the derogatory ventriloquizing of Black Americans by Freeman Gosden and Charles Correll's *Amos 'n Andy,* with the irony of actual African American performers Harry Scott and Eddie Whaley "blacking up" for BBC Radio. They were promoted as starring in a "Black-faced Minstrel Show" running from 1933 to 1949, and the *Radio Times* used the appallingly offensive N-word to promote the program when it started. If US drama was to be heard in Britain, it would be a celebration of high culture, such as Eugene O'Neill's *The Emperor Jones,* starring the British Guyanese Black actor Robert Adams in the title role (May 1937); Archibald MacLeish's *The Fall of the City* (October 1937); or the plays written by Norman Corwin. Morton Wishengrad's *The Battle of the Warsaw Ghetto* (NBC 1943) and Langston Hughes's *Booker T. Washington in Atlanta* (1945) have never been produced or heard on British radio though published in Erik Barnouw's edited volume *Radio Drama in Action* in 1945. In fact, Langston Hughes's script was commissioned by the Tuskegee Institute and CBS network but never produced because of Black-listing pressures from the House Committee on Un-American Activities starting in October 1944.

Langston Hughes's collaboration with D. G. Bridson in 1944 on a ballad opera exploring the friendship between African Americans going to war with the people of Britain, titled *The Man Who Went to War,* was produced from New York and live broadcast by shortwave to listeners in Britain; it has been archived by the Library of Congress. It would appear to be the first original play by a Black American writer to be heard in Britain and was certainly celebrated as a significant cultural and artistic event in the development of radio drama by D. G. Bridson in his autobiography, *Prospero and Ariel* (Bridson 1971: 109–12).

US scholars of radio drama recognize that Richard Durham at NBC's WMAQ in Chicago originated and wrote the series *Destination Freedom,* with the scripting and production of ninety-one episodes between 1948 and 1950. The series dramatized Black achievers such as Sojourner Truth, Denmark Vesey, Ida B. Wells, Ralph Bunche, and indeed, Langston Hughes. One episode, *The Heart of George Cotton,* was reproduced for the CBS Radio Workshop in 1957 and won a national award. It has been accepted that *Destination Freedom* is a significant series and event in US radio drama history, but, in my opinion, it needs to be elevated and recognized as one of the most important audio drama achievements in world radio history. Durham's achievement and output transcends any pigeonholing or ghettoization as one of the important Black American writers. He is one of the world's most outstanding dramatists across all media par excellence.

The publication and appreciation of fifteen of his scripts by Professor J. Fred MacDonald in 1989 began to amplify that the radio world had its middle twentieth-century equivalent of William Shakespeare toiling in Chicago's Bronzeville (MacDonald 1989; Williams 2015). There are no authors in the English-speaking world who have researched and written this breadth, depth, and quality of drama that addresses so many key aspects of the human condition. Durham's output was the equivalent of over thirty full-length stage plays or films. Their appeal, relevance, and thematic interest extends beyond Black American history to what were also at the time of writing and production key and urgent matters of world current affairs. He combined history, art, journalism, culture, politics, human rights, and drama to make a contribution in storytelling that had impact and represents a milestone in the literature of human struggle and progress.

In technique and artistic and literary expression, he demonstrated, advanced, and enhanced the creative possibilities of the audio drama genre. In *The Heart of George Cotton* (1948), Durham gave characterization and voice to the human heart, and this offered a unique creative perspective on the medical technique in surgery pioneered by Drs. Williams and Dailey. Durham also orchestrated the rhythm of heartbeats with cross-fading and coruscating of dialogue in different languages to bring a global outlook and understanding of the story. *Anatomy of an Ordinance* (1949) dramatized the struggle by Alderman Archibald Carey to improve housing conditions, and Durham characterized with voice and political and philosophical ontology the force of the Chicago slums. He made them metaphysical, gave them a single personality and a consciousness that became menacing, cunning, and the force of indifference, cynicism, injustice, and indeed evil. His ability to invest dramatic identity, characterization into inanimate forms, musical instruments, and social and biophysical phenomena shows how his understanding of the radio dramatic medium was supreme and originally creative. Durham could write for sonic imaginative reception and understood the phenomenology of the listener. His writing art in the sound medium was utterly exceptional, varied, and wide-ranging. The life of Louis Armstrong would resonate through the jazz characterization of trumpet sound; the story of baseball player Satchell Paige would be centered with musical exposition through folk ballad by Oscar Brown Jr. Now is the time to liberate the curriculum of radio and audio drama writing and scholarship to reference and draw inspiration from Durham's work.

Advice for Radio Dramatists—Experts 1985 to Present Day

William Ash's *The Way to Write Radio Drama*, published in 1985, set the scene for a series of books that to the present day explain and assert a confidence and explanation of how to achieve the best possible in a dramatic form now fast approaching its British centenary if we take the BBC's London station 2LO in the early 1920s as the starting point. His structured journey picks up on practical and theoretical concerns originated by Gordon Lea in 1926, Lance Sieveking in 1934, Felix Felton in 1949, and then Donald McWhinnie in 1959: Narrative and Dramatic form (Lea's self-contained or narrative play); The Nature of Radio Drama Compared with Visual Drama; Beginning the Radio Play; Characters, Dialogue, Sound Effects, and Music; Radio Drama Construction; The Script of Your Radio Play and What Happens to It; and Some Radio Plays. He finished with a few pages looking at other forms of radio dramatic writing in adaptation, features, and serials and politically discussed radio drama's future in the cultural and media industrial context. Intriguingly, one of the subtopics was "radio drama on cassette," a technological form now long redundant, though being independent of radio transmission and providing the listen-again performance of literature. This section in a way did prophesize the potential of internet plays and podcasting.

Ash's curriculum dovetails with critical narratology of drama and literature. It is not difficult to pinpoint and relate his advice on how to write radio plays with the theories of focalization (Bal 1996: 115–28), Ricœur's thoughts on "The Time of Narrating and Narrated Time" (Bal 1996: 129–44), and Hayden White's "The Value of Narrativity in the Representation of Reality" (Bal 1996:

273–85). Ash (1985) shows precision in his highlighting of post-structuralist, textual, and narrative possibilities in audio drama through his consideration of Harold Pinter's *A Slight Ache*:

> Listening to this play we have no difficulty in accepting that the old matchseller is not only a figment of the husband's and wife's imagination but also that this same fantastic creature is, at once, the shabby, menacing figure that threatens to replace the man and the sexually attractive figure that appeals to the woman; and furthermore, that man and woman have called this shadowy being into monstrous life by digging, under the most civil and urbane surface, into each other's and their own subconscious. Such a creature, the produce of the author's, the character's and our own imagination, all in dramatic relationship with each other, cannot be reproduced in any other medium— as attempts to stage this play have shown. (3)

Ash was the first how-to author to reference women radio dramatists and include extracts from plays by Rose Tremaine, Shirley Gee, Fay Wheldon, Gaie Houston, and Jennifer Philips, and he also discussed Bloke Modisani's *The Quarter Million Boys* as an example of how radio drama can deploy ridicule as a weapon in political writing that denounces racist tyranny (Ash 1985: 116). As a dramatist himself, he was the first writer to adapt some of the leading novels of Nobel Prize–winning Nigerian author Chinua Achebe for BBC Radio production with *Things Fall Apart* in 1984 and *Anthills of the Savannah* in 1995.

The future direction of academic and aesthetic analysis in Great Britain seems to be in the growth of synoptic practice and theoretical writing, with the intention of establishing a symbiotic relationship of theory informing practice and vice versa. That was certainly the intention of my book *Radio Drama: Theory and Practice* (1999), which predicted the potential of audio drama by internet and online distribution, and engaged narratological literary studies to the potential practice of ironic transposition in audio drama writing. Rattigan's *Theatre of Sound: Radio and the Dramatic Imagination* (2002) explored the interdisciplinary possibilities of studying the medium. A consideration of his diagram on "Transcodification of textual codes through performance and production into aural codes" (Rattigan 2002: 9) offered a remarkable diagrammatic representation of the relationship between playwright and listener as well as discussing the complexity of the bridging journey between audio-dramatic text and audio-performance text.

Guralnick retrieved Gordon Lea's appreciation of radio drama's potential as poetic literature in her 1996 study of Beckett, Pinter, Stoppard, and other contemporary dramatists on radio, *Sight Unseen*. She saw a constellation of dramatic expression that challenged the radio play in its ability to represent the visual, realized its limitation as an imperfect eye, celebrated its musical dimension, occupied and performed comfortably as the theater of the mind, and undoubtedly existed as a more worldly phenomenon linking the experience of the writer, producer, performer, and listener:

> From the delicatest ear in the mind of a playwright, a radio play repeats words as that ear wants to hear them: articulated, inflected, hence powerfully animated, yet safe from eclipse by theatrical apparatus. And at the sound of these words, an invisible audience listens intently, not only to the play but also to itself as expressed in the play's events and gestures, which perforce bear the stamp of whoever envisions them. Thus do the audience and the playwright become one, united in their effort to realize a work that, existing as a mutual "act of the mind," is what Stevens [a reference to Wallace Stevens's 1942 poem "Of Modern Poetry"] denominates poetry. (Guralnick 1996: 192)

Dr. Paula Knight in her 2006 thesis "Radio Drama: Sound, Text, Word; Bakhtin and the Aural Dialogue of Radio Drama" related the medium to Mikhail Bakhtin's theory of dialogism, polyphony, and heteroglossia. More recently, Dr. Farokh Shirazi (2018a, 2018b) has been investigating phenomenological understanding of intensively realized contemporary podcast audio fiction and the problem of what he calls a "semantic paradigm" in critically accounting and evaluating radio/audio drama's practice. Shirazi has successfully investigated how past practitioners and critiques of the medium have been hidebound by an over-preoccupation with visual metaphors for what is a listening experience. His development and expression of an original phenomenological discourse informs creatively about the artistic potential of podcast production of what has been regarded as radio drama, but may now require a new definition that combines sound and fictional storytelling with listen-again properties.

Decolonizing the Curriculum

Claire Grove and Stephen Wyatt's *So You Want to Write Radio Drama?* (2013) is regarded as the current go-to book and essential guide for aspiring sound and radio dramatists in the UK. The authors are rightly highly respected and award-winning practitioners in their field, underpinned with the authority of their outstanding BBC careers. They selected six landmark radio plays for reading and listening: *The War of the Worlds* by H. G. Wells, adapted by Howard Koch and Orson Welles (CBS 1938); *Under Milk Wood* by Dylan Thomas (BBC 1954); *Albert's Bridge* by Tom Stoppard (BBC 1967); *Hitchhiker's Guide to the Galaxy* by Douglas Adams (BBC 1978); *Cigarettes and Chocolate* by Anthony Minghella (BBC 1988); and *Spoonface Steinberg* by Lee Hall (BBC 1997). Few would argue this selection of worthy and significant canons of radio drama history.

Unfortunately, their ethnicity, class, and social and cultural hierarchy strikes the soundings of privilege. They are all high-achieving and elitist white men. Future how-to discussion and audio dramatic narratological scholarship needs to cast a much wider investigative, culturally expansive, and theoretically progressive approach. Much more needs to be done to elevate writing and production that has been neglected and gone unrecognized and analyzed in the past. Present BBC output now celebrates a mainstream of audio dramatic writing by Black and Asian playwrights such as Bonnie Greer, Winsome Pinnock, Kwame Kwei-Armah, Roy Williams, Lenny Henry, Benjamin Zephaniah, and Tanika Gupta. These and others are multiple new voices advancing and experimenting through the medium with new and thought-provoking political and sociopyschological imperatives, and exciting and innovative transcultural and sonic rhythms of speech and communication.

Works Cited

Ash, William. 1985. *The Way to Write Radio Drama*. London: Elm Tree Books.

Bal, Mieke. 1996. "Focalization." In *Narratology: An Introduction*, edited by Susana Onega and José Angel García Landa, 115–28, London: Longman.

Barnouw, Erik. 1945. *Radio Drama in Action: 25 Plays of a Changing World*. New York: Farrar & Rinehart.

Berkeley, Reginald. 1925. *The White Chateau*. London: Williams and Norgate.

Bridson, D. G. 1971. *Prospero and Ariel: The Rise and Fall of Radio: A Personal Recollection*. London: Victor Gollancz Ltd.

Burrows, Arthur R. 1924. *The Story of Broadcasting*. London: Cassel and Company.

Crayton, George. 1928. "X A Radio Play by George Crayton." *Radio Times* 21, no. 265 (October 26): 18.

Croker, Charles. 1928. "Speed—A Tragi-Comic Fantasy of Gods and Mortals by Charles Croker." *Radio Times* 18, no. 235 (March 30): 12.

Crook, Tim. 1999. *Radio Drama: Theory and Practice*. London: Routledge.

Felton, Felix. 1949. *The Radio Play*. London: Sylvan Press.

Gielgud, Val. 1933. *How to Write Broadcast Plays: With Three Examples: "Friday Morning," "Red Tabs" and "Exiles."* London: Hurst & Blackett.

———. 1946. *Radio Theatre: Plays Specially Written for Broadcasting*. London: MacDonald.

———. 1948. *The Right Way to Radio Playwriting*. London: Right Way Books.

———. 1957. *British Radio Drama*. London: George G. Harrap & Co.

Grove, Claire, and Stephen Wyatt. 2013. *So You Want to Write Radio Drama?* London: Nick Hern Books.

Guralnick, Elissa S. 1996. *Sight Unseen: Beckett, Pinter, Stoppard and Other Contemporary Dramatists on Radio*. Athens: Ohio University Press.

Guthrie, Tyrone. 1931. *Squirrel's Cage and Two Other Microphone Plays*. London: Cobden-Sanderson.

Jennings, Gertrude. 1934. "Divertissement—Five Birds in a Cage by Gertrude Jennings, the Scene Is an Underground Lift." *Radio Times* 44, no. 568 (August 17): 46.

Knight, Paula. 2006. "Radio Drama: Sound, Text, Word; Bakhtin and the Aural Dialogue of Radio Drama." PhD thesis, Goldsmiths, University of London.

Lea, Gordon. 1926. *Radio Drama and How to Write It*. London: George Allen & Unwin.

MacDonald, J. Fred, ed. 1989. *Richard Durham's Destination Freedom: Scripts from Radio's Black Legacy, 1948–50*. New York: Praeger.

Mackey, David R. 1951. *Drama on the Air*. New York: Prentice-Hall.

McWhinnie, Donald. 1959. *The Art of Radio*. London: Faber and Faber.

Mott, Francis J. 1928. "The Greater Power—A Drama for Broadcasting by Francis J. Mott." *Radio Times* 20, no. 259 (September 14): 26.

Rattigan, Dermot. 2002. *Theatre of Sound: Radio and the Dramatic Imagination*. Dublin: Carysfort Press.

Shirazi, Farokh Soltani. 2018a. "Inner Ears and Distant Worlds: Podcast Dramaturgy and the Theatre of the Mind." In *Podcasting: New Aural Cultures and Digital Media*, edited by Dario Llinares, Neil Fox, and Richard Berry, 189–208, London: Palgrave Macmillan.

———. 2018b. "'Play Don't Tell': A Phenomenological Critique of the Semantic Paradigm of British Radio Dramaturgy." PhD thesis, Royal Central School of Speech and Drama, University of London.

Sieveking, Lance. 1934. *The Stuff of Radio*. London: Cassell.

Sieveking, Lance, and Francis Bruguière. 1929. *Beyond This Point*. London: Duckworth.

Williams, Sonja D. 2015. *Word Warrior: Richard Durham, Radio and Freedom*. Chicago: University of Illinois Press.

2

"Stage" Directions in the Radio Script

A Transgeneric Narratological Approach

JANINE HAUTHAL

AS AN ART FORM where the written or printed script and its potential recording(s) or broadcast(s) reciprocally bear on one another, the radio script lends itself easily to a comparison with playtexts. Taking the similarity of their typographical layout as a starting point, this chapter sets out to compare radio scripts and playtexts by adopting a transgeneric narratological approach. Transgeneric narratology proceeds from the assumption that narratological categories (concerning, for instance, the representation of characters, time and space, narrative framing, narrative mediation and focalization) can be applied to the analysis of all literary genres, even though poems "do not seem to tell stories" and plays traditionally "do not seem to be mediated" (see Hühn and Sommer 2012: [4]). The present chapter extends transgeneric narratology's claim to radio scripts. In addition, it will seek to remedy the prioritization of performance in recent transgeneric and transmedial approaches to drama as well as in structuralist drama theory, which so far have paid little attention to the textual medium and the written playtext as an object of interest in itself and rather focused on drama as a scenically enacted, performed text.

The research for this article was financed by the Research Foundation—Flanders (FWO). I would like to thank Lars Bernaerts, Jarmila Mildorf, Pim Verhulst, and the participants of the Audioworkshops 2016–2018 at Ghent University, as well as the two anonymous reviewers for their generous feedback on draft versions of this chapter and for drawing my attention to some of the material discussed in this chapter.

Hence, previous scholarship in the field corroborates the need for a medium-specific perspective that differentiates between drama and theater, script and performance. In particular, the (implied) intermedial transition from page to stage poses a methodological challenge and tends to be either neglected or conceptualized in a problematic way.[1] Irina Rajewsky's theory of intermediality (2002: 19; 2005: 51–52) is particularly suited for the analysis of literary script genres as it allows one to conceptualize the implied transition to a different medium (*Medienwechsel*), for example from page to stage, as intermedial reference (*intermediale Bezugnahme*) qua system (*Systemreferenz*). Her theory also adequately emphasizes the *as if*-character (Als ob-*Charakter*) of intermedial references (2002: 39–40; 2005: 54–57), highlighting that such references "cannot *use* or genuinely *reproduce* elements or structures of a different medial system" but rather "*evoke* or *imitate* them," and "this inability to pass beyond a single medium" makes recipients aware of "a medial difference—an 'intermedial gap'" (2005: 55).

This distinction between script and performance appears to be equally crucial with regard to the radio play and the radio script. Yet, also the emerging field of audionarratology, which explores the radio play as a specific (narrative) genre of audiophonic art, so far has tended to adopt a transmedial approach, giving priority to studying sound, voice, silence, and music in radio plays and focusing on radio scripts as documents that underlie possible performances on the radio.[2] Therefore, based on the conclusive definition of the radio play as genre and medium by Lars Bernaerts (2016: 137–38; 2017: 115–16), this chapter will treat the radio script not just as the past or future projection of a specific recording or radio broadcast but as "a 'readable' medium *sui generis*" (Jahn 2001: 675) in order to problematize the neglect of the written/printed script for this artistic field. In so doing, this chapter takes a particular interest in linking the contested status of stage directions in drama to the radio play. For playtexts, stage directions tend to be conceptualized in two different ways. Conventionally, they have been attributed to the author

---

1. See, for instance, Roland Weidle's (2009) claim that applying the narratological concept of focalization to drama is problematic because of "drama's physical and visual nature and the material presence of the actors" (239). See also Manfred Pfister (1991) who—in his attempt to compensate for the outright neglect of the performative dimension of literary research up to the 1970s—defines the dramatic text "as a multimedial form of presentation" (6) and highlights "the collective nature of production and reception" (11). However, as Andreas Höfele (1991) has argued (11), a playtext merely *implies* a multimedial, collectively produced and collectively watched performance, which is why Rajewsky's theory of intermediality is better suited for the analysis of literary script genres than Pfister's multimedial model (see Hauthal 2009: 60–128).

2. See, for example, Mildorf and Kinzel (2016) as well as contributions to this volume by Siebe Bluijs on focalization and by Lars Bernaerts on narrative mediation in the radio play.

and regarded as illocutionary speech acts (*sensu* John Searle) or as instructions addressed to directors or performers (Korthals 2003; Zipfel 2001). Other narratological approaches to drama, by contrast, tend to conceptualize stage directions as a fictional discourse, uttered by a superordinate narrative agent or system and addressed to readers of the playtext.[3]

Following on these latter approaches, I hope to further demonstrate the potential of a transgeneric application of narratological categories first to playtexts from different periods and subsequently to three contemporary radio scripts, with autonomous[4] and ambiguous stage directions as my test case. Drawing on examples of contemporary radio plays in different languages, I will successively discuss Ursula Krechel's *Wenn man ein gleichschenkliges Dreieck auf den Kopf stellt* (*When One Turns an Isosceles Triangle Upside Down*; 2012), Samuel Beckett's *Cascando* (1963), and Harold Pinter's *A Slight Ache* (1959). Throughout the chapter, my comparison will point to genre-specific differences as well as to transgeneric similarities in the use of stage directions between playtext and radio script. In addition, I will address the question of how disparities and intersections between the two script genres may relate to medium-specific processes of production, distribution, and reception. I will begin by exploring how the use of autonomous and ambiguous stage directions in playtexts corroborates the need for a medium-specific perspective that differentiates between script and performance.

Stage Directions and the Intermedial Transition from Page to Stage

Stage directions, and the lack of stage directions in particular, can play a central role in foregrounding the playtext as a script that is *written to be performed* as well as the intermedial gap between script and performance. Strategies that can turn a playtext into a closet drama include experiments with the

---

3. See Jahn (2001), Schenk-Haupt (2007), and Weidle (2009). See also Carlson (1991) and, for a summary account of the debate with reference to recent meta- and postdramatic British plays, Hauthal (2009: 110–28; 2018b).

4. I take the term "autonomous" from Michael Issacharoff (1989), who applies it to stage directions that are "liberated from the referential constraints of the dialogue" (22). According to Issacharoff, they are "so named because they are manifestly intended for reading: they are in fact spurious stage directions, not meant to guide stage presentation or clarify nuances of the dialogue, or they explicitly contradict the dialogue" (20). Thus, the term echoes but is not equivalent to "literary autonomy," a notion closely linked to the idea of "the self-regulating or self-contained artwork" (Goldstone 2013: 4), which can variously be conceived in poetic, social, ideological, commercial, or aesthetic terms (see Dorleijn, Grüttemeier, and Korthals Altes 2007).

TOM THUMB *the Great.*

ACT I. SCENE I.

SCENE, *The Palace.*

Doodle, Noodle.

DOODLE.

URE, such a (*a*) Day as this was never seen!
The Sun himself, on this auspicious Day,
Shines, like a Beau in a new Birth-Day Suit:

That

(*a*) *Corneille* recommends some very remarkable Day, wherein to fix the Action of a Tragedy. This the best of our Tragical Writers have understood to mean a Day remarkable for the Serenity of the Sky, or what we generally call a fine Summer's Day: So that according to this their Exposition, the same Months are proper for Tragedy, which are proper for Pastoral. Most of our celebrated *English* Tragedies, as *Cato, Mariamne, Tamerlane,* &c. begin with their Observations on the Morning. *Lee* seems to have come the nearest to this beautiful Description of our Authors;

The Morning dawns with an unwonted Crimson,
The Flowers all odorous seem, the Garden Birds Sing

B

FIGURE 1. *The Tragedy of Tragedies* (Fielding 1731: 44)

The LIFE and DEATH of

This down the Seams embroider'd, that the Beams.
All Nature wears one univerſal Grin.
 Nood. This Day, O Mr. *Doodle,* is a Day
Indeed, (*b*) a Day we never ſaw before.
The mighty (*c*) *Thomas Thumb* victorious comes;
Millions of Giants crowd his Chariot Wheels,
(*d*) Giants! to whom the Giants in *Guild-hall*

Are

> *Sing louder, and the laughing Sun aſcends,*
> *The gaudy Earth with an unuſual brightneſs,*
> *All Nature ſmiles.*   Cæſ. Borg.

Maſſiniſſa in the new *Sophonisba* is alſo a Favourite of the Sun;
> ——— *The Sun too ſeems*
> *As conſcious of my Joy with broader Eye*
> *To look abroad the World, and all things ſmile*
> *Like* Sophonisba.

Memnon in the *Perſian Princeſs,* makes the Sun decline riſing, that he may not peep on Objects, which would prophane his Brightneſs.
> ———————*The Morning riſes ſlow,*
> *And all thoſe ruddy Streaks that us'd to paint*
> *The Days Approach, are loſt in Clouds as if*
> *The Horrors of the Night had ſent 'em back,*
> *To warn the Sun, he ſhould not leave the Sea,*
> *To Peep,* &c.

(*b*) This Line is highly conformable to the beautiful Simplicity of the Antients. It hath been copied by almoſt every Modern,

> *Not to be is not to be in Woe.*   State of Innocence.
> *Love is not Sin but where 'tis ſinful Love.*   Don Sebaſtian.
> *Nature is Nature,* Lælius.   Sophonisba.
> *Men are but Men, we did not make our ſelves.*   Revenge.

(*c*) Dr. B——*y* reads the mighty Tall-maſt Thumb. Mr. D——*s* the mighty Thumping Thumb. Mr. T——*d* reads Thundering. I think *Thomas* more agreeable to the great Simplicity ſo apparent in our Author.

(*d*) That learned Hiſtorian Mr. S——*n* in the third Number of his Criticiſm on our Author, takes great Pains to explode

this

FIGURE 2. *The Tragedy of Tragedies* (Fielding 1731: 45)

typographical layout, an unconventional amount of stage directions, and their narrative mode. Examples can be found, for instance, in *The Tragedy of Tragedies* (1731), a play by Henry Fielding in which he uses footnotes for annotations that not only break with the layout conventions of playtexts (see figures 1 and 2) but also form an impediment to the intermedial transition from page to stage, indicating that, already by the end of the Renaissance, plays were not just performed but also read (see Hauthal 2018a).

Almost two hundred years later, the sheer amount of stage directions turns the plays of George Bernard Shaw into closet dramas. *Heartbreak House: A Fantasia in the Russian Manner on English Themes* (1919/20), for example, starts with a long passage detailing the scenery, stage design, props, and costumes.

> The hilly country <u>in the middle of the north edge of Sussex,</u> looking very pleasant on a fine evening <u>at the end of September,</u> is seen through the windows of a room <u>which has been built so as to resemble</u> the after part of an old-fashioned high-pooped ship . . .
>
>   . . .
>
>   . . . A small but stout table of teak, with a round top and gate legs, stands against the port wall between the door and the bookcase. It is the only article in the room that suggests <u>(not at all convincingly)</u> a woman's hand in the furnishing. (Shaw 1921: 59–60; my emphasis)

As the highlighted sections show, spatiotemporal concretizations and references to intentions of the room's architecture are likely to be too specific for the theatrical mise-en-scène and can only be grasped by readers of the play. The frequent comments, moreover, can be attributed to a superordinate narrative agent or system (*sensu* Jahn and Weidle) and indicate a narrative mode that deviates from the conventional instructive mode of stage directions.

A similar superordinate narrative agent or system also features in Tom Stoppard's *Travesties* (1974) and becomes manifest, for example, in stage directions referring to the unreliability of the main character: "*A note on the above: the scene (and most of the play) is under the erratic control of Old Carr's memory, which is not notably reliable, and also of his various prejudices and delusions*" (Stoppard 1975: 27). As in the two previous examples, Stoppard's note, too, is only directly accessible to readers of the playtext, but not to audiences of a performance of the play. Therefore, based on Michael Issacharoff (1989), stage directions like the above can be described as "autonomous" (20–22): "Since they are not subordinate to the dialogue . . . , autonomous didascalia thus presuppose reading, which, in such cases, takes precedence over performance" (22). According to Weidle (2009), who also discusses this passage from Stoppard's *Travesties,* the stage directions "provide the reader with additional information that helps him or her to transcend the perceptive horizon of the characters" (235). It follows that stage directions of this kind can be read as instances of zero focalization (see Weidle 2009: 236–38) and of a superordinate narrative system (Korthals 2003: 273–74).

Gerda Poschmann's concept of "text theatricality" further helps to account for the challenge that autonomous stage directions pose. According to Poschmann (1997: 42–44), "text theatricality" characterizes playtexts that reflect on, or even undermine, the (implied) intermedial transition from page to stage. Indeed, the information about Old Carr's unreliability cannot be staged unaltered but needs to be "translated" into performance and, thus, can prompt recipients to reflect on possible stage performances.[5] The stage direction in question could, for instance, be read out loud by an actor. However, this actor would be just another (narrating) character. Consequently, the transition from page to stage would bring about a shift of function for this narrating instance, namely from that of a superordinate narrative agent, located on the level of narrative transmission and generating the narrative, to that of a merely intradiegetic narrator. Hence, the example shows how autonomous stage directions have the capacity to trigger recipients' reflections on the playtext's genre-defining intermedial gap between script and performance.

In my next example, taken from Martin Crimp's *Attempts on Her Life* (1997), such an effect potentially results from ambiguous or undefined stage directions:

> —3 a.m. Anne wakes up. Hears voice, lights cigarette. Appears in doorway. Dialogue.
> —Who was it, she says.
> —Nothing, he says.
> —Who the fuck was it, she says. End of dialogue.
> —And now she's angry, exactly: end of dialogue—and now she's angry. She's angry because she knows exactly who it is. (Crimp 2005: 211)

In the quoted passage, there are no indications as to who speaks (a man or a woman), how old this person is, and whether there are more than two

---

5. The self-reflexive potential of such autonomous stage directions presumably varies. While some readers of the playtext might simply "naturalize" (*sensu* Jonathan Culler) the information about Old Carr's unreliability by incorporating it into the overall fiction, directors and actors might become more aware of how this passage complicates the intermedial transition from page to performance.

speakers. While dashes indicate a change of speaker, character names and stage directions concerning the setting, or the delivery of lines, are missing. In this way, Crimp's playtext creates a textual ambiguity that cannot be translated into performance because directors of a theater production have to choose a definite number of actors and actresses with a (more or less) specific gender and age as well as a particular set.[6] With reference to Poschmann, these kinds of stage directions, again, can be described as manifestations of text theatricality because their indeterminacy or ambiguity reflects and impedes the (implied) intermedial transition from page to stage.

Turning to the radio script, the question is whether (or not) similar stage directions can be found in texts written to be recorded or broadcast on the radio. In the following, I will first concentrate on autonomous stage directions that potentially turn a radio script into a *closet radio play* (i.e., a published radio script without recording). Due to the medium-specific characteristics of production, distribution, and reception of the radio play, however, this term should be treated with caution. To begin with, in the field of drama, the term "closet drama" has specifically been coined for playtexts that are deemed "unstageable," while there is no institutionalized practice of publishing radio scripts that have not been broadcast, which is why—at least to my knowledge—there are no closet radio plays. Neither am I aware of a radio play whose publication and recording is temporally as dispersed as, for instance, in the famous example of Heinrich von Kleist's *Penthesilea*, where sixty-eight years passed between the play's publication in 1808 and its premiere in 1876. Quite on the contrary, most published radio plays postdate the recording and tend to be recording editions. Moreover, radio plays are often only produced once, which is why possibilities to compare different recordings are scarce (Beckett's radio plays are one of the few exceptions to this rule). In the last decades, an ever-increasing amount of radio plays tends to be produced either by the author him- or herself, or in close collaboration with the author, and very often—as in the case of Krechel's *Wenn man ein gleichschenkliges Dreieck auf den Kopf stellt*, to which the analysis will now turn—scripts tend to remain unpublished. My analysis of this radio script focuses primarily on its autonomous stage directions but also takes its 2013 recording into account in order to discuss how the script's *text aurality* complicates the intermedial transition from text to recording.

---

6. In performance, even an empty stage is not an undefined space but is likely to be perceived as a meaningful artistic choice.

Autonomous Stage Directions in Ursula Krechel's *Wenn man ein gleichschenkliges Dreieck auf den Kopf stellt*

In Ursula Krechel's *Wenn man ein gleichschenkliges Dreieck auf den Kopf stellt* (SWR 2013)—a radio play about the retrospective analysis of (dysfunctional) relationships between children and parents from the perspective of the now grown-up children—it is not only the amount but also the autonomous nature of the stage directions that arrest readers' attention. In the very beginning of this radio script, stage directions characterize the different voices by referring to bodily features: for example, "The woman with the disciplined elbows," "The woman with the exposed necks of tooth," and "The man with the nervous fingers" (Krechel 2012: 2).[7] The stage directions also make use of metaphors, as in "the voice of a singing bird" (2) and in "I imagine an inner bleeding, that penetrates into speech, that envelops all speaking, insalivates and also caresses it" (2).[8] Krechel's radio script also includes stage directions that formulate questions concerning the instruments to be used for the audio track, as in "(Ecstatic laughter, then really an unexpected, seemingly drippy music. Harp?)" (5) and "(A glassy music, very bright.... As instrument, a glass harmonium?)" (20).[9] Other stage directions begin with similar questions but continue with suggesting more far-reaching interpretations, as in "(Is the instrument, which could be heard after the story of the snow cave-reading, rather a wind harp? Or does the bright, drifty [sound] superimpose a teetering, scurrying, an alacrity?)" (22) and "Did one hear again a sound that is remotely reminiscent of a hoover? Or is this already a slight of hearing?)" (27).[10] In addition, there are stage directions that evoke synesthesia[11] or comment on characters' utterances. Two examples of this latter use of stage directions are, for instance: "The woman with the exposed necks of tooth: Don't make me laugh. (And then she laughs rather cruelly.)" (13) and "The woman

---

7. Here and elsewhere, translations are mine. The German original is included in the footnotes: "Die Frau mit den disziplinierten Ellbogen," "Die Frau mit den entblößten Zahnhälsen," "Der Mann mit den nervösen Fingern" (Krechel 2012: 2).

8. "Eine Singvogelstimme"; "Ich stelle mir ein innerliches Bluten vor, das in die Sprache dringt, das ganze Sprechen umhüllt, einspeichelt, auch umschmeichelt" (Krechel 2012: 2).

9. "(Verzücktes Lauschen, dann wirklich eine unerwartete, wie tropfende Musik. Harfe?)" (5); "(Eine gläserne Musik, sehr hell. ... Als Instrument eine Glasorgel?)" (20).

10. "(Ist das Instrument, das nach der Erzählung von der Schneehöhlen-Lektüre zu hören war, eher eine Windharfe gewesen? Oder überlagert sich das Helle, Verwehte mit einem Stöckeln, Trippeln, einer Eilfertigkeit?)" (22); "(Hörte man hier wieder ein Geräusch, das von fern an einen Staubsauger erinnerte? Oder ist dies schon eine Kränkung des Gehörs?)" (27).

11. See, for instance, the stage direction "One should almost be able to hear the animal smell" ("Man müßte fast den Tiergeruch hören können"; 30).

with the exposed necks of tooth: Yes? Yes? Yes? I don't think so, I don't really think so. (And this is exactly how she sounds like.)" (28)[12] Altogether, these examples demonstrate that the stage directions in Krechel's radio script are not subordinate to the dialogue and may be primarily intended for reading. Hence, they do not function as straightforward, unambiguous instructions but are "autonomous," in accordance with Issacharoff, thus foregrounding the literariness of the script.

Moreover, making use of the first-person singular pronoun twice, the stage directions entice readers of the radio script to identify this presenting agency with the author.[13] Thus Krechel self-reflexively foregrounds the textual medium of the script. Applying Poschmann's concept of text theatricality to the radio script and to the way Krechel thematizes the intermedial relation between text and recording, the autonomous stage directions in *Wenn man ein gleichschenkliges Dreieck auf den Kopf stellt* create what could be called "text aurality."[14]

The text aurality emerging from Krechel's use of autonomous stage directions becomes particularly palpable when the stage directions suggest that actors may speak them out loud:

> It is possible that the actors and actresses themselves speak out loud the stage directions which describe their character and detail their vocal performance. This would bring them more swiftly "into play" from the very beginning. They could also vary the stage directions and include their own names into the spontaneously changed text. (Krechel 2012: 3)[15]

If actors and actresses were to follow this suggestion, a commenting level would emerge that cannot be attributed to one of the fictional voices in the

---

12. "Die Frau mit den entblößten Zahnhälsen: Daß ich nicht lache. (Und dann lacht sie ziemlich gemein.)" (13); "Die Frau mit den entblößten Zahnhälsen: Ja? Ja? Ja? Ich glaube es nicht, ich glaube es nicht wirklich. (Und genau so hört sie sich auch an.)" (28).

13. "I imagine a body, beautiful and reduced to the extreme, but wide awake." ("Ich stelle mir einen Körper vor, schön und aufs Äußerste reduziert, aber hellwach."); "I imagine an inner bleeding, that penetrates into speaking" ("Ich stelle mir ein innerliches Bluten vor, das in die Sprache dringt"; 2).

14. I define aurality based on the *Oxford English Dictionary* as "relating to the ear or the sense of hearing" (https://en.oxforddictionaries.com/definition/aural). See also Beck (1999: 1.5) as well as Mildorf and Kinzel (2016): "The Latin word *auris* (Engl. *ear*), which forms the stem of *aural* and *auricular*, stresses the function of the hearing organ in sound perception" (5).

15. "Es ist möglich, daß die Schauspieler und Schauspielerinnen den Regie-Text, der sie und ihre Stimmführung beschreibt, selbst sprechen. Es würde sie von Anfang an eher 'ins Spiel bringen.' Sie könnten ihn auch variieren und im spontan veränderten Text ihren eigenen Namen nennen."

text but can be conceived as evidence for an overt presenting agency. At the same time, however, the suggestion also makes it possible to perceive the descriptions of the characters and their voices as a self-commentary, which—depending on whether the use of pronouns is changed or not—could be either figural or *ex persona*. If the stage directions were to be included in a recording of the radio play and speakers would not vary the use of pronouns, actors and actresses would refer to their character in the third-person singular. Consequently, listeners could have the impression that they are commenting on their voice roles from an external perspective, that is, *ex persona*. Moreover, since two of the unchanged sentences make use of the first-person singular pronoun, the ensuing shift between pronouns could have a self-reflexive function, making listeners aware of the tension between speaker and voice character, between text and recording. Therefore, a certain ambiguity would pertain to this self-commentary *ex persona*. Only a recording that decides for a unifying adjustment of the use of pronouns (so that the passages become a figural self-commentary) could reduce it. Hence, depending on the interpretative choices of the recording, the textual manifestation of an overt presenting agency could be transformed into a (more or less ambiguous and more or less self-reflexive) self-commentary.[16]

In the 2013 production of Krechel's play by the Südwest-Rundfunk SWR, the production team decided to follow the suggestion in the stage directions, having them spoken out loud by three speakers, namely "The woman with the disciplined elbows," "The woman with the exposed necks of tooth," and "The man with the nervous fingers" (0:00:00–0:00:30).[17] Since each speaker utters the stage directions that concern his or her character, the recording attributes the stage directions to the respective characters. Thus, acoustically, the recording unambiguously transforms the textual manifestations of an overt presenting agency into a figural self-commentary while, on the textual level, it retains the ambiguous mix between first- and third-person singular pronouns that potentially highlights the tension between speaker and role and creates

---

16. In general, Krechel's radio script does not shy away from self-reflexivity, as becomes evident toward the end of the play when "The man with the nervous fingers" addresses listeners directly in a metaleptic manner: "Dear listener, you have not heard me, this was an illusion, my sister, my ex-wife, my father-in-law have dragged, hauled me in front of the microphone, here I am, there I was, there I had been. You will never hear from me again" ("Lieber Hörer, liebe Hörerin, Sie haben mich nicht gehört, es war eine Illusion, meine Schwester, meine ehemalige Frau, mein Schwiegervater haben mich vor ein Mikrophon gezerrt, geschleppt, da bin ich, da war ich, da war ich gewesen. Sie hören von mir nie wieder"; 30).

17. Time indications refer to the SWR production from May 23, 2013 (directed by Hans Gerd Krogmann; speakers: Hedi Kriegeskotte, Hille Darjes, Christoph Bantzer, Hans Diehl).

the impression that the actors and actresses are commenting on their voice characters *ex persona*.

Compared to the script, three further alterations characterize the recording at hand and contribute to the creation of a fictional frame that the starting sequence is embedded into. To begin with, the three voices overlap and gradually intensify in volume (while, on page, the different voice characters are displayed one after/below the other). The initially low volume and the simultaneous arrangement of the three voices preclude listeners' understanding of individual utterances. The resultant musicalization of the speech accentuates the speakers' different voice qualities. At the same time, the overlapping and gradual increase in volume of the three voices creates a pattern of narrative progression and foregrounds the speakers' gradual "coming into play."

The recording, secondly, excludes the part of "the exalted teacher" ("Der hehre Lehrer"; Krechel 2012: 2), that is, the women's father and the man's father-in-law, so that only three of the four voices feature in the initial sequence. In addition, a third change from script to recording occurs when the utterances of the three speakers are interrupted and brought to a stop by a tapping sound. This tapping sound imparts a fictional frame to the scene as a whole, namely that of the moment at the beginning of a lesson when the pupils' chatter is silenced by the teacher. The tapping sound invites listeners of the radio play to retrospectively read the initial clutter of whispering voices *as* children's chatter. Thus, from the very beginning, the recording emphasizes the generational divide between the protagonists, which pervades the radio play as a whole. Fittingly, the chatter is followed by a speech of "The exalted teacher" before a call-and-response routine between the teacher and his pupils (i.e., the two women and the man) unfolds: "The exalted teacher: Morningchildren.—The woman with the disciplined elbows; the woman with the exposed necks of tooth; the man with the nervous fingers (in unison): Good morning, Mr. teacher.—The exalted teacher: Sit down." (Krechel 2012: 4; 0:00:43–0:00:50).[18] Adding the tapping sound to the original script turns out to be crucial as it transitions from the starting sequence (the stage directions of the script) to the ensuing fictional dialogue of the characters (the main text of the script) and brings the two elements together in one fictional scene, the start of a lesson led by "the exalted teacher." In other words, the added tapping sound retrospectively transforms the initial stage directions into main text. This is particularly noteworthy given the radically different textual level and pragmatic/fictional status of the main or "primary" text and the stage

---

18. "Der hehre Lehrer: Morgenkinder.—Die Frau mit den disziplinierten Ellenbogen; der Mann mit den nervösen Fingern; die Frau mit den entblößten Zahnhälsen (im Chor): Guten Morgen, Herr Lehrer.—Der hehre Lehrer: Setzen."

directions or "secondary text" in the original script—a difference the recording basically levels out. Hence, through fictional embedding, the recording suspends the autonomous character and text aurality that these stage directions had in writing. They are no longer manifestations of an overt presenting agency but are transformed into a figural self-commentary. At the same time, their ambiguity is reduced to a minimum through the fictional embedding that the additional sounds create.

Summing up: As manifestations of a superordinate narrative agent, the autonomous stage directions in Krechel's radio script trigger reflections on the intermedial gap between script and recording and challenge the (implied) intermedial transition. While the 2013 production of *Wenn man ein gleichschenkliges Dreieck auf den Kopf stellt* exemplifies a recording in which the text aurality of the autonomous stage directions is reduced, a possible future second recording might translate the text aurality differently, for instance by doing without the fictional embedding, or by having another (fifth?) voice utter the initial stage directions so that a level of narrative mediation emerges. The artistic choices of a possible future recording notwithstanding, it should have become clear that the narrative mode emerging in the "autonomous" manifestations of an overt presenting agency indicates an intermedial tension between text and recording, and thus indicates a transgeneric similarity between the script genres of playtext and radio script. In order to further develop this argument, the next section turns to a radio script that makes use of undefined or ambiguous stage directions, namely Samuel Beckett's *Cascando* (1963).[19]

Ambiguous Stage Directions in Samuel Beckett's *Cascando*

Samuel Beckett's *Cascando*—a radio play that can be read as a reflection on artistic creation and authorship—features two speakers, namely "OPENER" and "VOICE." An additional third instance is "MUSIC," whose utterances are shown as dots in the text (see the following).[20] The stage directions (i.e., the inquit formulas "OPENER:" "VOICE:" and "MUSIC:") introduce MUSIC as

---

19. See also Pim Verhulst's audionarratological exploration of *Cascando* in this volume.
20. When MUSIC and VOICE can be heard together, Beckett does not make use of a split page but annotates their "voices" in two parallel lines. This typographical representation of simultaneity (and the fact that both MUSIC's and VOICE's lines feature dots) would be worth exploring in more detail but exceeds the scope of this chapter. See, however, Caroline Kita's exploration of simultaneity in audio fiction in this volume.

a character alongside OPENER and VOICE.[21] None of the three, however, are defined in terms of age and gender. Only with regard to OPENER, the dialogue explicitly designates a male voice. This can be seen, for instance, when OPENER refers to what "they"—an undefined group of critics?—say about him (his work?):

> OPENER: So, at will.
>   They say, It's in his head.
>   It's not. I open.
> VOICE:—falls . . . again . . . on purpose or not . . . can't see . . . [. . .] . . . he
>   goes down . . . sea—
> OPENER (*WITH* VOICE): And I close.
>   *Silence.*
>   I open the other.
> MUSIC: . . . .
>   . . . .
> OPENER (*WITH* MUSIC): And I close.
>   *Silence.*
>   So, at will.
>   It's my life, I live on that.
>   *Pause.* [. . .]
>   What do I open?
>   They say, He opens nothing, he has nothing to open, it's in his head.
>   They don't see me, they don't see what I do, they don't see what I have,
>   and they say, He opens nothing, he has nothing to open, it's in his
>   head.
>   I don't protest any more, I don't say any more, There is nothing in my
>   head.
>   I don't answer any more.
>   I open and close. (Beckett 1968: 12–13)

The pronouns ("he" and "his") in this passage clearly indicate that "they" refer to OPENER as a man (and OPENER does not oppose this). OPENER, however, denies that VOICE is a voice in his head when he says, "It's not. I open" and claims, farther down, "There is nothing in my head." Only at a later point

---

21. Hence, through its use of inquit formulas, the script clearly suggests an equality of the three characters or voices. In a recording of *Cascando*, however, their relationship is likely to remain more ambiguous or to only gradually clear as listeners might (initially) misconceive or "naturalize" MUSIC's expression as mere (background) music despite the fact that OPENER explicitly states "I open the other" (Beckett 1968: 10).

in the text, one of OPENER's lines suggests that he considers changing his opinion and regarding both MUSIC and VOICE as voices in his head:

> OPENER: They said, It's his, **it's his voice**, it's in his head.
> *Pause.*
> VOICE:—faster... scudding... rearing... plunging... heading nowhere ... for the island... then
> no more... elsewhere... anywhere... heading anywhere... lights—
> *Silence.*
> OPENER: **No resemblance.**
> I answered, And that...
> MUSIC (*BRIEF*): . . . .
> . . . .
> *Silence.*
> OPENER: ... **is that mine too?**
> But I don't answer any more (Beckett 1968: 16; my emphasis)

Up to this point, the ambiguity of the text would make it possible for a recording to have VOICE spoken by a woman in order to underline OPENER's assertion that there is "no resemblance" between him and VOICE. However, both the first production in French on France Culture and the English version for the BBC Third Programme uniformly chose to have VOICE spoken by a man.[22] Having VOICE spoken by a man, both recordings implicitly answer OPENER's last question ("... is that mine too?") in the affirmative. Thus, not only do they reduce the ambiguity that predominated the script up to this point, but, from the beginning, they turn OPENER into an unreliable voice, a voice that (at first) denies that both VOICE and MUSIC are voices in his head.[23] Interpreting *Cascando* biographically, such recordings turn this radio play into a reflection of authorship that is clearly linked to Beckett. Admittedly, Beckett himself must have favored such interpretations—he was, after all, strongly involved in the French recording. Nonetheless, I hope to have shown that the radio script allows for different readings and recordings—for instance, for one that categorically refutes biographical interpretations by recording VOICE with a female speaker. Also, in theory, it would be pos-

---

22. The French production premiered on October 13, 1963 (L'Ouvreur: Roger Blin; La Voix: Jean Martin), the English version on October 6, 1964 (Voice: Patrick Magee; Opener: Dennis Hawthorne; director: Donald McWhinnie).

23. For a discussion of how sound perception facilitates narrative unreliability and ambiguity in radio drama and how this differs from written narratives, see the chapter by Jarmila Mildorf in this volume.

sible to have the same actor speak both VOICE and OPENER, which would reduce the script's ambiguity even further. Just like two existing ones, both these possible productions, however, would inevitably reduce the text's ambiguity by giving either an implicitly negative or an implicitly affirmative answer to OPENER's question concerning the identity of both VOICE and MUSIC. In other words, the ambiguity of stage directions in Beckett's *Cascando* clearly corroborates the need for a medium-specific perspective that differentiates between script and recording.[24] While in both the French and the English recording of Beckett's *Cascando* textual ambiguity is reduced, the 2000 recording of Harold Pinter's *A Slight Ache* (1959) provides a contrasting example.

The Ambiguity of Sound in Harold Pinter's *A Slight Ache*

Harold Pinter's *A Slight Ache* revolves around the fears and desires of a married couple (Flora and Edward), who invite a silent matchseller into their house. The play focuses mostly on the husband and his fears of the unknown, of growing old, and ends with the silencing of the husband and his taking the tray of matches from his wife, who has decided to adopt the matchseller as both her lover and child. *A Slight Ache* has been performed in two different media. A recording of the play premiered on BBC's Third Programme on July 9, 1959 (director: Donald McWhinnie, Edward: Maurice Denham, Flora: Vivien Merchant). One and a half years later, McWhinnie directed a theater production with three actors (in the roles of Edward, Flora, and the matchseller), which premiered on January 18, 1961, at the Arts Theatre, London. Note how in contrast to the later theatrical version of *A Slight Ache,* McWhinnie's recording only featured two speakers for the voices of Edward and Flora (the silent role of the matchseller was not performed by a speaker).[25] Several

---

24. In this volume, Verhulst presents a complementary argument concerning *Cascando,* which takes the work's genesis into account and elucidates whether (or not) OPENER can be regarded as a "generative narrator" in the sense of Brian Richardson (1988), as a character who is "ontologically distinct from the figures who emerge from or are engendered by his discourse" (209), namely VOICE and MUSIC. See also Tom Vandevelde's (2013) narratological analysis of this radio script, which ponders this and two additional possible conceptualizations of OPENER's role and their respective narratological implications.

25. However, listeners' expectations were thwarted since BBC publicity material "billed . . . a third character with the name of a fictitious actor" (Esslin qtd. in Stulberg 2015: 515). Indeed, the entry from July 29, 1959, in the BBC archive (https://genome.ch.bbc.co.uk/34ae196 12c484b33b99d68843f2ce5ee) lists David Baron, the stage name Pinter used between 1954 and 1960 (Raby 2009: xii–xiii). The entry, however, does not bill Baron in the role of the Matchseller but as "Barnabas," the name given to the character by Flora in the second half of the play (Pinter 1991: 8). Thus, listeners' expectations were even further thwarted "in order to enhance

scholars have compared the recording favorably to the theater production and discussed how the radio play, in particular, exploits the ambiguity of sound in order to create the sense of menace and conflict that is often seen as a defining characteristic of Pinter's work. Martin Esslin (1973), for instance, has praised the openness of the recording: "But in its radio form the play is bound to be more effective, because then it can remain open whether the central character, the matchseller, who never speaks, actually exists or is no more than a projection of the two other characters' fears" (87).[26] Victor L. Cahn (1993) likewise claims that

> the object of contention, the matchseller, reminds us of the disparity between the dramatic forms of radio and stage. On radio, a character who never speaks cannot make his presence felt, and we are ultimately left to question whether he exists at all. . . . On stage, however, the matchseller is tangible, a living being not quite realistic nor quite symbolic. The ambiguity is less subtle. (13)

The ambiguity of sound that critics like Esslin and Cahn have foregrounded in their analyzes of the play, however, contrasts sharply with the unambiguous stage directions of the published script, as the following extract from scene 1 demonstrates:

> FLORA: [. . .] I'll join you . . . later. (*She goes out.*)
> The MATCHSELLER *stands on the threshold of the study.*
> EDWARD (*cheerfully*): Here I am. Where are you?
> (*Pause.*)
> Don't stand out there, old chap. Come into my study.

---

the suspense of the play" (Esslin qtd. in Stulberg 2015: 515). Moreover, "Barnabas," as Stulberg (2015) has pointed out, is not only an equally fictitious name in the context of the play but also intertextually alludes to the process of renaming as chronicled in the New Testament (516). Barnabas (not to be confused with Barabbas) is first mentioned in Acts 4:36–37: "Joseph, a Levite from Cyprus, whom the apostles called Barnabas [which means 'son of encouragement'] sold a field he owned and brought the money and put it at the apostles' feet" (see http://www.biblica.com/bible/niv/acts/4/).

26. Several Pinter critics have made a similar point. Randall Stevenson (1984), for instance, writes: "Similarly, radio drama offers the possibility of leaving open any questions about the real or imaginary status of characters, as Pinter successfully illustrates in the mysterious figure of the matchseller" (45). See also the concurring statements by Mary Jane Miller, Rüdiger Imhof, and Elissa Guralnick, quoted in Jacob Stulberg's article (2015: 508). The latter, however, points out that Pinter "did not merely push back against the conventions of 'radio drama' as an abstract concept," but rather "challenged a specific set of practices in place at the 1950s BBC" (Stulberg 2015: 509).

(*He rises.*) Come in.

The MATCHSELLER *enters.*

That's right. Mind how you go. That's . . . it. Now. Make yourself comfortable. Thought you might like some refreshment on a day like this. Sit down, old man. (Pinter 1991: 22)

In the BBC 4 recording from October 13, 2000, directed by Ned Chaillet, featuring Pinter himself in the role of Edward alongside Jill Johnson in the role of his wife Flora, sounds of footsteps and of rustling clothes can be heard, but listeners cannot be sure whether these sounds are made by the silent matchseller or by the character of Edward, moving through the room (0:16:34–0:17:21). In other words, listeners can decode the sounds but not ascertain their source. Therefore, in contrast to the script, it remains unknowable to listeners of the recording whether Flora humors (or even shares) her husband's fear of the (nonexistent) matchseller—or whether the play as a whole is set in Edward's mind.

Even though the recording's paratexts suggest that a third actor was involved by listing Albert Stokes in the role of the matchseller,[27] this information should be treated with caution since Albert Stokes is (also?) a character in Pinter's radio play *A Night Out*, which premiered on BBC Third Programme on March 1, 1960 (Raby 2009: xiii). Therefore, it is likely that the practice of billing a third speaker in the BBC publicity material of the 2000 recording reiterates that of the radio play's premiere (see note 25). In addition, the recording's alterations of, and additions to, the script do very little to disambiguate sound. In the above scene, one such addition to the script includes Edward counting from 3 to 8 and then calling "Come in!" (0:16:39–0:16:53). Each number uttered by Edward is preceded by a stepping, thumping (or rather knocking?) sound. The regularity of these sounds makes it difficult to denote them as "footsteps." Is Edward really simultaneously counting the steps of the matchseller—or is he rather producing the tapping sounds himself? Or, are these latter sounds to be perceived as internally focalized, providing an insight into Edward's mind and lending a sense of "impending doom" to the nearing of the matchseller?

Similarly, at a later point in the (imagined or real) confrontation between Edward and the silent matchseller, again only readers of the radio script are clearly informed by the stage directions that the matchseller's "tray falls":

---

27. See http://genome.ch.bbc.co.uk/cc0d7d5a0ef340e1b31d44dc99783ef5.

EDWARD: [...] Well now, before the good lady sounds the gong for petit déjeuner will you join me in an apéritif? I recommend a glass of cider. Now... just a minute... I know I've got some—Look out! Mind your tray!
The tray falls, and the matchboxes.
Good God, what...?
(*Pause.*)
You've dropped your tray.
Pause. He picks the matchboxes up.
(*Grunts.*) Eh, these boxes are all wet. You've no right to sell wet matches, you know. Uuuuuuggh. (Pinter 1991: 25–26)

Indeed, in the 2000 recording, listeners can hear something fall (0:23:18–0:23:45) but cannot know what kind of object has caused this particular sound and whether it confirms the existence of the matchseller—or whether it is rather indicative of Edward's beginning psychosis and of the play being set in his mind. Only Edward's remark "You've dropped your tray" retrospectively explains and disambiguates the earlier sound, encouraging listeners to believe in the existence of the matchseller. Nevertheless, the ontological status of the sound (whether it is focalized through, imagined, or even produced by Edward or "real") remains uncertain.

Summing up: In *A Slight Ache,* Pinter—by building his radio play around a silent character and transforming the setting into a mindscape—challenges the conventions of the BBC's Drama Department at the time, which, as Jacob Stulberg (2015) points out in his article on "Pinter and the BBC," promoted a clear and coherent on-air style (509–10).[28] Moreover, the ambiguity of sound in the recording of *A Slight Ache* takes up a narrative function that the radio script only acquires implicitly, prompting listeners to perceive the play's setting as a mindscape and to regard the character of the matchseller as a symbol. Ultimately, if we consider the creation of a silent character as a self-reflexive way of challenging the (implied) intermedial transition from page to radio play, both script and recording foreground and reflect on genre- and medium-specific conventions and the intermedial gap between the two.

A similar relation between script and recording characterizes Beckett's *Embers* (1959). In this radio script, stage directions unambiguously inform readers of the ghost-like quality of the encounter between the protagonist

---

28. Both the recent date of the recording and the fact that Pinter was involved as an actor make it unlikely that the ambiguity of sound was accidental, for example a result of poor recording equipment. Moreover, according to Stulberg (2015), already the first recording for the BBC's Third Programme "stirred up a miniature tempest among the BBC's leadership" (503).

Henry and his wife Ada: "HENRY: [. . .] Are you going to sit down beside me?—ADA: Yes. (*No sound as she sits.*)" (Beckett 1970: 27) Even though, in the 1959 recording, indeed no sound can be heard when Ada sits down (0:17:46–0:17:48),[29] listeners, however, are likely to miss the absence of sound as—in contrast to the script—the recording does not make them explicitly aware of it. Moreover, as Jarmila Mildorf contends in this volume, reading about (the absence of) sounds affects recipients in a different way than (not) hearing the sounds themselves. Therefore, Ada's "unnatural" ontological status is less prominent in the radio play than it is in the script. Arguably, in *Embers*, the ambiguity of the recording's soundscape makes it more likely that listeners perceive the entire play as a mindscape, a dream or a reflection on artistic processes of composing and conducting,[30] while the radio script, starting with stage directions unambiguously referring to the "*sea scarcely audible*" (Beckett 1970: 21) as the source of the soundscape, only gradually unfolds a ghostly or dreamlike quality.

Conclusion

The examples discussed here have shown how central the relationship and intermedial tension between text and recording in radio scripts is and how it can be captured through a transgeneric narratological approach placing the text more center stage again. Considering the disparities and intersections between the two script genres of playtext and radio script as well as the related processes of their production, distribution, and reception from a narratological point of view, in particular, has helped to account for the autonomous nature of stage directions in radio scripts and to analyze them as overt manifestations of a superordinate narrative agent. Even though this chapter's focus was primarily on the transgeneric transfer of narrative theory, it also contributes to the project of a transmedial narratology (see most recently Thon 2016) based on the broader claim that its findings concerning radio scripts might apply to other, if not all, script genres.

---

29. Time indications refer to the 1959 production that was broadcast as part of BBC's Third Programme (Henry: Jack MacGowran; Ada: Kathleen Michael; director: Donald McWhinnie).

30. On the meta-musical dimension of orchestration in both *Embers* and *Cascando*, see Ojrzynska (2016).

Works Cited

Beck, Alan. 1999. "Is Radio Blind or Invisible? A Call for a Wider Debate on Listening-In." World Forum for Acoustic Ecology (WFAE). http://ecoear.proscenia.net/wfaelibrary/library/articles/beck_blindness.pdf.

Beckett, Samuel. 1968. "Cascando." In *Cascando and Other Short Dramatic Pieces*, 7–19. New York: Grove.

———. 1970. "Embers." In *Krapp's Last Tape and Embers*, 21–39. First published 1959. London: Faber & Faber.

Bernaerts, Lars. 2016. "Voice and Sound in the Anti-Narrative Radio Play." In *Audionarratology: Interfaces of Sound and Narrative*, edited by Jarmila Mildorf and Till Kinzel, 133–48. Berlin: De Gruyter.

———. 2017. "Hybride en multimodaal: Nieuwe genretheorie en het literaire hoorspel vandaag." *Cahier voor Literatuurwetenschap* 9: 113–25.

Cahn, Victor L. 1993. *Gender and Power in the Plays of Harold Pinter*. New York: St. Martin's Press.

Carlson, Marvin. 1991. "The Status of Stage Directions." *Studies in the Literary Imagination* 24, no. 2: 37–48.

Cascando. 1964. Directed by Donald McWhinnie, script by Samuel Beckett. Aired October 6, 1964, on BBC Third Programme.

Crimp, Martin. 2005. "Attempts on Her Life." In *Plays 2*, 197–284. London: Faber & Faber.

Dorleijn, Gillis, Ralf Grüttemeier, and Liesbeth Korthals Altes, eds. 2007. *The Autonomy of Literature at the Fins de Scièles (1900 and 2000): A Critical Assessment*. Leuven: Peeters.

Embers. 1959. Directed by Donald McWhinnie, script by Samuel Beckett. Aired June 24, 1959, on BBC Third Programme.

Esslin, Martin. 1973. *Pinter: A Study of His Plays*. First published 1970. London: Methuen.

Fielding, Henry. 1731. *The Tragedy of Tragedies, or, the Liee [sic] and Death of Tom Thumb the Great. As it is Acted at the Theatre in the Hay-market. With Annotations of H. Scriblerus Secundus*. London.

Goldstone, Andrew. 2013. *Fictions of Autonomy: Modernism from Wilde to de Man*. Oxford: Oxford University Press.

Hauthal, Janine. 2009. *Metadrama und Theatralität: Gattungs- und Medienreflexion in zeitgenössischen englischen Theatertexten*. Trier: WVT.

———. 2018a. "Text (und) Theatralität: Gattungs- und Medienreflexion frühneuzeitlicher Dramendrucke am Beispiel von Henry Fieldings *Tragedy of Tragedies*." In *Zur Druckgeschiche und Intermedialität frühneuzeitlicher Dramendrucke*, edited by Alexander Weber, 79–96. Berlin: LIT.

———. 2018b. "Towards a Narrative Aesthetic? The Scarcity of Stage Directions as (Text)Theatrical Challenge in Plays by Crimp, Ravenhill and Stephens." *Zeitschrift für Literaturwissenschaft und Linguistik* 48, no. 3: 541–59.

Höfele, Andreas. 1991. "Drama und Theater: Einige Anmerkungen zur Geschichte und gegenwärtigen Diskussion eines umstrittenen Verhältnisses." *Forum Modernes Theater* 6, no. 1: 3–23.

Hühn, Peter, and Roy Sommer. 2012. "Narration in Poetry and Drama." *The Living Handbook of Narratology*, edited by Peter Hühn et al. Hamburg: Hamburg University Press. http://lhn.sub.uni-hamburg.de/index.php/Narration_in_Poetry_and_Drama.html.

Issacharoff, Michael. 1989. *Discourse as Performance*. Stanford: University of California Press.

Jahn, Manfred. 2001. "Narrative Voice and Agency in Drama: Aspects of a Narratology of Drama." *New Literary History* 32: 659–79.

Korthals, Holger. 2003. *Zwischen Drama und Erzählung: Ein Beitrag zur Theorie geschehensdarstellender Literatur.* Berlin: Erich Schmidt.

Krechel, Ursula. 2012. "Wenn man ein gleichschenkliges Dreieck auf den Kopf stellt." Unpublished manuscript. Frankfurt: Verlag der Autoren.

Mildorf, Jarmila, and Till Kinzel. 2016. "Audionarratology: Prolegoma to a Research Paradigm Exploring Sound and Narrative." In *Audionarratology: Interfaces of Sound and Narrative,* edited by Jarmila Mildorf and Till Kinzel, 1–26. Berlin: De Gruyter.

Ojrzynska, Katarzyna. 2016. "Music and Metamusic in Beckett's Early Plays for Radio." *Beckett and Musicality,* edited by Sara Jane Bailes and Nicholas Till, 47–62. London/New York: Routledge.

Pfister, Manfred. 1991. *The Theory and Analysis of Drama.* First published 1988. Cambridge: Cambridge University Press.

Pinter, Harold. 1991. "A Slight Ache." In *A Slight Ache and Other Plays,* 7–40. London: Methuen.

Poschmann, Gerda. 1997. *Der nicht mehr dramatische Theatertext: Aktuelle Bühnenstücke und ihre dramaturgische Analyse.* Tübingen: Niemeyer.

Raby, Peter, ed. 2009. *The Cambridge Companion to Harold Pinter.* First published 2001. Cambridge: Cambridge University Press.

Rajewsky, Irina O. 2002. *Intermedialität.* Tübingen/Basel: A. Francke/UTB.

———. 2005. "Intermediality, Intertextuality, and Remediation: A Literary Perspective on Intermediality." *Intermédialités* 6: 43–64.

Richardson, Brian. 1988. "Point of View in Drama: Diegetic Monologue, Unreliable Narrators, and the Author's Voice on Stage." *Comparative Drama* 22: 193–214.

Schenk-Haupt, Stephan. 2007. "Narrativity in Dramatic Writing: Towards a General Theory of Genres." *Anglistik* 18, no. 2: 25–42.

Shaw, George B. 1921. *Heartbreak House: A Fantasia in the Russian Manner on English Themes.* Leipzig: Bernhard Tauchnitz.

A Slight Ache. 2000. Directed by Ned Chaillet, script by Harold Pinter. Aired October 13, 2000, on BBC 4.

Stevenson, Randall. 1984. "Harold Pinter—Innovator?" In *Harold Pinter: You Never Heard Such Silence,* edited by Alan Bold, 29–60. London: Vision.

Stoppard, Tom. 1975. *Travesties.* London: Faber & Faber.

Stulberg, Jacob. 2015. "How (Not) to Write Broadcast Plays: Pinter and the BBC." *Modern Drama* 58, no. 4: 502–23.

Thon, Jan-Noël. 2016. *Transmedial Narratology and Contemporary Media Culture.* London/Lincoln: University of Nebraska Press.

Vandevelde, Tom. 2013. "'I OPEN': Narration in Samuel Beckett's *Cascando*." *Samuel Beckett Today / Aujourd'hui* 25, no. 1: 253–65.

Weidle, Roland. 2009. "Organizing the Perspectives: Focalization and the Superordinate Narrative System in Drama and Theatre." *Point of View, Perspective, and Focalization: Modelling Mediation in Narrative,* edited by Peter Hühn et al., 221–42. Berlin: De Gruyter.

Wenn man ein gleichschenkliges Dreieck auf den Kopf stellt. 2013. Directed by Hans Gerd Krogmann, script by Ursula Krechel. Aired May 23, 2013, on SWR 2.

Zipfel, Frank. 2001. *Fiktion, Fiktivität, Fiktionalität: Analysen zur Fiktion in der Literatur und zum Fiktionsbegriff in der Literaturwissenschaft.* Berlin: Erich Schmidt.

3

Narrative Mediation and the Case of Audio Drama

LARS BERNAERTS

IN NARRATIVE THEORY, "mediation" is the term used for the narrative (rather than "medial") channels through which a story is presented to an audience. It stands for the way stories are presented to an audience, or more precisely, it is the ascription of agency to the narrative arrangement of signifiers. When processing a radiophonic narrative, the listener attributes a degree of narrative coherence to the flow of sounds and thereby assumes an organizational force. For now, mediation needs to be formulated in quite abstract terms, simply because the narrow sense of mediation as the anthropomorphic narrator or reflector cannot hold from a media-conscious point of view. In other words, for reasons that will become clear, I abandon the position that mediation is restricted to the idea of an identifiable mediating authority (a narrator).

In particular, this chapter discusses the nature, conventions, and devices of narrative mediation in the auditive art of the radio play, a term I will use as synonymous with "audio drama." It will focus mainly on one dimension of mediation, namely the narrative function, rather than another, the perspectival function. In the view that will be developed here, mediation structures the recipients' experience. At the same time, it emerges from their experience that the narrative is structured in a particular way. The multimodal structure of mediation—that is, the way the combined sign systems of audio drama are deployed and interpreted—relies on strategies of storytelling familiar from other media, such as film, drama, and literature. This approach acknowledges the medial, rhetorical, as well as the cognitive dimensions of mediation, and to that end it will turn to a range of postclassical narratologies. Before embarking upon a theoretical discussion of the intricacies of narrative mediation, I present two telling cases to indicate what exactly is at stake.

The Power of Mediation

The Mercury Theatre on the Air featuring Orson Welles performed a free interpretation of H. G. Wells's novel *The War of the Worlds* (1898) on October 30, 1938. As part of a weekly series of radio adaptations, the episode was preceded by, among others, Bram Stoker's *Dracula*, Arthur Schnitzler's *The Affairs of Anatol*, and Alexandre Dumas's *The Count of Monte Cristo* in the weeks before (Welles, Bogdanovič, and Rosenbaum 1994). Consequently, the audience would have been familiar with the conventions of audio drama. Still, the response to what later would become an international classic in the repertoire of radio drama was quite different, as we know. The story about the invasion of Martians allegedly caused panic among the listeners, perhaps precisely because of the way it deviated from familiar storytelling conventions. In a synthesis of the research into the well-documented reaction, the radio scholar Tim Crook (1999: 105–14) suggests a range of explanatory factors: the psychology of radio communication, the media historical background, the social-political moment inspiring anxiety (the world was on the brink of war), Orson Welles's deliberate aims and talent, the realist quality of the performance, and the programming schedule. From a narratological point of view, however, what stands out and undoubtedly added to the primary audience's response are the features of narrative mediation.

The invasion narrative of *The War of the Worlds* is mediated by a structure resembling that of the breaking news story: An entertainment program is interrupted by a series of news bulletins and live reports. However, the transmission of the story is further dependent upon a higher-order narrator, who presents himself at the beginning of the broadcast and then again—but "out of character"[1]—at the end of the piece. The narrator is announced as "the director of the Mercury Theatre and star of these broadcasts, Orson Welles" and introduces the story. In that capacity, he is similar to the narrator of a prologue in a play, who enters the stage before the action starts (Richardson 1988: 195). This particular narrator immediately ushers the listener into a fictional world and is also affiliated with the conventions of an extradiegetic novelistic

---

1. The character played by Welles is that of Richard Pierson, a professor of astronomy.

narrator. The audience is immersed in a "present" that is both familiar and strange:

> We know now that in the early years of the twentieth century this world was being watched closely by intelligences greater than man's, yet as mortal as his own. (00:37–00:50)

> In the thirty-ninth year of the twentieth century came the great disillusionment.
> Near the end of October. Business was better. The war scare was over. More men were back at work. Sales were picking up. On this particular evening, October 30, the Crosley service estimated that thirty-two million people were listening in on radios. (01:55–02:20)

The introduction is immediately followed by a weather forecast, which starts mid-sentence and establishes a following level of narrative mediation, based on the conventions of radio programming. By contrast, in accordance with novelistic conventions, the higher-order narrator frames himself as an authorial, retrospective narrator. Since the play is broadcast on October 30 (not coincidentally the day before Halloween), however, the narrator is located in a future vis-à-vis the story and the audience's temporal coordinates. The framed narrative is situated in a present that is signaled as past at the outset. On that level, the narrative is mediated by a narrative voice external to the invasion story but belonging to the same story world.

In the scenes that follow, the play switches from epic, diegetic conventions to a mimetic strategy of enacting the narrative. By adopting the format of a news bulletin, the events are presented directly to the narratee (i.e., the listener of the fictional radio broadcast) and the actual and authorial audience as defined by rhetorical narratology (Phelan 2018). More accurately, the piece uses the audiophonic and linguistic conventions of "breaking news" in a strict sense (a bulletin interrupting regular programming) and eyewitness reporting. In fact, "interruption" becomes a distinct rhetorical figure in *The War of the Worlds* that engenders an illusion of immediacy. Not just the programmed music by Ramón Raquello and his orchestra, but also witness reports are suddenly interrupted. What also contributes to the illusion of immediacy are electroacoustic effects, diegetic sounds, and the use of first-person present-tense narration in the eyewitness reports. For example, Carl Phillips, a correspondent at Grovers Mill, New Jersey, turns from a merely observing into an experiencing character while describing the Martian creatures:

> Good heavens, something's wriggling out of the shadow like a gray snake. Now it's another one and another one and another one. They look like tentacles to me. There, I can see the thing's body. It's large, large as a bear and it glistens like wet leather. But that face, it . . . Ladies and gentlemen, it's indescribable. I can hardly force myself to keep looking at it—so awful. The eyes are black and gleam like a serpent. [. . .] This is the most extraordinary experience. I can't find words . . . I'll pull this microphone with me as I talk. I'll have to stop the description until I can take a new position. Hold on, will you please, I'll be right back in a minute. (15:45–16:37)

Philips's present-tense narration and the concomitant frantic intonation and electroacoustic sound of the audio equipment immerse the listener into the scene. In that way, the play aspires to convey an immediacy of experience, for which it employs journalistic conventions of narrative mediation.

In short, it is safe to say that the narrative's principal rhetorical effects are contingent on the structure of narrative mediation. The strategies of mediation in *The War of the Worlds* demonstrate the way authority, reliability, and credibility are encoded in the mediation. Also, they are modelled on novelistic and journalistic conventions. In that connection, the radio play's mediation is characterized by the dynamics of remediation, as defined by Jay Bolter and Richard Grusin (2000). It trades on effects of hypermediacy and immediacy by, on the one hand, emphasizing the technological and material conditions (the audio equipment, the microphone, radio transmission) and, on the other hand, creating a strong sense of direct presence in the scene for the audience. I would argue that the frequent switches from announcer to reporter, the interruptions, and the references to the infrastructure of the radio are the equivalent of what Bolter and Grusin (2000) describe for new visual media (e.g., the multiplicity of windows in a computer interface): "The logic of hypermediacy acknowledges multiple acts of representation and makes them visible" (34). In *The War of the Worlds,* the multiplicity is made audible as part of the narrative mediation.

My second case is an international classic as well, albeit in another respect. The Dutch novel *Max Havelaar* was published in 1860, and its English translation by Roy Edwards became part of the Penguin Classics series. Known not just for its attack of the colonial system in the Dutch East Indies (today Indonesia) but also for its highly effective, complex narrative structure (Sötemann 1981; Vervaeck 2012), *Max Havelaar* shows us that the mediation is the message. The structure of an extradiegetic narrator (i.e., a narrator at the highest diegetic level; Genette 1980: 228) and two alternating intradiegetic narrators (i.e., situated within the story told by the extradiegetic narrator) with further embedded narratives echoes the hierarchical system of the colonial administration, which the novel mocks and protests against. When the novel undermines the established hierarchical structure of mediation, as we will see in a moment, it attacks the colonial system as well.

There are two adaptations for the ear, one of which was broadcast on May 15, 2010, by the Dutch public broadcaster AVRO and then distributed on CD. In the final scene of the radio play, the higher-order narrator Multatuli interrupts the narrative voice that was speaking, sends away all the other narrators, and stresses that the preceding narrative should be read as a charge against the Dutch for the way they treat the Javanese in the Dutch East Indies:

> Enough, my good Stern! I, Multatuli, take up the pen. You are not required to write Havelaar's life story. It is enough, Stern, you may go.
>
> I make no apology for the form of my book. It seemed suitable to me for the attainment of my object. I wanted to be heard. I wanted to be heard by politicians, who are obliged to keep an eye on the signs of the times . . . by merchants who have an interest in the coffee auctions . . . by ex-Governors-General in retirement . . . by Ministers in office . . . by preachers, who will say that I am attacking Almighty God . . . by the thousands of specimens of the tribe of Droogstoppel, who will be the loudest in joining in the chorus about the "prettiness" of my writings while they continue to go about their business . . . by the members of the House of Representatives, who ought to know what is going on in the great Empire beyond the seas which belongs to the Realm of the Netherlands.
>
> Yes, I will be heard!
>
> When this object is attained, I shall be satisfied. "The story is chaotic . . . its pace is too variable . . . striving for effect . . . the style is bad . . . no talent . . . no structure . . ."
>
> Right, right . . . all right! But . . . THE JAVANESE IS MALTREATED! (2010: track 9, 03:39–05:00)[2]

Contrary to the case of *The War of the Worlds*, the salient gesture of interruption *breaks* the illusion instead of contributing to it. In both cases, the interruption impacts the audience's experience of mediation. Here, the narrator Multatuli reveals himself as the narrator of the whole piece. Within the purview of the novel, this means that there was an extradiegetic narrator all along, but he remained hidden until the end. This reminds us that mediation

---

2. My own translation from the Dutch radio play is based on the English translation by Roy Edwards (Multatuli 1987: 317–19).

is also in flux during a reading; it is not only a product, as it is often described, but also a process. In the words of Jan Christoph Meister and Jörg Schönert (2009): "There is no one narrative instance; rather 'it' is something that is in flux and can change throughout every reading: it is a function, rather than a given" (14). Meister and Schönert are critical of narratology's tendency to neglect the process and to "re-interpret [the process] by way of stratificatory models" (14). In *Max Havelaar*, the narrator remains hidden, and so the experience of mediation shifts, although Genette's model[3] (1972) would have us identify a fixed extradiegetic narrator.

In my view, both the process and the a posteriori reconstruction are fundamentally relevant to the interpretation of a narrative. The listener of *Max Havelaar* is tricked into believing that the story is presented by the alternating narrators Batavus Droogstoppel and Ernest Stern. Only in that way can the novel demonstrate how the Dutch people are constantly tricked by the discourses of trade, liberal politics, and religion that legitimate the colonial abuses. It is the first narrator, Droogstoppel, that embodies these discourses, while Stern increasingly sides with the rebel Max Havelaar, whom he gets to know through a pile of manuscripts he is reading for Droogstoppel. In the course of the narrative, Stern becomes the ethically and rhetorically favored, though somewhat sentimental, narrator and Droogstoppel remains the sober but unreliable and morally suspect bourgeois. The reading process evoked by the processual dimension of mediation is thus key to the interpretation.

For the radio play, the language of the narrator is not the only channel through which narrative information is provided. To begin with, we hear not only words (language in a strict sense) but also a physical, distinctly male voice. We can hear a soundscape—sounds of nature, birds, insects—evoking the setting to which the main character of the novel belongs. We can hear extradiegetic music that runs as a thread through the whole piece and equally conjures up the *couleur locale* of the Dutch East Indies. All of these semiotic modes are part of the structure of narrative mediation in the sense that they convey narrative information and construct a view on the events and story world. This being the case, the question is how we can identify and approach narrative mediation in audio drama. While we would be tempted to analyze Multatuli as the extradiegetic narrator of the novel, the radio play urges us to think twice: If he is the mediating figure on the highest level,

---

3. In his *Discours du récit* (1972), Genette builds a theory of narrative discourse that differentiates between issues of voice (relations between the teller and what is told), mood (focalization and the representation of thought and speech), and tense (relations between the time of telling and that of the events in terms of order, duration, and frequency).

then where does the narratively relevant information of sound and music come from?[4]

A Media-Conscious Approach

In view of the issues raised by the two examples, it is necessary or at least worthwhile to revisit the notion of narrative mediation itself. The aim of this chapter is to reconsider it from the perspective of audio drama. Drawing on extant views in classical and postclassical narratology, the chapter explores what is typical of audio drama mediation, and how the case of audio drama even nudges us to recalibrate theoretical discussions on this topic. The underlying observation is that core concepts in narrative theory still bear the traces of the context in which they were first developed. Considering them from the vantage point of another medium (e.g., radio drama) or sensory channel (e.g., the aural), we can achieve a more solid and less biased theoretical framework.[5]

As Marie-Laure Ryan (2004, 2005) has explained, and as many others in transmedial narratology have demonstrated, media construct narratives in divergent ways, which is clear when one takes adaptations into account: "A core of meaning may travel across media, but its narrative potential will be filled out, actualized differently when it reaches a new medium" (Ryan 2005: 1). Yet, since classical narratology started as a language-based and more particularly a literary narratology, it exhibits a degree of media blindness, Ryan suggests. This bias affects the definition of mediation as well. Classical narratology often puts forward language-based narratives as the norm "because" they allow us to identify a narrator. In turn, narrators are often thought of as anthropomorphic instances. The "somebody" in James Phelan's rhetorical definition of a narrative ("somebody telling somebody else on some occasion and for some purpose that something happened"; Phelan 2018: 1) is easily taken to be a humanlike figure, and the primary association with the "telling"

---

4. What complicates the structure of mediation even more is the existence of a script, in which stage directions are included. The stage directions suggest yet another level of mediation. This complexity is further discussed in the chapter in this volume by Janine Hauthal.

5. Transmedial narratology and audionarratology will be major resources in this chapter, but notions from cognitive, unnatural, and rhetorical narrative theory will prove useful to approach mediation in audio drama as well. Rather than setting different narratological strands against each other, this chapter explores the compatibility of specific ideas and tools from these divergent strands in narrative theory (see Herman et al. 2012). In order to address narratological problems that are clearly delineated—such as narrative mediation in audio drama—such a multifaceted approach is beneficial.

in this definition is language, although Phelan himself explicitly includes narrative across media (such as the visual rhetoric of graphic novels). The means of communication need not to be verbal in the rhetorical definition. In those other media, the structure of mediation is different—events can be performed by actors on a stage or evoked by a sequence of diegetic sounds (a slamming door, a car engine, . . .) in a radiophonic piece—but that does not mean there is no narrative or no mediation at all.

In addition to this linguistic bias, audionarratology and sound studies have pointed out the visual bias of narrative theory (Mildorf and Kinzel 2016), which surfaces in omnipresent metaphors such as "perspective," "point of view," or "showing vs. telling." Even transmedial narratology is oriented toward visual and textual media (multimodal novels, graphic novels, video games, film). Listening to audiophonic narratives, however, we can become sensitive to the auditory counterparts of narrative concepts. In its technological and semiotic realization, audio drama shifts the attention from point of view to point of audition and from showing to sonically enacting. In a next step, we can use this awareness of auditory meaning-making to clarify, for example, the differences between auditory and visual focalization in novelistic fiction. What characters hear does not always chime with what they see, the omnidirectional nature of sound implies a different experience than a character's visual focus, and so on. The perceptivity required by the radio play can thus improve narratological precision in the analysis of other media as well.

The study of audio drama can aid in debunking the visual bias and can advance the media-conscious approach that has become dominant in narratology. What is interesting about the perspective of audio drama is not only the distinctiveness of auditory signification but also the range of multimodal strategies of narrative mediation. Audio drama exploits a variety of semiotic modes to regulate the narrative flow (including music, noise, silence, and voices) and it borrows conventions from media and genres such as film, music, the novel, and drama. Therefore, we need a dynamic, flexible model of mediation, which both acknowledges the range of narrative and semiotic modes constituting mediation and takes the listener's experience into account. To put the latter in necessarily circular terms: Mediation is a structure experienced by an audience, and at the same time the audience's experience of a narrative shapes mediation. In this context, "experience" is considered as temporal and doubled, as Jonas Grethlein (2018) conceptualizes it: It is temporal because it relies on memory and expectations; it is doubled because the experience of the reader is "directed toward the character's [and the narrator's] experiences" (284).

Mediation: Why Care?

If the narratological study of mediation may seem overspecialized at times, one should bear in mind that a lot is at stake when we turn this concept. The issue goes to the heart of narrative meaning-making and narratological inquiry. Let us consider some of these issues in relation to audio drama and the examples introduced earlier. First, mediation is intertwined with the authority of authentication. Lubomír Doležel (1998) conceptualizes "authentication" as the power to bring something into existence within a fictional world. A heterodiegetic narrator in a realist novel—a narrator who is not a character in the story he or she is telling—typically has this kind of power. In the example of *Max Havelaar*, the higher-order narrator exploits this power in a metaleptic gesture and poses as what Brian Richardson (2001) terms a "generative narrator" in the context of theater: "He generates a fictional world . . . in a manner similar to that of an omniscient narrator" (685).

Still, it is the audiophonic composition that holds sway in this respect. The piece starts, for example, with gamelan music that helps to set the scene in the East Indies and then fades into the sound of church bells. The church bells introduce the faithful Christian Batavus Droogstoppel. A subtle but corrosive narrative irony inheres in the analogy between the gamelan bells and the church bells into which they fade. This irony is not mediated by Droogstoppel, but by the ensemble of semiotic modes. The issue leads us to the idea that the study of mediation requires an insight into the semiotic makeup of a narrative. Semiotic modes work together to give the audience the impression that some force is organizing the experience of the narrative. The question, then, is to which degree we permit technical interpretations of what narration is and what narrators do. Narrative information does not only come from a narrative voice in a strict sense but can also be encoded in the typography and segmentation in a book, or the music and sound in a radio play. In the view that I wish to develop in this chapter, this means that we should acknowledge this interaction of semiotic modes as part of structures of mediation.

Second, in putting together pieces of narrative information and building an image of mediation, the role of the listener's experience and background knowledge is vital. The mediation in *The War of the Worlds*, for example, requires an understanding of radiophonic and journalistic conventions as it refers to the speech register and pragmatic and semiotic composition of the radio bulletin (Dunne 2005). If the reader is not familiar with these conventions, the effect and even the nature of the mediation are affected, as the story of the panic after the broadcast exemplifies. On that count, narrative mediation cannot be separated from the listening experience.

Finally, the two examples demonstrate that mediation can bring about different degrees of immediacy. In *The War of the Worlds*, the mediation is geared to the illusion of immediacy and presence. Similarly, radio plays that resemble drama in consisting only of dialogue afford this kind of experience, unlike radio plays in which the story is told by a narrator. This issue touches upon the classical distinction between mimetic and diegetic genres, which has been questioned with regard to drama (Richardson 1988: 197) and which is even more shaky when it comes to audio drama. Later in this chapter, I will return to the relevance of the narratology of drama for the study of radio plays.

The question of mediation matters because in individual narratives it is inextricably bound to ethical and epistemological positions, to questions of rhetoric, agency, knowledge, power, authority, credibility, and reliability. The rhetorical effects of *The War of the Worlds* rely on the audience's belief in the authority and reliability of news bulletins, reporters, professors, and even the broadcasting system as a whole. As I mentioned before, the metaleptic gesture in *Max Havelaar* is analogous to the main character's efforts to effect change in the hierarchy of the colonial administration. The analogy already demonstrates how mediation involves power relations.

There are also reasons to distrust a general concept of narrative mediation. Franz Stanzel's insistence upon the main differentiation between a teller mode and a reflector mode as options for mediation, for example, can obscure the distinction between the act of narrating and the center of perception, which is to say narration and focalization. From a Genettean perspective, we could perhaps simply do away with the vague term "mediation" and consistently opt for more precise descriptions of enunciatory and perspectival aspects of narrative.

Still, mediation is clearly relevant in the experience of the narrative's audience—the spectator, reader, listener. When we are listening to a radiophonic piece, we experience a succession and simultaneity of sounds in which we identify patterns, some of which are narrative. In this experience, these sounds are organized, presented to us. Also, mediation is useful as a heuristic category in narrative theory. As soon as we start describing the composition of narratives with their double chronology, the reordering of a fabula in a szujet (which is a defining principle, according to Genette and Chatman), we are positing a structure that organizes and presents configurations of characters and their actions in certain settings.

In the context of intermediality and transmedial narratology, the notion of mediation regains significance. Without having to equate mediation to mediality, one can see how the mediation of a narrative is realized not simply on the level of what Chatman in *Story and Discourse* (1978) calls transmission, but also on the level of "manifestation" or "actualization." This is the level of the substance of the expression in Chatman's terms, which depends on the medium. It concerns the "how" rather than the "what" of the narrative. In sum, mediation is an experienced structure that occurs across narrative media but that is also medium-specific in its realization. This idea brings us to the heart of the debates around the concept, to which I will now turn.

Mediation in Narrative Theory

As Jan Alber and Monika Fludernik show in their 2011 contribution to the *Living Handbook of Narratology*, mediation quickly became one of the founding concepts of classical narratology, but it is also a contested one. At the beginning of Franz Stanzel's *Theorie des Erzählens* (2001), mediation (*Mittelbarkeit*) is presented as a defining characteristic of narrative (*Erzählung*). In the wake of earlier German theories of the novel and epic fiction, in particular Käte Friedemann's 1910 study, Stanzel introduces mediation as the feature that distinguishes narrative from drama.

The idea that narrative mediation is bound to one particular medium and genre lives on in narrative theory up until today, not only in Stanzel's version but also in the version of narratologists such as Genette (also in *Nouveau discours du récit*, 1983) who restrict narrative to verbal transmission and identify "narrative with diegesis and drama with mimesis" (Chatman 1990: 110).[6] In a helpful and thorough synthesis of the discussions, Wolf Schmid (2010) distinguishes between "mediated" and "mimetic narrative texts." In the latter case, the "story is portrayed without a mediating narrative authority" (7). Here, too, the idea of mediation is restricted to that of a figure somehow explicit or present. From a transmedial perspective, however, the limited view is simply untenable. As Chatman (1990) puts it in *Coming to Terms*, the "double chronology" of narrative can be either enacted or recounted (110–11)—enacted as in drama, or recounted as in a novel. Both are narrative, both are mediated, since mediation goes hand in hand with narrative. However, it should be distinguished from the genetic function of invention. Invention is attributed to an author, who also "invents" the narrative mediation for his or her text. In the case of radio plays, the genetic function is distributed between the members of an entire production team.

If we understand mediation as a function and as a structure of experience, the narrating instance is not necessarily an anthropomorphic figure. In

---

6. For Genette (1972), the key elements of mediation are focalization or mode, narration or voice, and temporal ordering.

the case of cinema, which is an important point of reference for the medium of the radio play, Chatman (1990) sees the narrator as "the composite of a large and complex variety of communicating devices" (134). I concur with this view but suggest replacing "communicating devices" by "devices that regulate narrative experience." As Marisa Bortolussi and Peter Dixon (2001) and Luc Herman and Bart Vervaeck (2017: 614–15) have argued, the model of communication obscures the fact that it is the reader in his or her own context who constructs meaning from a text: "The so-called communication model is a legitimation of a readerly construction" (Herman and Vervaeck 2017: 614). Hence the notion of "experience" in my discussion (Herman and Vervaeck, for their part, argue for the concepts of "negotiation" and "circulation" as alternatives). It is presented here as a dialectic counterpart of "structure": Mediation is both structure and experience.

In accord with Chatman's view, Manfred Jahn (2003) has defined a theoretical agency for film narration that can be adapted for the analysis of mediation in audio drama, as it considers the technological and multimodal aspects of mediation while at the same time doing justice to the spectator's role. Here is his definition of a filmic composition device, or FCD:

> The theoretical agency behind a film's organization and arrangement, assumed to be guided by maxims of giving efficient, sufficient, and relevant information. The FCD selects what it needs from various sources of information and arranges, edits, and composes this information for telling a filmic narrative. A film shows us what the FCD has arranged for us to see. (§F4.1.2)

His proposal is also based on a communicative model, more specifically on H. P. Grice's pragmatic notion of the cooperative principle. This means that the sender is assumed to give appropriate, relevant, and reliable information that fits the nature of the conversation. Since the sender is abstract and absent, though, and the receiver is constructing this sender, it is desirable to take into account the receiver's expectations, mental models, and experience. To a certain extent, this approach will always remain hypothetical, but cognitive poetics and the results of empirical research do allow us to plausibly reconstruct the mental processes involved in comprehending the narrative of a radio play.

In keeping with Jahn's proposal, mediation in the radio play is also ascribed to a multimodal composition device, an assumed agency that arranges and presents narrative information through the available and selected semiotic modes. This composition device can be called audiophonic. Elsewhere in this book, Siebe Bluijs examines the implications of this model for how we analyze and interpret focalization in audio drama. For the radio play this means that narrative mediation emerges as an ensemble of available semiotic modes that make up the audiophonic composition device. In particular, as Götz Schmedes (2002) has theorized in *Medientext Hörspiel*, the main semiotic modes of audio drama are language, voice, music, sound, silence, montage, mix, and stereophony. Individual radio plays realize narrative mediation through a selection and combination of these modes.

As a consequence, mediation cannot be seen separately from the radio play's multimodality. It may be a sound effect, say reverberation, that conveys the size of a space that a narrator would describe in a novel. In fact, an entire story could be told through the reproduction of sounds with a reality effect, also known as the art of Foley. Montage and mix, techniques of cutting and editing also add to the way the mediation manifests itself. In *Max Havelaar*, the audiophonic composition device often mixes the voices of narrators and characters with sounds of nature and underscores emotional or otherwise meaningful passages with gamelan music. In that way, the mediation rhetorically leans toward the main character and the Javanese in this piece.

Elke Huwiler, who developed a narratology of audio drama in her 2005 book *Erzähl-Ströme im Hörspiel*, states that the radio play therefore has a "non-personalized narrating instance . . . that utters the acoustic (non-verbal) signs, as well as a focalizing instance that determines the 'perspective' from which the story is perceived by the hearer"[7] (103)—so a narrator similar to Jahn's composition device and a focalizer. What is missing in this view, however, is (1) an account of the dynamics of remediation, which strongly affects narrative mediation in the radio play, and (2) an account of the listener's cognitive response as part of the structure of mediation.

Audio drama exploits the conventions of mediation dominant in other media and genres. As a more marginal genre, the radio play is part of a whole network of genres and media from which it borrows and then transforms conventions. Due to its history as a relatively marginal genre, the radio play is strongly susceptible to the dynamics of remediation as described by Bolter and Grusin (2000). It derives its identity from the differences from and similarities to other media. A lot of radio plays import the conventions of drama, whereas others present themselves as movies for the ear, as dramatized novels or as spoken opera's (e.g., the German "Funkoper" in the thirties). A radio play can stage a succession of dialogues, as in theatrical plays; it can introduce the voice of a narrator external to the story world, as in a novel; it can realize mediation through music, mix, and montage, as in cinema—it is telling,

---

7. "nicht-personifizierte erzählende Instanz . . . , die die akustischen (nicht-verbalen) Zeichen äußert, sowie eine fokalisierende Instanz, die regelt, von welchem 'Blickwinkel' aus die Geschichte durch die Hörenden wahrgenommen wird."

on the one hand, that the adaptation of *Max Havelaar* is paratextually presented as an audio*film* (CD cover). On the other hand, a higher-order narrator interrupting the narrative with a metafictional gesture strongly reminds us of novelistic conventions and practices. For this reason, it makes sense to understand the narrator in *Max Havelaar* as a "framing storyteller" (Thon 2016: 159) and therefore consider the extradiegetic narrator as being in charge, as it were, of the non-narratorial representation as well.

So, the imported conventions also shape what a listener experiences as mediation in the radio play. Therefore, the radio play requires a flexible model of narrative mediation that takes this importation and transformation into account. In other words, we should differentiate between a technical, stratificatory, and heuristic analysis on the one hand and a cognitive, processual, and phenomenological analysis on the other hand.

Multimodality across Media and the Role of Experience

The multimodal composition can be conceptualized as part of the narrative mediation, as theorists have done for other media as well. In *Transmedial Narratology and Contemporary Media Culture*, Jan-Noël Thon (2016) discusses a number of these proposals, such as the idea of a "monstrator" (Groensteen) in the graphic novel (146–48) or the "intrigant" (Aarseth) in videogames (149). Thon himself is skeptical of the tendency to "attribute the representation of storyworlds to a 'narrating instance'" (151) that is not clearly defined and present. Still, in such cases of non-narratorial presentation, we cannot ignore that information relevant to the narrative progression is presented to us. In order to acknowledge this narrative function, we need to include it in our analysis of mediation.

By invoking discussions from film and transmedial narratology, I do not simply wish to "borrow insights from" other fields. My transmedial approach is informed by the intrinsic dynamics of the radio play: The genre displays a historically strong contiguity to other media (film, TV, literature, etc.), as I already mentioned. In that respect, the narratology of drama is of particular relevance as well. As several narratologists have argued in recent decades (Jahn 2001; Nünning and Sommer 2002; Rajewsky 2007; Richardson 1988, 2001), drama and narrative are not in any way opposed to each other. There is a strong tradition of including narrating instances on the stage (Richardson 2001), even beyond the "Episierung" in the wake of Brecht (Rajewsky 2007: 44). These scholars have described various types of narrative mediation in drama, including the anonymous organization of semiotic modes or the option of an actual narrator figure on stage. This reflection upon drama *as* narrative and upon narration in drama is partly transposable to the study of audio *drama*, where narrators can also be performed and where narrative can also be enacted rather than recounted. In sum, in accounting for the radio play's structure of mediation, it is logical and useful to turn to the narratology of film, drama, and literature rather than just adopting or imposing one particular medium-based model.

Let us add a final piece of the puzzle and complete the idea of mediation through a multimodal composition device as a structure of experience. In methodological terms, the view from transmedial narratology is only part of the story; a view from cognitive narratology has to supplement it, since narrative mediation comes into being in the audience's experience and in the act of attributing narrative agency, of ascribing a function of mediation to the work.

Monika Fludernik's view of mediation in *Towards a "Natural" Narratology* is based on such a cognitive approach. It goes beyond Stanzel's distinction between teller mode and reflector mode by situating all mediation in cognitive schemata and by liberating narrativity from the idea of plot and double chronology. There can be narrative without plot, but there will always be a form of mediation through the cognitive schemata of telling (cf. teller mode), experiencing (cf. reflector mode), viewing (cf. focalization), or reflecting (cf. consciousness). These schemata correspond to types of mediation distinguished in other narratological models such as the narrator, the reflector, and focalization. The most basic frame is that of experientiality itself, which denotes "the quasi-mimetic evocation of real-life experience" (Fludernik 1996: 12). The ultimate force of mediation and narrativity itself is the projection of human experience.

Narrativity equals "mediated experientiality," as Fludernik (2018) emphasizes again in a recent discussion of her earlier theory (340), and experientiality is distinct from "experience" in that it refers to the "dynamics of tellability and point" (343). In anchoring experientiality in the reader's embodied (quasi-) experience, she paved the way for theories of embodiment and narrative such as Marco Caracciolo's work. Caracciolo (2014) theorizes how the reader's mind and body in this respect co-create mediation. It is the embodied imagination of the reader that turns semiotic cues into characters' experiences, for example. Conversely, the material signs regulate the reader's experience, so that not just anything goes. The sounds of a radio play structure that experience *and* the structure is a result of the reader's projection of experience.

This account of how mediation works intends to bridge the gap between an objective ("structure") and a subjective ("experience") conceptualization, both of which are unsatisfying in itself. Though the proposal remains theoretical, the ideas are consistent with cognitive endeavors such as the cognitive linguistics that feeds Fludernik's theory or the philosophy of mind and enactivism prominent in Caracciolo's approach. Ideally, this proposal would be further substantiated with empirical findings. A lot of empirical work in narrative studies has been done in describing the cognitive processes of story and discourse comprehension (see, e.g., Graesser 1981; Kintsch 2010; Zwaan 1993), rarely including listening comprehension (see Kuzmičová 2016 on audiobooks), but to the best of my knowledge there is no empirically founded account of how narrative *mediation* (as opposed to the mental representation of events, characters, and space) is processed in listening. Still, the idea of mediation as experience and structure can be empirically tested along the lines Marisa Bortolussi and Peter Dixon (2003) sketched in their empirical study of narrative aspects. In their view, narrators emerge as readerly constructs based on "explicit attributions" and "inference invitations" (80–81) in narrative texts. This view, which they flesh out in their empirical work, can be adopted for future investigations of narrative mediation in audio drama as well.

Conclusion

To recapitulate, narrative mediation should be defined in a broad transmedial sense to include narratives traditionally seen as mimetic and even non-narrative, as opposed to narratives with a distinct and often humanlike narrator. In this broader definition, which is in keeping with a media-conscious approach and recognizes the transmedial occurrence of narrative concepts (see Thon 2016), mediation is experienced as a structure, an agency that regulates the flow of narrative information, which can be, but does not have to be, embodied by a distinct entity (either human or nonhuman).

Narrative mediation is a structure of experience *and* the experience of a structure. There is no useful way out of this circularity, since we want to acknowledge on the one hand the extent to which material and technological aspects contribute to mediation and on the other hand the experience of the audience in which it is ascribed. Narrative mediation in audio drama cannot be adequately described or understood if we restrict it to the presence of a humanlike narrator and to the words spoken by narrative voices. The mediation experienced by the radio play's audience emanates from a multimodal composition device. However, the audiophonic conventions of mediation strongly rely on the conventions familiar from other genres and media. Narrative mediation is thus not just audiophonic composition but always also a result of "re-mediation."[8]

8. I am grateful for the generous exchange of ideas with other authors in this book, of which this chapter has benefited. In particular, I wish to thank Janine Hauthal and Jarmila Mildorf for their thoughtful and helpful comments.

Works Cited

Alber, Jan, and Monika Fludernik. 2011. "Mediacy and Narrative Mediation." In *The Living Handbook of Narratology*, edited by Peter Hühn et al., Hamburg: Hamburg University Press. https://www.lhn.uni-hamburg.de/node/28.html.

Bolter, Jay David, and Richard Grusin. 2000. *Remediation. Understanding New Media*. Cambridge: The MIT Press.

Bortolussi, Marisa, and Peter Dixon. 2001. "Text Is Not Communication: A Challenge to a Common Assumption." *Discourse Processes* 31, no. 1: 1–25.

———. 2003. *Psychonarratology: Foundations for the Empirical Study of Literary Response*. Cambridge: Cambridge University Press.

Caracciolo, Marco. 2014. *The Experientiality of Narrative: An Enactivist Approach*. Berlin: De Gruyter.

Chatman, Seymour. 1978. *Story and Discourse. Narrative Structure in Fiction and Film*. Ithaca: Cornell University Press.

———. 1990. *Coming to Terms: The Rhetoric of Narrative in Fiction and Film*. Ithaca: Cornell University Press.

Crook, Tim. 1999. *Radio Drama: Theory and Practice*. London: Routledge.

Doležel, Lubomír. 1998. *Heterocosmica: Fiction and Possible Worlds*. Baltimore: The Johns Hopkins University Press.

Dunne, Anne. 2005. "Radio News and Interviews." In *Narrative and Media*, edited by Helen Fulton, Rosemary Huisman, Julian Murphet, and Anne Dunn, 203–17. Cambridge: Cambridge University Press.

Fludernik, Monika. 1996. *Towards a "Natural" Narratology*. London: Routledge.

———. 2018. "*Towards a 'Natural' Narratology* Twenty Years After." *Partial Answers* 16, no. 2, 329–47.

Friedemann, Käte. 1969. *Die Rolle des Erzählers in der Epik*. First published 1910. Darmstadt: Wissenschaftliche Buchgesellschaft.

Genette, Gérard. 1972. *Figures III*. Paris: Seuil.

———. 1980. *Narrative Discourse: An Essay in Method*. Translated by Jane E. Lewin. Ithaca: Cornell University Press.

Graesser, Arthur C. 1981. *Prose Comprehension beyond the Word*. New York: Springer-Verlag.

Grethlein, Jonas. 2018. "More than Minds: Experience, Narrative, and Plot." *Partial Answers* 16, no. 2: 279–90.

Herman, David, James Phelan, Peter J. Rabinowitz, Brian Richardson, and Robyn Warhol. 2012. *Narrative Theory: Core Concepts and Critical Debates*. Columbus: The Ohio State University Press.

Herman, Luc, and Bart Vervaeck. 2017. "A Theory of Narrative in Culture." *Poetics Today* 38, no. 4, 605–34.

Huwiler, Elke. 2005. *Erzähl-ströme im Hörspiel: Zur Narratologie der Elektroakustischen Kunst*. Paderborn: Mentis.

Jahn, Manfred. 2001. "Narrative Voice and Agency in Drama: Aspects of a Narratology of Drama." *New Literary History* 32: 659–79.

———. 2003. "A Guide to Narratological Film Analysis." In *Poems, Plays, and Prose: A Guide to the Theory of Literary Genres*. English Department, University of Cologne. http://www.uni-koeln.de/~ame02/pppf.htm.

Kintsch, Walter. 2007. *Comprehension: A Paradigm for Cognition*. Cambridge: Cambridge University Press.

Kuzmičová, Anežka. 2016. "Audiobooks and Print Narratives: Similarities in Text Experience." In *Audionarratology: Interfaces of Sound and Narrative*, edited by Jarmila Mildorf and Till Kinzel, 217–37. Berlin: De Gruyter.

Max Havelaar. 2010. Directed by Marlies Cordia, script by Melissa Prins based on the novel by Multatuli. Hoorspelfabriek.

Meister, Jan C., and Jörg Schönert. 2009. "The DNS of Mediacy." In *Point of View, Perspective, and Focalization: Modeling Mediation in Narrative*, edited by Peter Hühn, Wolf Schmid, and Jörg Schönert, 11–40. Berlin: De Gruyter.

Mildorf, Jarmila, and Till Kinzel. 2016. "Audionarratology: Prolegomena to a Research Paradigm Exploring Sound and Narrative." In *Audionarratology: Interfaces of Sound and Narrative*, edited by Jarmila Mildorf and Till Kinzel, 1–26. Berlin: De Gruyter.

Multatuli. 1987. *Max Havelaar or The Coffee Auctions of the Dutch Trading Company*. Translated by Roy Edwards. London: Penguin.

Nünning, Ansgar, and Roy Sommer. 2002. "Drama und Narratologie: Die Entwicklung erzähltheoretischer Modelle und Kategorien für die Dramenanalyse." *Erzähltheorie transgenerisch, intermedial, interdisziplinär*, edited by Vera Nünning and Ansgar Nünning, 105–28. Trier: Wissenschaftlicher Verlag Trier.

Phelan, James. 2018. "Authors, Resources, Audiences: Toward a Rhetorical Poetics of Narrative." *Style* 52, no. 1–2: 1–34.

Rajewsky, I. O. 2007. "Von Erzählern, die (nichts) vermitteln. Überlegungen zu grundlegenden Annahmen der Dramentheorie im Kontext einer transmedialen Narratologie." *Zeitschrift für französische Sprache und Literatur* 117, no. 1: 25–68.

Richardson, Brian. 1988. "Point of View in Drama: Diegetic Monologue, Unreliable Narrators, and the Author's Voice on Stage." *Comparative Drama* 22, no. 3: 193–214.

———. 2001. "Voice and Narration in Postmodern Drama." *New Literary History* 32, no. 3: 681–94.

Ryan, Marie-Laure. 2004. Introduction to *Narrative across Media. The Languages of Storytelling*, edited by Marie-Laure Ryan, 1–40. Lincoln: University of Nebraska Press.

———. 2005. "On the Theoretical Foundation of Transmedial Narratology." In *Narratology Beyond Literary Criticism: Mediality, Disciplinarity*, edited by Jan-Christoph Meister, 1–24. Berlin: De Gruyter.

Schmedes, Götz. 2002. *Medientext Hörspiel: Ansätze einer Hörspielsemiotik am Beispiel der Radioarbeiten von Alfred Behrens*. München: Waxmann.

Schmid, Wolf. 2010. *Narratology: An Introduction*. Berlin: De Gruyter.

Sötemann, A. L. 1981. *De structuur van Max Havelaar. Bijdrage tot het onderzoek naar de interpretatie en evaluatie van de roman*. Groningen: Wolters-Noofdhoff,.

Stanzel, Franz K. 2001. *Theorie des Erzählens*. Göttingen: Vandenhoeck und Ruprecht.

Thon, Jan-Noël. 2016. *Transmedial Narratology and Contemporary Media Culture*. Lincoln: University of Nebraska Press.

Vervaeck, Bart. 2012. "Seeing the Real: Word and Image in *Max Havelaar*." In *150 Jahre Max Havelaar. Multatuli's Roman in neuer Perspektive*, edited by Jaap Grave, Olf Praamstra, and Hans Vandevoorde, 17–39. Frankfurt am Main: Peter Lang.

The War of the Worlds. 1938. Directed by Orson Welles, script by Howard E. Koch based on the novel by H. G. Wells. CBS Radio.

Welles, Orson, Peter Bogdanovič, and Jonathan Rosenbaum. 1994. *This Is Orson Welles*. New York: Da Capo Press.

Zwaan, Rolf. 1993. *Aspects of Literary Comprehension: A Cognitive Approach*. Amsterdam: Benjamins.

4

Earwitnessing

Focalization in Radio Drama

SIEBE BLUIJS

IN HIS FAMOUS STUDY on the medium of the radio, Rudolf Arnheim (1936) elaborates on the possibility of representing subjective experience by purely acoustic means in the (at the time relatively new) art form of the radio play:

> With the help of distance it is possible to introduce a perspective vector in the dramatic situation similar to the "shooting-angle" in photography and film. By certain sounds coming from near at hand while simultaneously others come from farther away, the listener is given, so to speak, a definite observation post within the scene, from which he gets a subjective grasp of the situation. (86)

In this passage, Arnheim brings up several issues related to focalization in radio drama.[1] His choice of words also points to some of the potential problems that arise when the narratological concept is applied to the radio play. To an extent, these problems are inherent to the term's genealogy. As Shlomith Rimmon-Kenan (2002) points out, the concept of focalization is "not free of optical-photographic connotations" (72). The term "focalization" is derived from media such as photography and film, making the term's visual bias hard

---

1. The term had not been coined at the time the book was published, but precursory concepts such as *point of view* and *reflector* (James 1972) were already in use (see Niederhoff 2011).

to avoid (Bal 2009: 147). Describing a purely acoustic phenomenon, Arnheim circumvents visual terminology by using more encompassing terms like "observation post" and "subjective grasp." But at the same time, he also references visual media to consider perspective in the radio play.

As Arnheim's term "perspective vector" indicates, the subjective point of audition is suggested through the relative position of sounds within the acoustic "space."[2] The dimensions of this space are most optimally suggested when different sounds are presented simultaneously. In Arnheim's time, the acoustic space of a radio play was projected on a one-dimensional axis: In monaural sound, reproduction sounds could only be positioned relative to the acoustic "foreground" and "background." Technological advancements (particularly the introduction of stereophony) have expanded this space into a multidirectional sound experience. Arnheim emphasizes that in radio drama, a complex amalgam of auditory layers is created through the editing and the superimposition of various sounds. This chapter builds on approaches that differentiate among these layers by examining auditory signs such as sound effects, volume, and stereophonic mixing to understand how these elements are employed to suggest a "perspective vector" of the narrative.

Audionarratology

Although the genre has existed for almost a century now, radio drama has been largely overlooked by narratology. Recent publications—including the current volume—are signs that the tide is turning (see also Huwiler 2005a; Mildorf and Kinzel 2016). The emergence of "audionarratology" fits into a larger trend within narratology of increasing attention to narrativity in a variety of media (Ryan 2014). Considering the radio play's connection to different media and genres (see Bernaerts 2017), it is not surprising that theory on the radio play draws from different traditions. Film narratology is perhaps the most obvious starting point for a narratology of the radio play.

Film—an art form that roughly emerged at the same time as the radio play—has been within the purview of narratology for several decades. In this tradition of film narratology, narrative sound elements have been prominent objects of study. Leading film narratologists have extensively paid attention

---

2. R. Murray Schafer (1993) points out that spatial terms gain different meanings in relation to sound, as space is determined differently in sound than in the visual realm (31). Chion (2009) offers a similar observation when he states that sound—unlike the visual shot—lacks a clear frame (226). These scholars emphasize that with regard to sound, space is not a container, but rather a dimensional effect that is manifested *in* sound.

to film's auditory dimension. David Bordwell (1985), for instance, theorizes the filmic possibility of temporal simultaneity through the overlap of sound events (77) and pays attention to sound as a means of suggesting off-screen space (120). Like Bordwell, Edward Branigan (1992) understands sound alongside other filmic techniques in relation to narrative functions. Seymour Chatman (1978) pays attention to the auditory channel's possibility of presenting a divergent temporality from the visual channel to evoke "partial or split flashbacks," the most commonly used device in this regard being the filmic voice-over (64). Following these film scholars in his handbook on film narratology, Peter Verstraten (2008) distinguishes an auditory narrator from a visual narrator—both of which are embedded in the narration of the encompassing "filmic narrator" (more on the implications of this distinction in the following). Other film theorists have even put sound center stage in their analysis. John Belton and Elisabeth Weis (1985) provide an overview of the theoretical discussions on film sound and offer an account of innovative uses of sound in film history, as well as suggestions for aspiring filmmakers.[3] Michel Chion (2009) has argued that a film's visual aspects cannot be considered separate from the audiovisual. He even takes the "sound" of "silent" cinema into consideration, arguing that this latent or implied sound layer continues to have an effect in the era of sound film.

Radio play scholars have turned to film studies to understand acoustic phenomena. Tim Crook (1999), for example, has adopted Chion's vocabulary of film sounds for the radio play (81–89). Throughout his book on radio, Arnheim (1936) uses film as a framework to understand the particularities of radio drama. These references to film (studies) are not surprising, since there are clear similarities between film and radio drama: The arrangement of events in the radio play, for example, is analogous to the montage techniques in film. But although film and radio drama share a number of equivalent storytelling devices and organization principles, radio drama cannot simply be understood as "film without images" (nor as "theater for the blind," as the genre has also been referred to). Sonic equivalents of filmic elements such as camera choices (such as tracking shots, pans, close-ups) or editing choices (such as cuts, dissolves, fade-outs) are not so easily transferable to the medium of the radio play.

Therefore, as Elke Huwiler (2016) explains, "a narratological methodological model for analysing audio drama must include special terminology for describing the medium-specific features of this art form" (101). She provides

---

3. It should be pointed out that a lot of sound innovations that became well-known through film and television were first developed for the radio.

such a model, based on Götz Schmedes's exposition of radio drama's semiotic elements, in her book *Erzähl-Ströme im Hörspiel* (Huwiler 2005a). These elements are voice, music, noise, fading, cutting, mixing, the (stereophonic) positioning of the signals, electroacoustic manipulation, original sound (actuality), and silence (Huwiler 2005a: 57; Schmedes 2002). Huwiler emphasizes the important distinction between voice and language. Language refers to the words a character or the narrator uses, whereas voice connotes more specific material qualities including intonation and pitch, or a character's accent. With her emphasis on the medial aspects, Huwiler opened the radio play to postclassical narratology. She stresses that her model does not aim to offer a definitive exposition of the semiotic elements in relation to narrative devices, since, as she argues (following Bordwell), "every acoustic sign can in principle assume any narrative function within a specific context" (Huwiler 2016: 103). Therefore, "in a narratological analysis of a radio play the functions of the different features can only be described within the scope of that particular play" (Huwiler 2005b: 53; see also Huwiler 2005a: 224).

In her book, Huwiler (2005a) introduces the concept of focalization to the radio play. She provides several examples of the representation of subjective experiences by the characters, shifts in focalization, and the difference between the focalizing instance and the focalized object. The subtitle of Huwiler's book—*zur Narratologie der elektroakustischen Kunst* (*Towards a Narratology of Electroacoustic Art*)—indicates that the topics of her study require elaboration. This chapter wants to further develop these insights by exploring different kinds of focalization in the radio play (external/internal, successive/simultaneous focalization). In a theoretical discussion and four case studies, it examines questions such as: How can internal and external focalization be distinguished in the radio play? How can different narrative levels be determined through auditory effects? How can transitions between internal and external focalization be realized through sound? Is it possible to present external and internal focalization simultaneously in the radio play? The field of sound studies is helpful since it provides a clearer grasp of specific sound phenomena and offers a specialized terminology to understand focalization in the radio play. And, as indicated, film narratology provides a model that includes other elements than language, and it has paved the way in its attention to narrative sound elements.

In the second part of this chapter, I will turn to four examples of Flemish and Dutch radio plays to demonstrate how focalization is suggested by means of (a combination of) medium-specific elements. The examples display four different kinds of focalization in the radio play, which also increase in complexity. In order of appearance, these are (1) static and exclusively external,

(2) exclusively internal (with shifts between two internal focalizers), (3) shifts between external and internal, and (4) simultaneously external and internal. The final radio play in particular showcases the constraints and affordances of the medium, as it employs several semiotic elements of the radio play simultaneously to evoke internal and external focalization at the same time. The analysis of how focalization is achieved through acoustic means offers an entrance point for interpreting the narrative of these radio plays.

Defining Focalization in the Radio Play

Huwiler points out that the purely auditory nature of the radio play calls for a revision of the narratological terminology. Considering the "perspective vector" in radio drama, is it perhaps better to distinguish auditory focalization, or "auricularization" (a term borrowed from William Nelles), as Bartosz Lutostański has argued (2016: 120)? I would like to make a case for the term "focalization" in the radio play. As the selected case studies make clear, the senses are often interfused. Furthermore, "focalization" is an overarching term for experiences that extend beyond a sensory paradigm and include remembering and projecting (Bal 2009: 150).[4] Rimmon-Kenan (2002) has claimed that the term "has to be broadened to include cognitive, emotive and ideological orientation" (72). Crook (1999) points out that auditory signals can evoke images in the mind when he writes that radio drama "is auditory in the physical dimension but equally powerful as a visual force in the psychological dimension" (8). Or, as Jarmila Mildorf and Till Kinzel (2016) put it: "Is there perhaps a mutual cognitive influence or even interdependence between sound and image in certain kinds of aural genres and formats?" (13).

To focus solely on instances of auditory focalization leaves out other acts of focalization that are expressed in (or translated into) sound. In other words: Since radio drama is a purely auditory medium, subjective experience is always expressed in sound, but the nature of this subjectivity is not necessarily related to the sense of hearing (by the characters or by the narrator). Avoiding the term "focalization" in fear of its visual connotations runs the risk of enforcing the misconception that the radio play is a blind medium (see Crook 1999: 53–54; Hand and Traynor 2011: 35–36). Instead, the medium-specific qualities

---

4. As Alessandra Calanchi (2015) points out, the realm of the imaginary is infused with occularcentric terminology—the term "imagination" itself being a case in point: "While it may seem difficult to 'imagine' or 'visualize' with our ears, it is certainly possible to think of a sound. Well, it is curious that we do not have a verb in the English or American language to define this 'acoustic imagination,' an expression which is used by scholars but is an obvious oxymoron" (12).

of the radio play call for a reevaluation of the presumed visual bias of focalization. For instance, focalization is associated with the optical notion of "bringing into focus." As one of the case studies (*Vernissage*) illustrates, however, the human ear is able to "focus" its attention as much as the eye.

The difference between focalization, perspective, and point of view is a controversial topic within narratology (Hühn, Schmid, and Schönert 2009; Nieragden 2002). Central to this debate is Mieke Bal's revision of Gérard Genette's term (Niederhoff 2014). Genette's (1988) concept of focalization is famously based on a differentiation between "who is *telling*" and "who is *perceiving*" (64). Genette never precisely defined the term, but Henrik Skov Nielsen (2013) has extracted the following definition: "Focalization = restriction of access to point of view" (75; see also Nieragden 2002). This definition differs from Bal's (2009) definition, which conceptualizes focalization as "the relation between the 'vision,' (which includes other modes of perception) the agent that sees, and that which is seen" (149).

Bal's differentiation of a focalizing subject (focalizer) and a focalized object indicates that she understands focalization and narration in relation to power structures. She clarifies the relation between narrator and focalizer in terms of embeddedness: The narrator tells a story, the content of which is a "vision," either from the narrator or one of the characters (Bal 1981b: 44–45). With regard to the medium of the radio play, however, this relation of embeddedness gives rise to an important question: If a radio play conveys a narrative through various sonic elements, who or what can be considered the "narrator"? Bal's (2009) definition of a narrative "text" is a helpful starting point:

> A *narrative text* is a text in which an agent or subject conveys to an addressee ("tells" the reader) a story in a particular medium, such as language, imagery, sound, buildings, or a combination thereof. (5)

Bal's emphasis on the medium is of importance here. The subject or agent that conveys a story in a radio play does so purely in sound (coincidentally one of the media Bal mentions above). Rather than a sound décor that is mimetic or entirely realistic, the radio play is conventionally composed of sound elements that are meaningful in relation to the narrative (Hand and Traynor 2011: 143; McWhinnie 1959: 24; see also Huwiler 2016: 100).

Film narratology provides a model that includes semiotic elements other than language into the act of narration. As Manfred Jahn (2003) explains: "A film narrates not by speaking but by arranging and composing information from various sources" (F4.1.2.). He introduces a theoretical agent, the filmic composition device (FCD), that "selects what it needs from various sources of information and arranges, edits, and composes this information for telling a filmic narrative. A film shows us what the FCD has arranged for us to see" (F4.1.2.). In his narratological model, the FCD is an overarching entity that embeds all the other narrative levels. In analogy to the FCD, one can posit an audiophonic composition device (ACD) for the radio play: a theoretical agent that narrates by arranging and composing sonic layers and auditory elements (see also Bernaerts in this volume). I would like to emphasize that the ACD functions primarily as a theoretical entity; it is not to be confused with the author (of the script) or the director of the radio play, nor is it an "implied author." Rather than a pragmatic concept for a narratological model, the implied author is a "semantic category," and as such belongs to a different realm (Bal 1981a: 209). By introducing the theoretical entity ACD, I wish to avoid the intentional fallacy, the idea that there is an (anthropomorphic) agent "behind" the text who is ultimately responsible for the arrangement of elements. In my view, the mental projection of an implied author runs the risk to "naturalize" inherent tensions and contradictions that may exist within the text. The use of the ACD, on the other hand, allows for ambiguities and contradicting interpretations to exist together.[5]

Although the film narratologist Peter Verstraten does not mention Jahn, he suggests a similar narratological model for film. He makes a distinction between a narrator on the visual level and a narrator on the auditory level (Verstraten 2008: 129). He then introduces a narrator on a higher narratological level that regulates these two narrators. This narrator is "responsible" for any coordination between these two sublevel narrators: The film's soundtrack can complement, reflect on, or counter the information on the visual level. Verstraten claims that film is distinct from literature precisely because the auditory track can diverge from the visual track. A character can visually be the object of focalization and at the same time be the subject of focalization on the auditory level (Verstraten 2008: 147). As I will aim to show, however, film is not unique in its ability to present focalization that is *simultaneously* external and internal. Sensory discrepancies are also possible *within* the auditory dimension.

Of particular note in this regard is Bal's notion of "double" and "ambiguous" focalization. When the external focalizer "looks over the shoulder" of the

---

5. In this regard, my definition of the ACD deviates from Jahn's (2003) notion of the FCD, as he writes: "The viewer approaches the filmic data on the assumption of encountering a well-formed composition guided by maxims of giving efficient, sufficient, and relevant information. As a matter of fact, as film viewers we will actively exploit expectations in these matters, especially when we are facing difficult, incomprehensible, or illogical data" (F4.1.1.). Jahn's terminology, however, is still very useful for the purposes of my research because it avoids anthropomorphic connotations.

internal focalizer—a situation analogous to free indirect speech, as Bal indicates—Bal (2009) suggests the term "double" focalization (163). Focalization is "ambiguous" when it is difficult to decide to which narrative level focalization should be assigned (163). Focalization can function like this in the radio play: As we shall see in the examples, the decision whether focalization is external or internal cannot always be conclusively made. However, this is not the same as simultaneous focalization in the radio play as I understand it. Simultaneous focalization refers to two (or more) sound events that can be attributed to either the external or the internal focalizer that are presented at the same time. This is not possible in (conventionally typeset) literature, because of the text's linear nature. The sound medium offers means to present two individual kinds of focalization simultaneously.

The radio play consists of individual "sound events" that make up the overall composition—or the narrative "sound field" (see Vandevelde 2015: 58–59). These sound events are presented by the ACD, but they can be filtered through the perception of a narrator or a character on the level of the story. Because the radio play's "language" consists of sound, internal focalization should be understood as a particular treatment of this sound. Rimmon-Kenan's (2002) understanding of focalization as a "transposition" of the "overall language" of the narrative is helpful in this regard:

> In itself, focalization is non-verbal; however, like everything else in the text, it is expressed by language. The overall language of a text is that of the narrator, but focalization can "color" it in a way which makes it appear as a transposition of the perceptions of a separate agent. (84)

Rimmon-Kenan understands focalization (which, as she points out, is in itself "non-verbal") as a "color" that is added to the "language" of the radio play. In film, one can think of framing devices, the use of different lenses, optical superimposition, and literal color to achieve such a subjective effect (Verstraten 2008: 108). With regard to sound, this color can be compared to an acoustic filter. The *Guide to Everyday Sounds* understands subjective hearing in analogy to a filter: "The human hearing system, from the external ear to the brain, is itself a filtering process. Subjectivity also intervenes as a filter that is influenced by the degree of familiarity with sound situations, memory, and possible connotations" (Augoyard and Torgue 2005: 49). The authors offer a description of such a filter: "A filtration effect is perceived when the frequency of a sound that we are accustomed to or that we have heard previously is modified" (48).

In the radio play, such filtration effects are often suggested to emphasize or reveal what Sam Halliday (2013) calls the narrative's "para-sonic factors." In his study of the representation of sound in modernist (written) literature, he explains these factors as "sound's social connotations, its relationships with other senses, and—perhaps most importantly of all—the qualitative dimension that means certain sounds are actually of interest to people, things they actively seek out or shun" (12). These "para-sonic" factors are emulated in the radio play by means of (for instance) electroacoustic manipulation or the stereophonic positioning of the channels to suggest internal focalization. Therefore, when we are listening to a radio play, we should ask: Is a particular sound presented as it would be heard in the world of the story, or is the sound filtered through a character's attention? And, since focalization goes beyond the realm of the auditory (while it is expressed in sound), we also need to ask: Is the sound perhaps the result of something else—a translation into sound of what a character sees, feels, smells, or remembers?

Cocktail Party Effect

In Mark Insingel's radio play *Vernissage* (*Exhibition Opening*) (VRT 1977), the listener hears a soundscape of voices at an art gallery. Initially, the listener is not able to distinguish the individual conversations. Then, by adjusting the volume and by means of fading in, the ACD brings individual voices to the stereophonic center, like a camera zooming in on individual elements. Now, the listener is able to hear what the guests are saying one by one. The background sound, consisting of people talking, establishes a unifying soundscape against which these expressions are uttered. The voices in the room are nondistinct characters—portrayed by ten voices, both male and female. The radio play presents what has been called the "cocktail party effect" by the cognitive scientist Colin Cherry (1953). This effect concerns the ability to focus on specific sound events within a soundscape. It is named after the ability to pay attention to a conversation at a crowded party.

Subjectivity plays an important role in this effect. When a particular word or sound is uttered that is of interest to the listener (her name, for instance), she will—deliberately or involuntarily—turn her attention to the source of that sound. In *Vernissage*, the listener is put in the auditory position of someone at the party, eavesdropping on people's conversations. In the introduction to the script, Insingel (1975) writes that the radio play concerns "the double and ambiguous theme of art and women (in a comparable situation: on display and possibly for sale)" (59).[6] The voices fading in and out of the stereophonic center alternately talk about the artworks and the women in the room. These

---

6. All translations from the radio plays are mine, unless otherwise indicated.

topics are connected in the act of the appraising look. Consider the following sequence of utterances by the voices fading into the stereophonic center:

: A cheap collection of intentions
: It is shocking, everybody is looking at them.[7]
: But it is out of place
. . .
: There are several ladies without a bra, even some where the nipples are clearly—
: But the sensuality, the eye-candy, if I may put it like that, is included in the whole of the appearance. [1:07–1:35] (Insingel 1975: 60–61)

The language of art criticism is juxtaposed with statements about the women at the exhibition. Often it is not clear whether the voices are talking about the artworks or the women. For instance, "It is shocking, everybody is looking at them" can refer to the braless women or the scandalous art. The same is true for a sentence like "If you look around you what is on display—." As words like "cheap" and "on display" indicate, *Vernissage* aims to demonstrate that the gazes directed at art and women are both connected in their effects of commodification. The economy of the gaze is a recurring element in Insingel's radio work ("hoorteksten," or hearing texts).[8] The connection between looking at art and women goes beyond mere analogy. As one of the voices puts it, "Art is an alibi": Looking at art is a culturally accepted continuation of the estimating gaze of which women are the object, the radio play suggests. Because of the purely auditory nature of the radio play (its metaphorical "blindness"), the listener's own gaze is averted or circumvented (see also Hill 1996: 112). The listener is put into a position of someone who has an ear for the problematic aspects of the gaze: By listening in on people's conversations, she is able to draw (invisible) connections between the individual statements.

In *Vernissage*, the ACD presents a selection of auditory impulses by (literally) bringing them to the center of attention. As Arnheim already theorized, the relative positioning of sounds within the acoustic space is a particularly effective means to convey a "point of audition" in the radio play. In his article on perspective in radio drama, Lutostański (2016) understands focalization as

---

7. The word "ernaar" in "Iedereen kijkt ernaar" is ambiguous and can refer to both neutral and gendered objects of observation.

8. Insingel (1981) predicted that literature has a future through auditory channels: "It is a matter of time before books are being sold on records or tapes, like musical pieces, executed in the interpretation of a certain (audio) director" (51). *Wanneer een dame een heer een hand drukt* (*When a Lady Shakes Hands with a Gentleman*; 1975), a collection of "hearing texts" meant to be performed on the radio, is a manifestation of this idea.

a position from which the sound is heard, and this position is first of all connected to the location of the microphone (120). Lutostański (2016: 119) follows Bordwell (1985: 9) when he understands the recording device as a stand-in for an invisible witness. In *Vernissage,* the perspective is static throughout the radio play—there are no indications that the focalization shifts between narrative levels or between characters; the microphone acts precisely as an invisible witness. What is "told" in this radio play is entirely "colored" by the focalizing entity. The listener is put into a passive position from which the problematic aspects of the gaze are exposed. There is, however, another side to the coin: Listening in on people's conversations also turns into a meddlesome act that makes the listener complicit in the glaring looks and the gossip that are exchanged at the party.

Tel

The position of the microphone (equivalent to the camera's point of view) is perhaps the most straightforward way to establish a subjective "perspective." However, as film narratologists have demonstrated, focalization can also be suggested by means of other semiotic elements such as visual effects, mixing, and editing. The same is true for auditory focalization. Pol Hoste's radio play *Tel* (an abbreviation for *Telephone*) (VRT 2002, original scenario 1987) provides an example of (shifts in) internal focalization through the use of electroacoustic manipulation. The radio play represents a telephone conversation between a mother and her son. At first, we hear the mother's voice through a telephone speaker (with slight distortion); the son's voice is heard without the added electroacoustic effect. This indicates that the event is filtered through the perception of the son: The listener hears the mother just as the son hears her. The son tries to explain to his mother that he does not like her opening question: "How are you?" The mother does not understand why she is not allowed to ask a simple question. After a musical intermezzo, the electroacoustic effects are reversed: The woman's voice is heard clearly and we hear the man at the other end of the telephone line. This reversal can be compared (but is not equivalent) to the shot-counter-shot in film: It is as if there are cuts between shots of the characters talking into a telephone. In radio drama, however, this shot-counter-shot technique is much less conventional.

The shifts in focalization between the characters mirror their argument. The act of focalization is thematized throughout the radio play: The mother constantly asks her son to consider the matter from her point of view, and vice versa. The electroacoustic treatment of the characters' voices suggests that a subject's perspective determines his or her worldview, which can never be entirely shared by another subject. The characters do not gain access to each other's motives: The other remains a voice at the other end of the telephone line. The medium of the telephone is metaphorically employed to depict their relationship: Mother and son are able to hear each other (Greek *phone*: "voice, sound"), but there remains an unbridgeable distance (Greek *tele*: "distant"). The inability to put oneself into the other's position is also indicated by the constant emphasis on the phatic function of language: "Are you still listening?" both characters ask several times (which can also be understood metafictionally as an address to the listener of the radio play). The other answers affirmatively, but the fact that the other's voice remains heard through the distortion of the telephone speaker points to a persistent break in communication. In the final minute of the radio play, the son reluctantly tells his mother he is doing all right. There is no indication that he has converted to telling the truth, however, because the treatment of the voices is unchanged.

The son brings up aspects of auditory focalization when he says: "There are countless ways to find out how somebody feels. I mean, when I hear somebody talking, I notice instantly how he or she is doing. I hear that, I don't have to ask such a thing, it's not necessary at all, but you always explicitly want to hear it from me" [6:16–6:35] (Hoste 1987: 3). The listeners indeed recognize mood in the characters' voices: They hear depression and exhaustion in the son's voice (with an element of whining), and concern and indignation in his mother's, and irritation and despair in both. In her analysis of a thematically and structurally similar German radio play—in which a man and a woman give a subjective account of their relationship—Huwiler (2005b) elaborates on the meaning of the voice in relation to the narrative:

> The narrative function of the voice to indicate subjectivity and a focalized view of events is nowhere explained by the words of a narrator or character in the play, yet it becomes clear to the listener purely from the alterations of the voices during the unfolding of the story. (53)

Likewise, the alternating electroacoustic effects on the voices in the radio play are an indication of the subjective presentation of the situation. The listener is only offered a constant alternation of perspectives in which the other character's voice is embedded.

Without Subtitles

In *Zonder onderschriften* (*Without Subtitles*) (KRO 1971), written by Jeroen Brouwers, focalization seems to be more ambiguous. The radio play concerns the seventieth birthday of Aga, a deaf woman who lives with her husband. Her hearing impairment gives rise to isolation and feelings of paranoia. She thinks the Nazis are coming after her and that people try to steal her possessions. Her family members laugh at her paranoid claims. In the first moments of the radio play, we hear Aga's internal monologue as she reflects on what she sees on the television screen. Because this radio play presents a deaf protagonist, silence is a clear indicator of internal focalization. The lack of background sounds signals to us that we are inside the head of the deaf woman (she focalizes). As focalization shifts from internal to external, there is a change in the soundscape. The sound of a television fades in and we hear her family members enter the room. The position of the microphone, however, remains static. Whether we hear Aga's inner thoughts or she is interacting with her surroundings, her voice sounds the same. Sonically speaking, there is no change in the "treatment" of Aga's voice. There is no change in electroacoustic effects, and Aga's voice is consistently mixed in the middle of the stereophonic spectrum (in both channels). The other characters are mixed left and right, depending on their position relative to Aga. Throughout the radio play, the microphone is located very close to Aga, equivalent to the (extreme) close-up in film. The microphone can register, so to speak, the dialogue at the party with the same accuracy as Aga's inner thoughts.

The position of the microphone establishes a static frame: This effect makes Aga's isolation all the more tangible. We are locked inside Aga's head (as she is), but at the same time we also hear more than she is able to (since we know she is deaf). We can hear her family mocking Aga: They say she has got "a screw loose" and that there is "no connection" in her brain. The most important indication of focalization in this radio play is the story's activation of a mimetic framework. Since the radio play draws on mimetic conventions, the listener assumes that Aga's deafness functions according to real-life stipulations. We know it is impossible that Aga is the only focalizer throughout the narrative: Aga is unable to hear her family members because of her hearing condition, but the listener hears the other characters clearly. This assumption is connected to the radio play's semiotic elements: Where we would expect silence, we hear voices.

Because Aga is literally at the center of our attention, the static position of the microphone has the effect that we are put into her position, but we also hear more than Aga is able to. It is impossible to determine whether focalization is external or internal (To what extent does Aga hear what we hear? To what extent do her family members hear Aga?). There are no "attributive signs" (Bal 2009: 162) that indicate shifts in levels of focalization. Hence, focalization in this radio play seems to be "ambiguous" (in the sense Bal refers to [2009: 162–63]). But because both possibilities (external or internal) exclude the other (from a mimetic standpoint), "ambiguous focalization" is an inadequate categorization. Focalization can therefore best be assigned to a position "in between" external and internal.

Score in Decibels

In its hundred-year history, the radio play has introduced several famous (temporarily or situationally) blind(ed) characters.[9] Richard Hughes's *A Comedy of Danger* (1924), often considered the first radio play in history, is indicative of the genre's preoccupation with blindness. In the radio play, a group of people find themselves in a cave without a source of light. The characters are put into the position of the listener: They have to interpret the events without visual aid. Deaf protagonists, on the other hand, are relatively underexplored in the radio play. That a deaf character offers interesting possibilities and challenges to the radio play maker is illustrated by the previous radio play under scrutiny in this chapter, but even more so by Christine Kraft's *Partituur in decibels* (*Score in Decibels*) (VRT 1982). The radio play introduces Michiel, a seventeen-year-old boy with a hearing impairment, who is obsessed with everything concerning sound recording. He spends his days playing his collection of recordings at a loud volume, to the dismay of his mother.

In the conversations Michiel has with his parents and a neighbor kid, we can hear him speaking in a manner that is typical of people who have been deaf all their life. When Michiel is left alone in his room with his sound system, we hear his inner thoughts. There is a lot of reverb on his voice, a conventional acoustic manipulation to evoke the perception that the listener is inside the character's head. The voice we hear is completely different from the voice we heard earlier: There are no more signs of the effects of his hearing impairment on his speech. In the background of the soundscape, we hear Igor Stravinsky's orchestral work *The Rite of Spring* (1913), which is playing on the radio in the story world. In the foreground, we can hear Michiel's inner voice

---

9. Other famous examples in British radio drama include the blind narrator Captain Cat in Dylan Thomas's *Under Milk Wood*, the blind seer Peter in Louis MacNeice's *The Dark Tower*, and the metaphorical blindness of Edward in Harold Pinter's *A Slight Ache* (Drakakis 1981: 21).

wondering whether the sounds he vaguely hears represent human speech or music.

At the start of the piece, when a lonesome bassoon is playing, Michiel asks himself why the person speaking on the radio is talking so softly. Then the rest of the orchestra starts playing. Through the visual indications on the stereo Michiel becomes aware of the amplitude distortion of the sound. At first, he thinks the person is screaming, then he wonders whether maybe a choir is singing. He then realizes that he can ask his mother. The word "mother" is repeated by his inner voice (with the added reverb). The same word, expressed in Michiel's voice as it is being heard by the other characters, is faded into the mix on top of this inner voice. This points to a shift in focalization from internal to external with regard to Michiel: He turns from focalizer to focalized. In the superimposition of his two voices, external and internal focalization are presented simultaneously for a brief moment.

The transition from internal to external focalization does not affect the sound layer in which the music is heard. Stravinsky's piece is heard at the same volume level and with the same clarity throughout the transition of the scenes. The music is intradiegetic, since Michiel plays it on his sound system, but the sound is not focalized by him. In contrast to Michiel, we are able to hear that the sound system is playing music and not spoken words. We simultaneously hear Michiel's inner voice—an indication of internal focalization. Because Michiel's thoughts are presented as he "hears" them in his head, the listener experiences the character's isolation from the acoustic world. But because we simultaneously hear the externally focalized sound of the music, we also fail to fully understand Michiel's condition and his obsession with the sound. The confrontation between these two positions is narratively productive: Like his parents, we cannot put ourselves into his position entirely.

Michiel's obsession with sound ties in with the radio play's central existential and epistemological topics. When his mother asks why Michiel just doesn't read a book instead of being preoccupied with sound, his answer discloses that Michiel defines his subjectivity in relation to his deficiency: "If I were to read I wouldn't hear anything. Only in sound do I know and feel for sure that I am deaf." By extension, Michiel's rejection of literature in favor of sound can be regarded as a poetic statement: The radio play, too, is often defined through a lack (of visual information), but—as *Partituur in decibels* demonstrates—the radio play manages to convey meaning in ways that are impossible in literature.

After his mother has resolved the problem, Michiel continues to listen to his sound system. Again, internal and external focalization are superimposed:

We hear the music and Michiel's inner thoughts. Then, all of a sudden, a noise interferes with the music. Michiel reckons that a moped or a motorcycle is responsible for the disturbance of his sound perception. From the next scene, we learn that his mother's vacuum cleaning is the cause of the noise. The sound of the vacuum cleaner and its "translation" into Michiel's perception are presented simultaneously. The soundscape of this scene can be distinguished into four distinct layers that are distributed among the channels as such:

1. The "realistic" sound of the vacuum cleaner in the right channel
2. The distorted sound of the vacuum cleaner in the left channel
3. Michiel's inner voice reflecting on his inability to understand what is going on in the foreground
4. Stravinsky's *Rite of Spring* playing in the background

The complexity of the soundscape is matched by the narrative complexity: Several kinds of focalization are presented together. The sound of the vacuum cleaner and the music (1 and 4) cannot be focalized by Michiel. The distorted sound and Michiel's inner voice (2 and 3) are logically only heard by him. The four sound events are heard by the listener simultaneously. It should be pointed out that the sound field is easily naturalized by the listener. Even if the listener is not an experienced radio play listener (or is not familiar with radio play conventions), she is likely able to differentiate the sound layers and identify each sound event in relation to the story (see also Huwiler 2005b: 54).[10] Martine Huvenne (2012) makes a similar argument with regard to film sound. In her phenomenological approach to the film's soundtrack, she concludes that when the listener is interpellated multiperspectively, she is in several acoustic environments at once. With regard to images, such a superimposition of spaces is recognized as unconventional. But because of sound's inherent simultaneousness no defamiliarization takes place, because this effect is instantly naturalized by the listener (Huvenne 2012: 75).

Conclusion

The examples in this chapter show that the radio play raises several interesting questions with regard to the concept of focalization. The radio plays under

---

10. A recent radio play workshop with high school students at Ghent University serves as an illustration. The students claimed that neither of them had heard a radio play before. Still, after listening just one time to the radio play, they were able to give a detailed outline of the events and managed to attribute specific sounds to the subjective experience of the characters.

scrutiny present various examples of focalization by means of semiotic elements that are medium-specific for the radio play (the stereophonic position of the signals, volume, fading and mixing, the use of electroacoustic manipulation, etc.). As this chapter has demonstrated, the radio play has a range of elements at its disposal to evoke sensory activities like hearing and seeing, and cognitive categories like remembering and projecting—in short, the full range of subjective experience. The radio play is effective in suggesting such "filters" by means of sound alone. Therefore, the analysis of focalization in the radio play challenges the presumed "visual" bias of the terminology of focalization. Specialized terms like "auricularization" are too narrow to understand the full range of filters that the radio play is able to evoke. Attention to focalization in a broader sense acknowledges that the senses are often interfused (sound can create "images in the mind," for instance). Furthermore, a closer look at focalization unveils the specific affordances of the radio play, particularly in the medium's possibility to present several sound events and semiotic elements at the same time.

The survey of different kinds of focalization explored in this chapter is not exhaustive. One can, for instance, entertain the possibility of two kinds of internal focalization presented simultaneously. Another possibility is the indication of shifts between focalizing characters against the background of an externally focalized sound layer. This chapter has also only touched upon a selection of the semiotic elements of the radio play used to suggest focalization (particularly electroacoustic manipulation and the stereophonic positioning of the channels). A more systematic overview of how elements like music, voice, mixing, and silence function in relation to focalization is a topic that deserves further investigation. Additional research into the particularities of double, ambiguous focalization versus simultaneous focalization is needed as well. Finally, more work remains to be done regarding the distinction between radio plays that employ a mimetic framework in their suggestion of focalization and radio plays that challenge that framework.

As we have seen, the semiotic elements that the radio play maker has at her disposal are analogous to, but do not coincide with, visual devices for narration in film, such as editing and the superimposition of images. Studying radio drama from a transmedial perspective is a two-way street. Film narratology provides a model that considers focalization in an art form that (also) uses auditory elements. At the same time, a closer look into audio drama's unique characteristics enhances our understanding of the auditory channel in film and other media that use audiophonic elements. One can, for instance, think of the possibility of disjointed, ambiguous, or simultaneous focalization within the soundtrack of a film.

Works Cited

Arnheim, Rudolf. 1936. *Radio.* Translated by Margaret Ludwig and Herbert Read. London: Faber & Faber.

Augoyard, Jean-Francois, and Henry Torgue, eds. 2005. *Sonic Experience: A Guide for Everyday Sounds.* Translated by Andra McCartney and David Paquette. Montreal: McGill University Press.

Bal, Mieke. 1981a. "The Laughing Mice: Or: On Focalization." *Poetics Today* 2, no. 2: 202–10.

———. 1981b. "Notes on Narrative Embedding." Translated by Eva Tavor. *Poetics Today* 2, no. 2: 41–59.

———. 2009. *Narratology: Introduction to the Theory of Narrative.* 3rd. rev. ed. Toronto: University of Toronto Press.

Belton, John, and Elisabeth Weis. 1985. *Film Sound: Theory and Practice.* New York: Columbia University Press.

Bernaerts, Lars. 2017. "Hybride en multimodaal: nieuwe genretheorie en het literaire hoorspel vandaag." *Cahier voor Literatuurwetenschap* 9: 113–25.

Bordwell, David. 1985. *Narration in the Fiction Film.* Madison: University of Wisconsin Press.

Branigan, Edward. 1992. *Narrative Comprehension and Film.* London: Routledge.

Brouwers, Jeroen, and Jos Joos. 1970. *Zonder onderschriften.* Aired April 26, 1970, on BRT 3.

Calanchi, Alessandra. 2015. "Searching for Sounds in U. S. Literature: A Multisensorial, Multidisciplinary Project." *European Scientific Journal* 3: 10–21.

Chatman, Seymour. 1978. *Story and Discourse: Narrative Structure in Fiction and Film.* Ithaca: Cornell University Press.

Cherry, Colin. 1953. "Some Experiments on the Recognition of Speech, with One and with Two Ears." *The Journal of the Acoustical Society of America* 25, no. 5: 975–79.

Chion, Michel. 2009. *Film, a Sound Art.* Translated by Claudia Gorbman. New York: Columbia University Press.

Crook, Tim. 1999. *Radio Drama: Theory and Practice.* London: Routledge.

Drakakis, John, ed. 1981. *British Radio Drama.* Cambridge: Cambridge University Press.

Genette, Gérard. 1988. *Narrative Discourse Revisited.* Translated by J. E. Lewin. Ithaca: Cornell University Press.

Halliday, Sam. 2013. *Sonic Modernity: Representing Sound in Literature, Culture and the Arts.* Edinburgh: Edinburgh University Press.

Hand, Richard J., and Mary Traynor. 2011. *The Radio Drama Handbook: Audio Drama in Practice and Context.* London: Continuum.

Hill, Mary Louise. 1996. "Developing 'A Blind Understanding': A Feminist Revision of Radio Semiotics." *The Drama Review* 40, no. 3: 112–20.

Hoste, Pol. 1987. "Tel." *Dietsche Warande & Belfort* 132, no. 8: 2–7.

Hoste, Pol, and Martine Ketelbuters. 2002. *Tel.* Aired April 23, 2002, on VRT.

Hühn, Peter, Wolf Schmid, and Jörg Schönert, eds. 2009. *Point of View, Perspective, and Focalization: Modeling Mediation in Narrative.* Berlin: Walter de Gruyter.

Huvenne, Martine. 2012. *Het geluid als een innerlijke beweging in de overdracht van een ervaring in de film, een fenomenologische benadering.* Amsterdam: Vossiuspers UvA, Amsterdam University Press.

Huwiler, Elke. 2005a. *Erzähl-Ströme im Hörspiel: zur Narratologie der elektroakustischen Kunst*. Paderborn: Mentis Verlag.

———. 2005b. "Storytelling by Sound: a Theoretical Frame for Radio Drama Analysis." *The Radio Journal* 3, no. 1: 45–59.

———. 2016. "A Narratology of Audio Art: Telling Stories by Sound." In *Audionarratology: Interfaces of Sound and Narrative*, edited by Jarmila Mildorf and Till Kinzel, 99–116. Berlin: De Gruyter.

Insingel, Mark. 1975. *Wanneer een Dame een Heer de Hand Drukt. . . .* Amsterdam: Malperthuis.

———. 1981. *Woorden zijn Oorden*. Haarlem: In de Knipscheer.

Insingel, Mark, and Jos Joos. 1977. *Vernissage*. Aired March 8, 1977, on BRT 1.

Jahn, Manfred. 2003. "A Guide to Narratological Film Analysis." In *Poems, Plays, and Prose: A Guide to the Theory of Literary Genres*. English Department, University of Cologne. http://www.uni-koeln.de/~ame02/pppf.htm.

James, Henry. 1972. *Theory of Fiction*. First published 1908. Edited by J. E. Miller. Lincoln: University of Nebraska Press.

Kraft, Christine, and Michel De Sutter. 1982. *Partituur in decibels*. Aired May 2, 1982, on BRT 1.

Lutostański, Bartosz. 2016. "A Narratology of Radio Drama: Voice, Perspective, Space." In *Audionarratology: Interfaces of Sound and Narrative*, edited by Jarmila Mildorf and Till Kinzel, 117–32. Berlin: De Gruyter.

McWhinnie, Donald. 1959. *The Art of Radio*. London: Faber & Faber.

Mildorf, Jarmila, and Till Kinzel, eds. 2016. *Audionarratology: Interfaces of Sound and Narrative*. Berlin: De Gruyter.

Niederhoff, Burkhard. 2011. "Perspective—Point of View." *The Living Handbook of Narratology*, edited by Peter Hühn et al. Hamburg: Hamburg University. http://www.lhn.uni-hamburg.de/node/26.html.

———. 2014. "Focalization." In *Handbook of Narratology: Volume 1*, 2nd ed., edited by Peter Hühn, Jan Christoph Meister, John Pier, and Wolf Schmid, 197–205. Berlin: Walter de Gruyter.

Nieragden, Goran. 2002. "Focalization and Narration: Theoretical and Terminological Refinements." *Poetics Today* 23, no. 4: 685–94.

Rimmon-Kenan, Shlomith. 2002. *Narrative Fiction*. 2nd ed. London: Routledge.

Ryan, Marie-Laure. 2014. "Narration in Various Media." In *Handbook of Narratology: Volume 1*, 2nd ed., edited by Peter Hühn, Jan Christoph Meister, John Pier, and Wolf Schmid, 468–88. Berlin: Walter de Gruyter.

Schafer, R. Murray. 1993. *Voices of Tyranny, Temples of Silence*. Indian River: Arcana Editions.

Schmedes, Götz. 2002. *Medientext Hörspiel. Einsätze einer Hörspielsemiotik am Beispiel der Radioarbeiten von Alfred Behrens*. Münster: Waxmann Verlag.

Skov Nielsen, Henrik. 2013. "Naturalizing and Unnaturalizing Reading Strategies: Focalization Revisited." In *A Poetics of Unnatural Narrative*, edited by Jan Alber, Henrik Skov Nielsen, and Brian Richardson, 67–93. Columbus: The Ohio State University Press.

Vandevelde, Tom. 2015. "The Modernist Soundscape: Towards a Theory of the Representation and Perception of Sound in Narrative." PhD thesis, Leuven, Katholieke Universiteit Leuven.

Verstraten, Peter. 2008. *Handboek Filmnarratologie*. 2nd rev. ed. Nijmegen: Uitgeverij Vantilt.

5

Simultaneity and the Soundscapes of Audio Fiction

CAROLINE A. KITA

IN HIS NOW CANONICAL 1977 WORK, *The Soundscape: Our Sonic Environment and the Tuning of the World,* composer and scholar R. Murray Shafer (1994) coined the term "soundscape" to describe the "acoustic environment" or the universes created through the perception of sound (3). The term has since become accepted parlance to describe the worlds created in audio fiction by voices, music, noise, and silence. Yet, as Jarmila Mildorf and Till Kinzel (2016) have noted, although the term is derived from the visual descriptor "landscape," soundscapes are composed of ephemeral acoustic acts that "cannot easily be demarcated" (4). They do not directly represent a particular place, but rather evoke an image of it in the listener's mind by drawing on a recognizable language of acoustic signifiers. In audio fiction, where the listener must depend solely on the aural sense to discern plot, setting, and characters, this critical difference raises important questions. What is unique about the symbolic and representational forms of sound? And what other models might help us to conceptualize the way that audio fiction soundscapes take shape and create meaning?

In the following, I propose reading audio fiction soundscapes as *audiotopias*. Audiotopias, according to Josh Kun (2005), describe "sonic spaces of . . . utopian longing, where several sites normally deemed incompatible are

---

The author would like to thank Nicola Georgia Peinemann of NDR Kultur/Radiokunst and Sönke Treu of the Rundfunkarchiv NDR for their assistance in accessing the original recordings and scripts for the radio dramas examined in this article.

brought together" (23). Like the *heterotopia*, from which it is derived, audiotopias are real, a construction of the material reality of sound, yet also unreal, evoking imagined spaces and places in the mind of the listener. Their multiplicity is a product of the ambiguous nature of sound, where a single acoustic act can reference an infinite number of literal and metaphorical meanings. The listener is thus forced to engage with numerous meanings and perspectives at once. As a result, audio fiction soundscapes, like Foucault's (1984) mirror, "exert a counteraction" on the position that the listener occupies (4), encouraging reflection on, and deconstruction of, the self. Audiotopia thus describes both the form and function of the audio fiction soundscape—its ability to create multilayered, heterogeneous worlds in which culture can be "contested and consolidated" (Kun 2005: 22).

This chapter focuses on two German radio dramas from the mid-twentieth century, Heinrich Böll's *Tapping Signals* (*Klopfzeichen*; NDR 1962) and Jan Rys's *Border Crossers* (*Grenzgänger*; NDR 1960), to demonstrate how audio fiction exploits the soundscape's ambiguous, multilayered nature—using simultaneity as a technique to create contemporaneity (being in two time frames in the same moment) and bilocation (being in two spaces at once) as a narrative construct. This is achieved through narrative stacking, where shifts between narrative levels are made evident to the listener through sound signals, the audiopositioning of the listener, and the manipulation of vocal quality and sound. These elements orient the listener within a particular level of the sound world, but they can also blur boundaries by claiming reference points in another time or space. As the receptor of these sound signals, the listener becomes a participant in and co-creator of the different, simultaneous worlds that compose the soundscape as audiotopia.

Sounding Space and Time: Audio Fiction as Audiotopia

Studies of radio traditionally begin by describing it by what it is *not* or what it *cannot do*. The radio does not show us anything; it is a "blind" medium, and must therefore compensate for this lack of visual stimulus (Verma 2012: 9). However, with the acoustic turn in literature and cultural studies, there has been an increasing interest in developing a new vocabulary to articulate the form and function of audio narratives, and to emphasize their distinctive attributes. The soundscape stands in the center of such debates, for, in audio fiction, it is the primary means by which setting, characters, and plot are made manifest to the audience. Of course, sound plays a critical role in film, television, and stage plays as well, but it almost always serves an ancillary function to the visual. The soundscapes of radio plays, however, often serve not only a "naturalistic" or mimetic function but also a thematic function; that is, the sounds that compose them can represent not just an object or character but also an abstract idea—a memory of a specific place or time, for example.[1] As these sounds are repeated, manipulated, or transformed throughout the radio play, they take on new meanings on a thematic level and create dramatic effect.

Emily Thompson (2004) has drawn attention to the fact that the soundscape consists of not only the materiality of the sounds themselves but also the culture of listening, that is, the listener and the way that he or she perceives the sonic environment (1). The listener plays a particularly important role in the soundscapes of audio fiction, where the complexity of a soundscape is not necessarily determined by the number of sounds, but rather by their ability to evoke a set of "psychic associations" in the listener's mind (Verma 2012: 47). This is achieved by the way that sounds are articulated both individually and within the larger structure of the soundscape. Marshall McLuhan (1994) famously compared the effect of the radio to speaking in a dark room. In the darkness, he claimed, the "gestural qualities" of the word return, revealing textures and layers of meaning that are "stripped away" on the printed page (303). These gestures, perceived in terms of a distinct acoustic quality created by the speaker or manipulated through electroacoustic technology, prompt the listener to make connections between the sound and its potential signifiers in his or her own mind. Moreover, not just words, but any sound can, in the context of the radio play soundscape, develop associative meanings. In this way, the soundscape has the potential to evoke a seemingly endless number of story worlds.

The many possible meanings imbedded in each distinct element of the soundscape allow for radio drama to create new relationships between the temporal and spatial, the real and the imaginary. For this reason, Gregory Whitehead (2001) has described the soundscape of the radio as "a place of constantly shifting borders and multiple identities . . . a no-place" (89). Radio producer René Farabet elaborates on this idea by describing the unique properties of radio sound space according to Foucault's concept of heterotopia. Farabet writes that the radio as heterotopia creates "an other space, a place cut into the real, and, however, aside . . . a possible place of impossible encounters . . . a borderland place, marginal and tangential to my universe" (Farabet, qtd. in El Haouli 2001). In his essay "Of Other Spaces," Foucault (1984) describes the heterotopia as a counter-site "in which the real sites, all other real sites that can be found within the culture, are simultaneously represented, contested and inverted" (3). The heterotopia finds its counterpart in the utopia, the site with "no real place," that presents society either "in a perfected form,

---

1. For more on the mimetic and thematic as elements of the construction of character in narrative, see Phelan (1996: 29).

or else society turned upside down" (3). Foucault writes of the mirror as both heterotopia and utopia, a "placeless place," that creates a virtual space from which the one can look back on the present moment from a new vantage point—a place for the reconstitution of the self (4). The soundscape functions similarly to the mirror as a place of self-discovery. By activating emotional reactions and memories of past experiences in the listener's mind, the soundscape echoes the listener's own hopes, aspirations, and nightmares. Moreover, without the distractions of the visual or other senses, the soundscape's purely acoustic nature offers the potential to expose inner truths located deep in the listener's psyche, giving the impression that the experiences it evokes are more immediate, more real, than the "real world" itself.

Although Foucault himself did not directly address the auditory mode in his essay on heterotopia, Josh Kun has drawn upon this idea, referring to the worlds created by sound as "audiotopias" (see above).[2] The soundscape is audiotopia in its ephemeral, utopian existence, in which it echoes the realities of each of its listeners and offers a space for examining their own past and future. Because each individual listener imagines the space uniquely in his or her own mind, the soundscape becomes a space of difference, where many spaces are imagined simultaneously through the impetus of a single acoustic act. These spaces, which in reality might be considered incompatible, exist in the soundscape side by side.

The writers and producers of audio fiction draw upon the ambiguous, multilayered nature of the acoustic realm, building the coexistence of multiple realities into the very stories that they relay to us. One way that they exploit the audiotopian space of the soundscape in their narratives and engage the listener is to evoke simultaneous narrative action—the experience of being in two temporal or geographic realms at once.

Simultaneity in Narrative: The Inevitable Loss of Immediacy?

Events in a narrative are considered simultaneous if they "are isochronous or occupy exactly the same temporal interval" (Margolin 2014). This effect can be achieved in narrative in a variety of ways, through concurrent acts of speech, or when two different levels of narration interact. In prose narratives, the shifts between levels of narration are often cued by one or more narrators who acti-

---

2. Lauri Siisiäinen, however, indicates that Foucault was highly attuned to the "auditory-sonorous" nature of language. In "Language to Infinity" (1963), Foucault refers to the self-reflexivity of language in terms of the "murmur," again evoking the image of the mirror that he would elaborate upon in "Of Other Spaces" (Siisiäinen 2013: 12–13).

vate the reader's awareness of impending transitions between story worlds. In film or on the stage, visual transitions (fades in and out, lighting cues) might provide such indications of "intercutting," or signaling to the reader or audience that they are somewhere else or in another time. However, these transitions also create a delay effect, for by their very signaling, they shatter the immediate experience of concurrent narratives. Indeed, it is possible to present two narratives at once visually by dividing the text on the page, splitting screen in film, or partitioning the stage in the theater. Yet, the reader can only absorb one narrative at a time, and while a viewer of a play or movie might be able to *see* two scenes at once and still understand the action, to *hear* simultaneous speech or sound creates a cacophony that poses barriers to comprehension (Margolin 2014). Furthermore, while one might suggest contemporaneity or bilocation in cinematic and theatrical representation by indicating one world acoustically while visually displaying another, the radio play is unique in that it creates simultaneity through a single channel—the world of sound.

In the audio narrative, the soundscape can allow for nearly imperceptible shifts between levels of narration, temporal frames, and discursive spaces, initiated only by acoustic association. That is, these transitions are often not explicitly narrated, but merely suggested by familiar sounds that the listener has been trained (either by their frequent occurrence in everyday life or by their repetitive usage in the context of the audio narrative's world) to link with a particular person, place, thing, or feeling. Werner Wolf (2013) claims that the anti-immersive effect generated by the shifting between story worlds can be countered by "a high degree of emotional involvement in the story world" (125). The radio soundscape facilitates immersion by engaging and manipulating highly personal, emotive connections between sound and signifiers in the mind of the listener. By focusing the listener's attention on particular elements of the soundscape through positioning of the microphone or electroacoustic manipulation, or through the use of acoustic leitmotifs with referents in multiple levels of the narrative, the listener can be transported between different geographical and temporal realms through a single acoustic act. In this way, soundscapes are able to create the seemingly elusive experience of being in two places or two times at once.

The idea of simultaneity is a common trope in fantasies and stories of dreams and the unconscious, which typically feature the transgression of borders between the "real world" and the imagination. William Nelles (2002) refers to such shifts between modes of being, between reality and the unconscious, as "ontological" or "horizontal" framing (344). Marie-Laure Ryan (2002) further develops this concept by describing the different movements between levels of narration, not as frames, but rather as stacks. Stacks describe the form of narratives that employ constant fluctuations between discourse levels, both illocutionary (between multiple speakers or narrators) and ontological (between multiple realms of reality and/or fiction). The stack, unlike the frame, is dynamic in nature, and allows for the interaction and interpenetration of narrative worlds. While the stack is also found in prose narratives, it takes on a distinctive form in the acoustic realizations of audio fiction. Unlike frames, which are generally considered to be rigid (one crosses into an inner level and then returns to the outer level), stacks allow for the "contamination of levels," in which events in the "real world" might exact influence on the "diegetic world" and vice versa. Stacks also allow for the simultaneous transgression of both illocutionary boundaries (marked by the introduction of new speakers) and ontological boundaries (marked by the crossing into a new system of reality) (Ryan 2002: 366–67).

The following two examples of radio plays from postwar Germany reveal how audio fiction soundscapes employ stacking to embed multiple narratives and create the impression of simultaneous action occurring across space and time. However, unlike in prose narratives, where shifts between stacks are signaled by narrative cues, the crossing between temporal and spatial realms in these radio dramas are marked only through acoustic leitmotifs that maintain a referent in each of the worlds represented. Thus, it is in the acoustic soundscape that one achieves the full effect of simultaneity, as the borders between story levels appear to collapse in on one another. In Heinrich Böll's *Tapping Sounds*, the sound of tapping on the wall marks a threshold between two temporal realms, echoing both in the past and in the present moment. In Jan Rys's *Border Crossers*, a similarly banal sound, the clinking of glasses, accentuated by drastically reduced background sounds and accompanied by the manipulation of speakers' voices, allows for the experience of bilocation, being in two spaces at once. In both radio plays, the listener plays a critical role, for he or she is not just an observer, or "earwitness" (Shafer 1994: 8), but also a sounding board, a participant in the story's action and co-creator of these multiple realities.[3]

Transgressing Temporal Frames in Audio Fiction: Heinrich Böll's *Tapping Sounds*

Heinrich Böll's radio drama, *Tapping Sounds* (*Klopfzeichen*; 1956/1962), provides a powerful example for the way that audio fiction creates the contemporaneous experience of past and present through the use of sound signals,

---

3. See Bluijs in this volume.

which function in the text as acoustic leitmotifs.[4] In Böll's script, the sound of tapping is initially presented to the listener as an aural counterpart to illocutionary transgressions, or the intercutting of dialogues that occurred in the past but impinge on the story in the present time. However, in the 1962 production of Böll's play by the North German Radio (NDR), directed by Fritz Schröder-Jahn, the tapping signal gathers associative meanings in the mind of the listener, and it takes on a new function as a marker of an ontological border crossing as well, marking the shift between multiple simultaneous realities. The tapping engages the listeners directly in the narrator's own experience of time, so that they become a part of this other realm, where the past and present exist in the same moment.

The permeable boundaries between past and present in *Tapping Signals* are made evident first through the intercutting of the protagonist's voice with dialogues from the past. The main character is a man, around forty-five years old, who has recently returned from prison and explains that he awakens sometimes in the middle of the night, waiting for the sound of tapping. As the drama progresses, the soundscape comes to constitute two different realms that the man "inhabits" simultaneously: his home at the present time and the prison where he was incarcerated in the recent past. Shifts into the past are indicated in the radio play script by illocutionary transgressions, such as the following, when the man is interrupted by the voices of his fellow inmates, a man named Julius and a priest, whose cells were on either side of him.

> MAN: Julius lay in the cell to the right of mine, the priest in the cell to the left of mine, and I had to pass Julius' tapping on to the priest and the priest's on to Julius. Answer from the priest, question from the priest, answer from Julius . . . (*erratic taps, then*)
> PRIEST: Do you reject the devil? (*taps*)
> JULIUS: I reject him.[5]

The embedding of these dialogues indicates another level of the story, taking place in a past time. Throughout the radio play, the man seems to move back

---

4. R. Murray Shafer (1994) uses the term "signal" to refer to "foreground sounds . . . [that] are listened to consciously." They function as a kind of code that must be deciphered. These sounds differ from "keynotes," or the archetypal sounds of a landscape, and "soundmarks," which refer to a "community sound which is unique or possesses qualities which make it specially regarded or noticed by the people in that community" (9–10).

5. Mann: Julius lag in der Zelle rechts von meiner, der Priester in der Zelle links von meiner, und ich mußte Julius' Klopfzeichen an den Priester, die des Priesters an Julius weitergeben. Fragen von Julius, Antworten des Priesters, Fragen des Priesters, Antworten von Julius . . . (*Unregelmäßiges Klopfen, dann*) / Priester: Widersagst du dem Teufel? (*Klopfen*) / Julius: Ich widersage. (Böll 1961: 156–57).

and forth through these different temporal realms, as the dialogues from the past continually infringe on his perception of the present.

Describing the dynamic movement between story worlds in a "stacked" narrative, Ryan refers to the actions of "pushing down" and "popping up," calling to mind the image of a stack of trays in a cafeteria. When a new tray (or layer of narrative) manifests itself, it pushes the previous one down. When this element is removed, the previous one pops up to the top (Ryan 2002: 372). One sees a similar movement in *Tapping Sounds,* as the man's memories of his time in prison push the primary narrative (that of him preparing for a First Communion party with his wife) further down, so that the past seems to be "present." Yet the real present, the primary narrative, does not stay down for long—instead, it continually "pops up" to the front of his consciousness.

The ambiguity of time in *Tapping Sounds* is further emphasized by the soundscape of the radio drama's 1962 production, which remains relatively static. The most prominent noise is the sound of tapping, which claims a referent in both levels of the narrative. Its first occurrence in the present moment follows the narrator's opening lines: "Sometimes I awaken in the middle of the night and await the tapping sounds" (*Klopfzeichen* 1962: 0:11–0:28).[6] The listener hears a rhythmic sequence of three taps, six taps, four taps, and one tap, separated by brief pauses, muted but with a slight reverberation effect. The taps are heard again when the man reminisces about the conversations between Julius and the priest that he mediated. In this second occurrence, which takes place in the recent past, the listener hears the call and answer of more rapid, punctuated taps. These tapping sounds are slightly louder but retain the same acoustic quality as the first and are therefore easily recognizable from the opening sequence (2:18–3:00). Yet, in his next lines, the man identifies the very same tapping we just heard as the sounds of his wife kneading the dough for a cake that she is baking for the party the next day (3:26–3:38). Thus, the tapping serves throughout the radio play as a "transition-signaling device," but it does the opposite of a narrative cue, which, according to Ryan (2002), is intended to "enable readers to properly construct the stack, identify the discourse referents, and orient themselves among the levels of the semantic domain" (379). Instead, it indicates a moment of threshold between the past and the present—it signals a shift, but also holds the listener in the in-between space, because it resonates in both realms.

With the strategic use of tapping as a leitmotif, Böll disrupts the listeners' perceptions of space and time. Reflecting on the continuous sound of tapping

---

6. Mann: Manchmal erwache ich mitten in der Nacht und warte auf die Klopfzeichen (Böll 1961: 156).

that he hears, the man remarks to his wife, "One can fall in time [*in die Zeit fallen*], just like in a hole; everything there is present, past and future—and you don't know whether the past is present or the present is the future. It is one."[7] The man's description of "falling in time" echoes in the "stacking" of the narrative, which continually "pushes down" the stack by putting the past at the forefront of the story, and then allows the present moment or primary narrative to "pop up." Meanwhile the sound of knocking remains a persistent reminder that the borders of time are illusory and that in the mind, all events can be experienced simultaneously.

Finally, the soundscape of *Tapping Sounds* does not just speak of the mental state of its protagonist; it creates this experience for the listener as well, who is immersed in both realms. At one point in the story, the man attempts to explain to his wife what the taps mean and why he continually hears them: He demonstrates the sound for her, tapping the words "I believe" ("*Ich glaube*"). In this scene, the tapping belongs to the primary narrative level and the man, his wife and we as listeners can hear it. Yet, their dialogue is interrupted just minutes later by the murmuring voice of Julius repeating the Catholic confession of faith overlaid with the sounds of tapping, that matches the rhythmic pulse of the words.

>   MAN: And you are surprised, when I tap on the wall at night in my dreams . . . you are surprised, when I lie awake and wait for the tapping sounds? [. . .]
>   (*Longer tapping, shorter and longer signals in alternating order*)
>   JULIUS: . . . died and buried, on the third day raised from the dead.
>   WOMAN: I am often afraid because it appears to me as though you were standing—standing *aside* from our world. You tap against walls that don't belong to our world, give signals to people that I don't know, and I'm afraid that you will never return to our world. (*Klopfzeichen* 1962: 19:00–19:30).[8]

---

7. Mann: Man kann in die Zeit fallen, wie in ein Loch; da ist alles gegenwärtig, vergangen und zukünftig—und du weißt nicht, ob das Vergangene Gegenwart oder das Gegenwärtige Zukunft ist. Es ist eins (Böll 1961: 159).

8. Mann: Ja. Und du wunderst dich, wenn ich nachts im Traum gegen die Wand trommle? [. . .] wenn ich wach liege und auf die Klopfzeichen warte . . . / (*Längeres Klopfen kurzer und langer Zeichen in wechselnder Reihenfolge*) / Julius: . . . gestorben und begraben, am dritten Tage wieder auferstanden von den Toten. / Frau: Ich habe oft Angst, weil es mir so erscheint, als stündest du—stündest *neben* unserer Welt. Du klopfst gegen Wände, die nicht zu unserer Welt gehören, gibst Signale an Menschen weiter, die ich nicht kenne, und ich fürchte, daß du nie ganz in unsere Welt zurückkehrst (Böll 1961: 162–63).

When the wife breaks in to respond to her husband, it is unclear whether she has heard Julius's voice and the taps that accompany it. The listener, who at many times in the play is the only one (other than the man) who can hear the tapping sound, thus becomes complicit in the creation and sustaining of his reality, his "world apart." Only with a listener does the man's world, and its overlapping layers of past and present, exist outside of his own mind. In this way, the listener serves, like the man tapping on the walls of the prison, as a "sounding board" (*Resonanzboden*; 164), or receptor of sound and creator of its meaning. As we shall see, a similar technique is employed in Jan Rys's play *Border Crossers*, which further develops this experience of simultaneity by using, in addition to acoustic leitmotifs, audiopositioning, and the manipulation of voice to indicate the transgression of ontological narrative boundaries and the experience of multiple spaces at one time.

Simultaneous Space: Jan Rys's *Border Crossers* (1960)

The soundscapes of Jan Rys's 1960 radio drama, *Grenzgänger*, or *Border Crossers*, like Böll's drama, appear on the surface to be naturalistic, featuring sound signals that are easily recognizable to the listener, such as clinking glassware and opening and closing doors. Yet, as in *Tapping Sounds*, these sounds also mark thresholds between multiple realms, merging reality with the imaginative realm of "what could be." The soundscape created for the production by NDR, directed by Ludwig Cremer, allows for these spaces to converge, creating the conditions for the listener to imagine these worlds existing simultaneously.

Border Crossers opens with an elderly man sitting in a Viennese coffeehouse. The year is around 1960 and the man, Vrazil, is a Czech national living in a nearby refugee camp. He is waiting for a fellow countryman, named Liska, to play a game. Vrazil and Liska's game appears simple at first—they sit together in the coffeehouse and imagine what it would be like to cross back over the border to their homeland, retracing the steps they took when they fled years before. But as the conversation progresses, it becomes clear that there is much more at stake in this game than a trip down memory lane. As they imagine crossing the geographical border between Austria and Czechoslovakia, they enter a kind of no-man's-land between the reality of the present moment and their memory of the past.

As in *Tapping Sounds*, a formal aspect of *Border Crossers* is narrative stacking. However, while Böll's play presented a series of contemporaneous moments, ranging from the past to present, Rys's play moves between two simultaneously experienced geographical realms, the coffeehouse and the border lands. *Border Crossers* draws the listener's attention to this fact through narrative intercutting, such as when the waiter in the coffeehouse interrupts the discussion between the two characters. These illocutionary transgressions remind the listener that they are not, as it might sound like from their dialogue, wandering through a frontier at night, but rather sitting at a table in the coffeehouse. One such point of rupture of the imaginary realm occurs at a critical moment in the narrative of the border crossing, as Vrazil believes that he recognizes someone at the train station:

> VRAZIL: Hello there! Here comes Paluch towards us, an old acquaintance of mine. He's waving!
> LISKA: He knows what we're up to. For the love of God, did you tell him something?
> VRAZIL: Only hinted, nothing more. He is trustworthy.
> LISKA: One can never know that for sure, he could be a spy.
> VRAZIL: Impossible.
> LISKA: One can never trust any of our people. Somewhere along the line everyone is pressured by their past, even Paluch collaborated at some point, it doesn't matter with whom. Have you already forgotten? Tell him that we are driving to the mountains, on vacation or whatever, tell him that. (*Coffeehouse noises return*)
> WAITER: Here is your water, gentlemen.
> LISKA: Thank you.
> WAITER: Has he calmed himself down?
> LISKA: I told you, don't worry about it, stop being so curious. (*Sound fades out*) So, what happened?
> VRAZIL: I sent him away (*Grenzgänger* 1960, 12:11–13:00).[9]

The quick cut to the waiter serving water to Liska and expressing his concern for Vrazil's health is accompanied again by the sound of clinking glasses. This interruption breaks up the clearly defined world of the border-crossing

---

9. Vrazil: Hallo. (*Erklärt dann*) Da rennt Paluch auf uns zu, ein alter Bekannter von mir. Er winkt. Er weiß Bescheid / Liska: Umhimmelswillen, haben Sie ihm etwas erzählt? / Vrazil: Nur angedeutet, nichts mehr. Er ist zuverlässig. / Liska: Das weiß man nie genau, er könnte ein Spitzel sein. / Vrazil: Ausgeschlossen. / Liska: Keinem von unseren Leuten darf man trauen. Irgendwo drückt jeden seine Vergangenheit, auch Paluch hat mal kollaboriert, egal mit wem. Schon vergessen? Sagen Sie ihm, daß wir in die Berge fahren, zur Erholung meinetwegen, sagen Sie ihm das. (*Die Kaffeehausgeräusche kehren zurück*) / Ober: (*kommt*) Sehr wohl, das Wasser für die Herren, bitte. / Liska: Danke / Ober: (*leise*) hat er sich beruhigt? / Liska: Ich habe Ihnen gesagt: kümmern Sie sich nicht drum, seien Sie nicht neugierig. / (*Akustik gleitend wegblenden*) Liska: Also, was ist los? / Vrazil: Ich habe ihn weggeschickt (Rys 1960: 13).

"game," abruptly forcing Liska (and the listener) back into "reality" by popping the coffeehouse narrative to the top of the stack. The fading away of the coffeehouse noise a minute later brings Liska (and the listener) back to the other level, the action at the border.

While in Böll's play, the sound of tapping marked the transition between temporal realms, *Border Crossers* employs the sounds of clinking glassware to indicate shifts between locations—the coffeehouse and the borderlands. A footnote in the published text of the radio drama indicates that the sounds in the play should never be clearly identifiable. Their meaning should become apparent only in their interpretation through words, or the dialogue of the play.[10] The ambiguity of these sound signals is revealed as Vrazil and Liska are crossing the border territory, an open field laden with land mines and other traps.

> LISKA: Be still, I know my way around here. Follow two steps behind me. Don't fall out of line, there are lime pits along the way, they are rugged, mostly empty tin cans in them and other trash. Go slowly, mind the edge.
> VRAZIL: Strange. How does the stuff get here?
> LISKA: I don't know. Trash is everywhere. Be quiet.
> . . .
> LISKA: Man, Vrazil! Be careful! The tin cans make a hell of a noise. (15:20–15:44)[11]

The sound that Liska identifies as tin cans can quite easily be identified as the clinking of silverware or glasses in the coffeehouse heard a few minutes previously when the waiter arrived. Thus, these sounds have one referent in the narrative on the border and another in the coffeehouse. However, these sounds appear this time with no introduction or cue that the waiter is nearby. The listener is prompted by the sound to make such associations between the sound and the coffeehouse, even while the dialogue is telling them that the clinking refers to something else (tin cans), in another place (the border terri-

---

10. "Geräusche können erfahrungsgemäß nie restlos klar identifiziert werden, erst durch das Wort werden sie gedeutet" (Rys 1960: 14).

11. Liska: Still verhalten, kenn mich hier aus. Sie folgen mir mit zwei Schritt Abstand. Nicht aus der Reihe tanzen, da gibt es Kalkkuhlen, die sind schroff, meist leere Konservenbüchsen drin und anderer Unrat. Langsam gehen, auf den Rand achten / Vrazil: Komisch. Wie kommt das Zeug hierher? / Liska: Weiß nicht, Unrat gibt es überall. Leise. / . . . / Liska: Mensch, Vrazil, passen Sie auf: die Konservenbüchsen machen einen Höllenlärm (Rys 1960: 14–15).

tory). The soundscape dissolves the boundaries between stacks as the sounds point toward two different narrative frames.

The listener is able to accept both realities because of the effect of immersion, achieved in the radio drama through the "intimate" audiopositioning of the listener. "Intimate" audiopositioning, often created in early radio drama by placing the speakers close to the microphone, encourages the listener to sympathize with the speaking character's experience (Verma 2012: 65). In *Tapping Sounds,* the listener was "positioned" to align with the voice of the man and to hear the sounds that he heard. Similarly, in *Border Crossers,* the listener's focus is on Vrazil and Liska. Yet, the sense of intimacy created by audiopositioning is here perhaps even more pronounced because, other than their voices, the soundscape is nearly silent. Any other sounds that would "authenticate" the border crossing they are describing, the train, the bus, the street sounds of their hometown, are conspicuously missing from the "sound stage," placing the listener's focus only on their dialogue, or the sounds that the characters hear and interpret within the particular world they accept as reality in that moment. As Vrazil's voice becomes increasingly hoarse and his breath more labored over the course of the play, the arduous journey of the border crossing becomes ever more real for the listener.

Yet, just as the listener becomes settled into this close relationship to the characters, another acoustic shift occurs in the soundscape of *Border Crossers,* which creates a third level in the narrative stack—a play within the play within the play. According to Ryan (2002), this effect is typically achieved in prose fiction by the "double crossing of boundaries," when the "author makes believe to relocate himself in a new system of reality by overtly pretending to be one of its members" (368). By this act of impersonation, the author crosses both an illocutionary boundary (introducing a new speaker) and an ontological boundary (introducing a new reality). In *Border Crossers,* Liska takes on the role of the "author" of this next narrative level, inserting himself as a new character by manipulating his voice. Again, this alteration is not marked in the text, but is evident to the listener through the soundscape, in the change of the quality and sound of his voice, letting us know that we are in a new narrative level.[12] The growing distance between this "world" and the previous one is further emphasized by the use of reverberation, the electroacoustic manipulation of the soundscape.

In this scene, Vrazil and Liska arrive in their hometown, but their game has become complicated by the fact that Vrazil's vision of home is still shaped

---

12. As Elke Huwiler (2005) notes, the sign system of voice is to be differentiated from the sign system of language because it describes not the words themselves but rather the tone of voice, idiolect of the character, pronunciation, and intonation (53).

by his idealistic memories of the past, while Liska has adopted a realistic, pragmatic idea of the home that awaits them—one that openly conflicts with his partner's view. The two characters act out a scene, supposedly in front of Vrazil's old apartment, where Liska claims that a new tenant now lives. Vrazil, who cannot conceive that his house would not be empty as he left it, speaks to the current tenant, whose responses are either acted out or described by Liska:

> VRAZIL: Excuse me please, do you know a Mr. Vrazil?
> LISKA: No, never heard the name.
> VRAZIL: He is well known.
> LISKA: That could be.
> VRAZIL: He lives behind this door
> LISKA: Impossible.
> VRAZIL: Why is that?
> LISKA: Not so loud, he gets impatient, he raises his eyebrows. You must be more polite.
> VRAZIL: Allow me just one more question, please. What are you doing in this apartment?
> LISKA: This is his home, man, can't you understand that?
> VRAZIL: His home? Since when?
> LISKA: He thinks about it, gradually he remembers. Vrazil, he's the one who ran away. Left everything in a lurch, his room, his furniture, his curtains, his radio, everything. Is up and away and never heard from again.
> VRAZIL: But I had to leave!
> LISKA: He's going away, turns around again downstairs, shrugs his shoulders. The apartment house door closes. (*Grenzgänger* 1960: 39:40–41:09)[13]

Vrazil's voice sounds distant, betraying a slight reverberation (*mit leichtem Hall*), while Liska's voice is manipulated by the actor himself, changing in tone, pace, and rhythm as he shifts between his roles as the stranger in Vrazil's apartment into the interpreter of this man's body language and verbal

---

13. Vrazil: Entschuldigen Sie, bitte: kennen Sie einen Herrn Vrazil? / Liska: Nein, den Namen nie gehört. / Vrazil: Er ist bekannt. / Liska: Mag sein, / Vrazil: Er wohnt hinter dieser Tür. / Liska: Unmöglich. / Vrazil: Wieso? / Liska: Nicht so laut, er wird ungehalten, verzieht sein Gesicht. Sie müssen höflicher sein. / Vrazil: Gestatten Sie noch eine Frage, bitte: was machen Sie in dieser Wohnung? / Liska: Er ist dort zu Hause, Mann. Begreifen Sie denn nicht? / Vrazil: Zu Hause? Seit wann? / Liska: Er denkt nach, allmählich erinnert er sich. Vrazil, das ist doch einer, der abgehauen ist. Hat alles im Stich gelassen hat, sein Zimmer, seine Möbel, seine Gardinen, sein Radio, alles. Ist auf und davon, nichts mehr gehört. / Vrazil: Ich habe doch weglaufen müssen. / Liska: Er geht, unten dreht er sich noch einmal um, zückt die Achseln. Die Haustür schlägt zu. (Rys 1960: 25).

response, and finally back to his role as Vrazil's partner in the game. When playing the stranger, Liska's voice takes on a cruel, almost mocking tone. As narrator, he speaks almost under his breath, with a quick pace that accentuates the tension of the moment. His ability to role-play allows him to transgress illocutionary and ontological boundaries, to become a new speaker or narrator in another "reality," yet he also continues to play himself, the one that exists in the other layers of the narrative stack as well. Thus, he exists simultaneously inside and outside of the episode, serving both as actor and commentator.

In *Border Crossers*, the listener serves as a sounding board for the competing realities of both protagonists. Liska retains a clear grip on reality, manifest in his ability to shift up and down through the different levels of the narrative. Like the man in *Tapping Signals* who "pops" the narrative stack, moving from past to present, Liska frequently pops up to the upper levels of the narrative to speak to the coffeehouse waiter or to comment on the action of the game. Yet Vrazil, over the course of the play, becomes increasingly unable to return to the real world, falling deeper into the lower levels of the narrative. Vrazil's outburst at the end of the apartment scene marks a point of rupture with reality. In the final sequence of the play, Liska returns to the coffeehouse and calls for the waiter to bring a glass of water to bring Vrazil to his senses, but it is too late (57:50–58:04). Even though Vrazil's body has never left the coffeehouse, he believes that he is on the banks of the river in his hometown. His death thus marks a point of narrative "contamination" as the story world of the "lower level" of narrative stack exerts its influence on the "upper level" of real life (Ryan 2002: 383). Meanwhile, the listener, who has been privy to the world of the coffeehouse and the adventure of the border crossing has, along with Vrazil and Liska, existed the entire time in both spaces simultaneously.

Conclusion

The radio dramas of Böll and Rys reveal the soundscape's unique capabilities to create new relationships between the temporal and spatial, the real and the imaginary through the evocative power of sound. By their ability to juxtapose sonic realms and to relay them simultaneously to the listener through acoustic leitmotifs, audiopositioning, and manipulation of voice, radio play soundscapes thus function as acoustic heterotopias, or audiotopias. Stimulating the imagination, they call upon associative memories and invite the listener to deconstruct and graft spaces, both real and imaginary, onto one another. In this way, soundscapes hold a footing in the real world, while at the same time they push the boundaries of these spaces and redefine their dimensions and constituent elements. In the radio play, time is both fluid and ephemeral, yet the repetition of acoustic leitmotifs gives a sense of accumulated, or "stacked," time, in which past, present, and future times merge into one. Finally, the soundscapes of audio fiction turn the listener into a "sounding board" upon which particular sounds and their references resonate, creating the sense of simultaneously experiencing multiple spaces and temporal realms. As spaces "aside," the soundscapes of audio fiction offer new modes of telling that are exclusive to the auditory medium.

Works Cited

Böll, Heinrich. 1961. "Klopfzeichen." In *Hörspiele*, 156–65. Frankfurt am Main: Fischer.

El Haouli, Janete. 2001. "Radio: The Art of Sonorous Space." *The Online Contemporary Music Journal* 7.

Foucault, Michel. 1984. "Of Other Spaces: Utopias and Heterotopias." Translated by Jay Miskowiec. *Architecture/Mouvement/Continuité*: 1–9.

Grenzgänger. 1960. Directed by Ludwig Cremer, script by Jan Rys, performed by Willi Tenk-Trebitsch, Ernst Stankovski, and Wilhelm Walter. NDR Hamburg.

Huwiler, Elke. 2005. "Storytelling by Sound: A Theoretical Frame for Radio Drama Analysis." *The Radio Journal—International Studies in Broadcast and Audio Media* 3, no. 1: 45–59.

Klopfzeichen. 1962. Directed by Fritz Schroeder-Jahn, script by Heinrich Böll, performed by Wolfgang Wahl, Jo Wegener, Albert Johannes, Günter Briner, and Konrad Mayerhoff. NDR/SWR.

Kun, Josh. 2005. *Audiotopia: Music, Race and America*. Berkeley: University of California Press.

Margolin, Uri. 2014. "Simultaneity in Narrative." In *The Living Handbook of Narratology*, edited by Peter Hühn et al. Hamburg: Hamburg University. https://www.lhn.uni-hamburg.de/node/46.html.

McLuhan, Marshall. 1994. *Understanding Media: The Extensions of Man*. Cambridge: The MIT Press.

Mildorf, Jarmila, and Till Kinzel. 2016. "Audionarratology: Prolegomena to a Research Paradigm Exploring Sound and Narrative." In *Audionarratology: Interfaces of Sound and Narrative*, edited by Jarmila Mildorf and Till Kinzel, 1–26. Berlin: De Gruyter.

Nelles, William. 2002. "Stories within Stories: Narrative Levels and Imbedded Narrative." In *Narrative Dynamics: Essays on Time, Plot, Closure and Frames*, edited by Brian Richardson, 339–53. Columbus: The Ohio State University Press.

Phelan, James. 1996. *Narrative as Rhetoric: Technique, Audiences, Ethics, Ideology*. Columbus: The Ohio State University Press.

Ryan, Marie-Laure. 2002. "Stacks, Frames and Boundaries." In *Narrative Dynamics. Essays on Time, Plot, Closure and Frames*, edited by Brian Richardson, 366–86. Columbus: The Ohio State University Press.

Rys, Jan. 1960. *Grenzgänger*. Hamburg: Verlag Hans Bredow-Institute.

Schafer, R. Murray. 1994. *The Soundscape: Our Sonic Environment and the Tuning of the World.* Rochester: Destiny Books.

Siisiäinen, Lauri. 2013. *Foucault and the Politics of Hearing.* London: Routledge.

Thompson, Emily. 2004. *The Soundscapes of Modernity: Architectural Acoustics and the Culture of Listening in America, 1900–1933.* Cambridge: MIT Press.

Verma, Neil. 2012. *Theater of the Mind: Imagination, Aesthetics, and American Radio Drama.* Chicago: The University of Chicago Press.

Whitehead, Gregory. 2001. "Radio Play Is No-Place. A Conversation between Jerome Noetinger and Gregory Whitehead." In *Experimental Sound and Radio,* 89–94. Cambridge: MIT Press.

Wolf, Werner. 2013. "'Unnatural' Metalepsis and Immersion: Necessarily Incompatible?" In *A Poetics of Unnatural Narrative,* edited by Jan Alber, Henrik Skov Nielsen, and Brian Richardson, 113–41. Columbus: The Ohio State University Press.

PART II

NARRATIVE GENRES AND NARRATIVE EXPERIMENTS IN AUDIO DRAMA

6

"There ain't no sense to nothin'"

Serial Storytelling, Radio Consciousness, and the Gothic of Audition

HARRY HEUSER

> "Do you see the story? Do you see anything?"
> —The voice of Charlie Marlow in Joseph Conrad's *Heart of Darkness* (1899)

"THE STUDENT OF RADIO DRAMA in any of its phases should, first of all, know something about the medium," the writer of a 1951 "radio drama" handbook instructed his readers. Radio, he insisted, is a "heterogeneous product," a "composite of industrial, artistic, and sociological forces," and a "variegated patchwork of advertisers, broadcasters, educators, governing boards, and listeners" (Mackey 1951: 3–4). Considering that few of us today tune in by twisting the proverbial dial, the event of listening, especially to recordings of broadcasts from decades past, is complicated by our estrangement from the systems whose codes and conventions were once understood or at least familiar but now need to be recovered—and listened out for—so that their structures and strategies may remain readable instead of becoming dematerialized along with their medium of origin. Are we still listening to radio plays if we are not cognizant of the radios *in* such plays? My shortest answer, arrived at after long deliberation, is a resounding "no." The essence of radio plays is not sound. It is radio.

The aim of this essay is to raise the level of radio-consciousness—and listener self-consciousness—among those of us who choose to engage with narratives devised for sound-only broadcasting. Granted, narratology as a field has diversified greatly since Seymour Chatman argued, in *Story and Discourse* (1978), that "narratives" are "structures independent of any medium" (20). But whether theorists concur with that statement or refer us to others who deem it to be an "overstatement" (Elleström 2019: 7), they still tend to consider the medium of radio mainly in the abstract. Marie-Laure Ryan's (2004) assertion that radio "offers different narrative possibilities" than other media gets scant support in *Narrative across Media* (18). Any number of "radio plays" could be cited as examples of what Chatman (1978), who lumped them together with "bardic chants" and "musical narratives," referred to as "transposability" (28, 20). Indeed, the most widely discussed US American radio play is an adaptation. And yet, what sets the *Mercury Theatre on the Air* production of "The War of the Worlds" (1938) apart from H. G. Wells's narrative (first published serially in 1897) is its self-reflexive treatment of the medium for which it was readied. Yesterday's science fiction was transformed into an up-to-the-minute commentary on an invasion in progress, as the version for listening not only adapted the source material but also appropriated the conventions of live broadcasting, as reflected in its structure as a series of sporadic news flashes. And while the listener response was such that broadcasters deemed that particular performance unfit for radio, proscribing subsequent restagings, self-reflexivity continued to be a defining characteristic of plays for radio.[1]

Radio plays are the product of what Walter J. Ong (1982) refers to as the age of "secondary," "more deliberate and self-conscious orality" of the electronic age, an orality "based permanently on the use of writing and print" (136). While the concept of "secondary orality" has its limitations, as radio plays are aural rather than exclusively oral, the notion of "self-consciousness" is useful to our understanding of the tensions underlying such performances. Adapted though it was for stage, screen, and print, Lucille Fletcher's 1943 radio thriller "Sorry, Wrong Number," for instance, was lauded as "perfect" for the medium because it is essentially a play about being stuck at the receiving end of telecommunication, about listening without being heard.[2] The particular sequence I audited for my reading of Carlton E. Morse's serial *I Love a Mystery* (*ILaM*)—elements of which were reworked for film and television, as novel and comic (Harmon 1992: 74–77)—is similarly self-reflexive. Although this does not become clear until the sequence draws to a conclusion, its reflections on radio being essential to the mystery, there are indications along the way that *ILaM* is discursive about its medium.[3] My reading attempts to reflect—

---

1. See, for instance, my discussion of radio adaptations of stage plays and my reading of Archibald MacLeish's "The Fall of the City," as well as the radio plays of Norman Corwin, who "transformed radio's self-consciousness into an artistic project" (Heuser 2013: 296).

2. The statement was made in an 1945 article published in *Life*, as quoted in Matthew Solomon (1997: 30). See also Heuser (2013: 233–37).

3. While Morse was not responsible for the screenplays of the three *ILaM* B-movies produced by Columbia Pictures, he did revive *ILaM* for a projected series of novels, only one of which, *Stuff the Lady's Hatbox*, was published in 1988 by Morse's own Seven Stones Press.

and reflect on—the experience of picking up on them. Radio-conscious listening means being on the "watch," like the narrating narratee of Joseph Conrad's *Heart of Darkness*, for "the sentence, for the word"—as well as the sound—that might provide "the clue to the faint uneasiness" inspired by a narrative seemingly "shap[ing] itself without human lips in the heavy night-air" (Conrad 1996: 42–43). That "clue" may well lie in the fraught act of sense-making, of translating and transcribing, a process whose "uneasiness" radio playwrights—and writers of thriller programs in particular—self-consciously passed on to the listener.

This essay, then, seeks to make a case for audionarratology as an aid to "clued-in" listening. By that I mean listening switched on not only to any number of silenced narratives—and radio serials, which used to be more central to the daily lives of US Americans than motion pictures or pulp fiction, are still reverberating largely out of academic earshot—but also to broadcasting and its histories, to fellow listeners across the disciplines and beyond, as well as to our listening selves. Being mindful of the medium enables us to appreciate the extent to which our "uneasiness" was engendered by radio writers whose reflexive texts gave rise to what I call the "gothic of audition."

"Law don't get out this way much"

"There was nothing else on the air quite like *I Love a Mystery*," cultural historian Russell Nye (1970) declared. The serial struck him as the "most singular of the adventure-mystery type," a combination of the "better hard-boiled dick story and the adventure pulps" (403–4). Billed on the air as an "adventure-thriller," *ILaM* distinguished itself as "one of a kind" (Dunning 1998: 339) by virtue of being derivative. Its perceived strangeness and apparent unconventionality rests in our appreciation of its creator's thorough acquaintance with the industry and the conventions of radio storytelling.

ILaM's composite nature is rendered audible in the accents of its three central characters—the Easterner Jack Packard, the Texan Doc Long, and the Britisher Reggie York—even though the outbreak of the Second World War and the death of the actor who originated the role of Reggie necessitated changes to the original design, with new sponsors demanding further adjustments.[4] The titles of many of the sequences signaled that the trio were no ordinary crimefighters. References to tropes such as "castle," "werewolf,"

---

4. For instance, Jack Packard's last name was omitted from announcements when the Ford Motor Company became *ILaM*'s sponsor; see Grams (2003: 148).

and "vampire" aligned Morse's adventures to the Gothic, a genre familiar to listeners of horror anthologies such as *The Witch's Tale* (1931–35) or *The Weird Circle* (1943–44). Other titles recall the fictions of H. Rider Haggard, B. Traven, or Dashiell Hammett, suggesting the series' roots in adventure stories and detective fiction. When a codger named Jumping Dick warns Jack, Doc, and Reggie in chapter 3 of "Bury Your Dead, Arizona" that "law don't get out this way much" (Morse 1949a: ch. 3), he gives voice to our sense of dislocation when confronted with a narrative that, generically speaking, is all over the place. "Don't be surprised if one of these days Morse has [his characters] fighting some deadly spies from Mars," one journalist quipped. "On *I Love a Mystery* anything can happen, and does" (Alvin 1940: 16).

When Morse first gained recognition as a radio writer in Chicago, where the serial format was pioneered in the late 1920s and early 1930s, he let on (revealed or pretended) that he did not always plot his plays in advance; rather, his narratives responded to "new and unexpected opportunities for enlarging and strengthening the original plot" (Morse 1932: 40). While this is a romanticization of the process of writing for commercial broadcasting, *ILaM* could be more responsive to the "unexpected" since it was not the carefully controlled product of so-called "dialoguers," anonymous writers who were briefed on a storyline by the creators of daytime serials to "hack out the appropriate dialogue" (Field 1958: 325). Whether or not my reasoning here is complicit in Morse's romanticization by attributing the "unexpected" to an author's design, the ultimate-conclusion serial—unlike the telos-resistant "soap operas" that invite us to speculate what happens next without giving us reason to demand certainty about how it all ends—is well suited to the architecture of gothic narratives, which, as Linda Bayer-Berenbaum (1982) puts it, tend to delay the climax by replacing it with "ever-developing contingencies" (24). The promise of resolution propels the mystery; the potential for boundlessness promotes the adventure. It is by way of the listener's negotiation between both impulses—propulsion and protraction—that the finite chapter play generates its thrills.

Although *ILaM* eventually discloses the natural or hyperphysical occasion of each case, Morse's mysteries are "fantastic" in Todorov's (1973) sense of the word. Rather than being an "autonomous genre," the fantastic is "located on the frontier" of the "marvelous and the uncanny"; it "lasts only as long as a certain hesitation" (41). Pushing forward and drawing back, *ILaM* is proposed as a waltz, its musical curtain being Sibelius's "Valse Triste" performed on an organ. Whether it manages "to pull the listener into a vortex of darkness and danger," as one reader has it (Barfield 1996: 157), depends on our individual responsiveness. Still, the theme music, framed by the sounds of a train whistle incongruously giving way to the noise of screeching tires, sets us up for a romp of flight and pursuit—a sonic existence in transit.

What *ILaM*'s aural signature and title signal as well is that its writer claimed authorial control over the journey. Unlike thriller series such as *I Deal in Crime* (1946–1947), *I Fly Anything* (1950–1951), or *I Was a Communist for the FBI* (1952–1954), *ILaM* has no first-person narrator. The "I" of *ILaM*, the declared lover of mysteries, is Morse himself, who, unlike countless "dialoguers," regularly received on-air credit for his work as writer and director. Listeners, in turn, are invited to echo the sentiment expressed and to claim the program as theirs. As far as he possibly could, Morse kept the sponsor out of the equation. The fifteen-minute slot generally set aside for serials made that easier than the thirty-minute format—to which *ILaM* was tailored for parts of its run—as the former was not punctuated by a commercial halfway through the broadcast. Even if, in our readings of radio plays, we tune out the commercial—or, as in my case, rely on transcriptions from which commercials were excised—we should bear in mind that the spots reserved for them not only structure the narratives we do read but also define the relationship between broadcast audience and radio writer. Morse's titular *I* makes personal what, to sponsors and radio executives, is business as usual.

ILaM's signature collage is completed by the expository sound of a clock striking the hour of the action, after which a narrator recapitulates the events leading up to the scene thus set:

> Seven o'clock in the evening in a backstreet hotel somewhere in San Diego. A few minutes ago, Jack Packard and Doc Long, hearing a girl crying in the next room, investigated, and found her lying on her bed, head buried in her arms. She wasn't upset by their unexpected appearance but warned them away from her. She babbled that she was possessed of the Richard's curse, and that she brought death and disaster to any and all who would help her. Jack and Doc have finally calmed her to some degree of coherence. (Morse 1949b: ch. 2)

Morse (1944) called the "lead-in" the "greatest bugaboo the serial writer has to face"; a defining feature of radio serials, it was a "necessary evil demanded by the sponsor" (119), who makes use of single-voiced narration to create awareness of an advertiser's authorizing role in the production. The above example is transcribed in its entirety, demonstrating how deftly Morse dispensed with broadcasting's narrative policing, just as *ILaM*'s narratives tended to relegate actions taken by law enforcement officials—unvoiced and rarely mentioned—to the lapses between chapters.

That time is of the essence in commercial broadcasting is brought to mind by the clock's metallic chimes. Each program being forced into a grid of salable slots, network timetabling greatly contributed to formularized storytelling. The popular success of *ILaM* was, in part, the result of Morse's efforts to counter the predictability of that grid. The length of sequences varied, allowing for narrative arcs whose reach was more difficult to determine. *ILaM* also bridged sequences so that a character other than the protagonist trio could become story-arc resilient. After slapdash wrap-ups that are little more substantial than the lifted veil of Ann Radcliffe's *The Mysteries of Udolpho* (1794), threads of unraveled clues intertwist with new ones, freeing the abovementioned victim of "The Million Dollar Curse" to join Jack, Doc, and Reggie on their next adventure, "Temple of Vampires."

That strategies like these lend both realistic continuity and romantic contingency to an unfolding narrative is difficult to appreciate when segments or chapters are read in isolation. Charlie Marlow's question whether his crew could "see the story" should also be asked by academics whose writings are presumably designed to make us see, or hear, the narratives of which they speak but whose efforts to get at the big picture are often frustratingly austere. To gain a better sense of *ILaM*'s seriality, the following reading of "The Thing That Cries in the Night" (Morse 1949c), one of the fifteen-chapter segments of *ILaM,* seeks to approximate the experience of serial listening—as distinguished from listening to serials—by auditing chapters consecutively.[5]

At the height of the blogging phenomenon, I sought to encourage serial listening by inviting readers of my journal to reflect on their evolving journey via comments posted in the interstices between chapters as they had been broadcast, Monday through Friday, on US network radio back in 1949 (Heuser 2005). I am conscious that such fidelity to a plot in the process of unraveling complicates the task of drawing meaningful conclusions from what I hear, and that my reading in installments may be read as me stalling; but the advantage of adopting a process narrative lies in its potential to render the listening event—our act of unfolding a narrative—more transparent than it would be otherwise. Since the advent of social media and on-demand streaming services, "serialized narratives" have had a "remarkable resurgence," as Tore Rye Andersen and Sara Tanderup Linkis (2019) point out, "not least as a result of the digitalization of the culture industry" (84). And yet, the diversification

---

5. Broadcast live via NBC affiliates between November 20 and December 8, 1939, under the sponsorship of Fleischmann's Yeast, "The Thing That Cries in the Night" was produced again a decade later, when it aired, by transcription and mostly without sponsorship, on the Mutual network between Halloween and November 18, 1949; the latter version is discussed here.

of means by which radio narratives can be accessed makes it difficult for us to gain the understanding of "the evolution of the serial narrative form" that researchers seek (103), let alone to appreciate the impact a particular medium has on the content and form of serial narratives, as well as on our experience of them.

It should be acknowledged that the recordings I audited are far from authoritative. Only six of *ILaM*'s forty-odd sequences have survived virtually intact, and that in omnibus editions eliminating most of the introductory narratives as well as commercials. Not that this makes them less pure than broadcasts that are subject to atmospheric disturbances and the vagaries of everyday life impinging on the receptiveness of an audience all too frequently considered in the abstract, an unresponsiveness to acts of listening that audio-narratology can help and should strive to overcome.

No abstraction is implied in the term "auditor," proposed here to differentiate latter-day listeners, including my tinnitus- and hearing loss-suffering self, from the intended audience and actual tuners-in on whose experience and conditioning the radio gothic drew to such an extent that it calls for a contextualization to make its strategies of disorientation readable.

"What are we waitin' for?"

Aside from its signature collage and lead-in, recordings of which are not extant, "The Thing" opens with the humming of propellers indicating the interior of an aircraft. Quite literally, the story declares itself to be underway in the very process of exposition. The subsequent dialogue discloses that Jack (voiced by Russell Thorson), Doc (Jim Boles), and Reggie (Tony Randall) are returning to Los Angeles to enjoy the reward money from a previous assignment. Upon disembarking at Burbank, they respond to the surprise of being met by the chauffeur of an unsolicited limousine. Unable to resist the as yet unnamed "armful of girl" in the back seat, Doc has the last word in the matter: "Let's climb in. What are we waitin' for?" The line serves as a "tag," or cliffhanger, for the first chapter.

Morse (1944) dismissed as perfunctory the contrivance of an announcer's intrusive urging to "Listen tomorrow for the most hair-raising and exciting blah, blah." He held that a "tag" needed to be a "logical conclusion" to the scene preceding it (119). In keeping with plot and characterization, Doc Long's "What are we waitin' for?" is such a "logical" response. Having spent the duration of the flight attempting to relive his recent exploits via a newspaper article that eulogizes him as "the modern Tarzan," Doc fails to live up to the image created of him in print. "Pooh!" an unimpressed stewardess taunts him. "My folks live on a mountain ranch up in Washington. My mother scares mountain lions out of her chicken yard by shushing her apron at them." The bathos of comic deflation achieved through this reprocessing of storylines in repeated acts of editing and editorializing counteracts the erosion of the serial's thrill value. To anyone so puerile and thin-skinned, being seduced to ride in a stranger's sedan may be as hazardous as hunting vampires.

Not every auditor will be convinced that the limousine is the only stretch here. A contemporary reviewer of one such first installment of an *ILaM* sequence argued that the "characters were rather laboriously 'set' and the plot a long time moving an inch and a half" but, acknowledging that serials "are almost impossible to evaluate fairly on a single hearing," allowed for the possibility that the "lead-into sections of the continuity" might be "rapidly succeeded by something a little easier to chew on" (Landry 1939: 26).

The second chapter opens with Jack, Doc, and Reggie responding to their arrival in the mansion of one Randolph Martin, a potential client who is as yet little more than a name. The purpose of their stay is undisclosed, as Jack—summing up what transpired during the trip from the airport—has not gotten "one bit of information" out of the siren whose presence enticed them to step into the limousine. In the absence of soundscaping, it is the dialogue that furnishes the house, and the lexical *meubles*, however thinly scattered and slight, suggest an interior remote from the modern world of airplanes and automobiles. The house, as Jack describes it, is "overflowing with the refinements and niceties of an old family," with "signs of the family tree almost everywhere." What Bakhtin (1990) refers to as the "chronotope of the gothic castle" in his reading of Ann Radcliffe's *The Mysteries of Udolpho* applies to the architecture of Morse's serial at this point in time. Providing "very little new information," description consists of "suggestive bits" belonging to the "realm of the mysterious" (Bakhtin 1990: 245–46).

Also among the "suggestive bits" is a reference to "silk sheets," which Doc singles out with excitement. Before they can decide whether, in Jack's words, to "stay here long enough to sleep between any kind of sheets," the men are approached by a distraught young woman who appeals to them in a tremulous voice: "Look. Somebody slashed me." Asked to identify her attacker, she whispers that "they" did it, and that "they" are trying to kill her, offering nothing in stead of those pronominal placeholders. Dressing the woman's wounds, it is "apparent" to Jack "that the family tree is beginning to show signs of decay." "Rotten clean down to the root," Doc agrees. And yet, the power failure of language to shed light on matters makes it difficult to get to the dark heart of the Martin mystery. Might secrecy be the root of their rottenness?

Granting no access to the inner worlds of any one character—a conventionalized psycho-narrative exploited in soap operas through interior monologues—"The Thing" is set up as an onomastic poser in which auditors are encouraged to ponder whether the Martins are saints or sinners, whether their Christian cloaks truly suit or whether, if *nomen* be omen, they might grow into them. Ostensibly adhering to the conventions of radio serial dialogue in which, as Dunning (1998) points out, the "constant repetition of names" was designed to leave "no doubt" as to the identity of participants in a dialogue (463), "The Thing" turns the familiarity of repeated names into a strategy of estrangement. The wounded woman is Charity (voiced by radio stalwart Mercedes McCambridge), one of three sisters living in the Martin mansion, the others being Faith (the "armful" in the limousine) and Hope. "Whoever heard of naming girls Faith, Hope, and Charity?" Doc protests. "Sounds like a Texas camp meeting." That Charity begs and Faith demands to be called "Cherry" and "Fay," respectively, suggests at least a nominal rebellion against the imposition—or imposture—of a "rotten" lineage.

There is also a brother, Job, the three comrades are being told by Fay, but wherein his misfortunes lie and whether they are undeserved is as yet impossible to determine, even though it may dawn on auditors receptive to his queerness, which is hinted at in Fay's description of Job as a "good-natured drunk" who "hates girls" as well as Job's audible pleasure at being steadied by Jack's "nice firm hand." To a queer reader such as myself, this amounted to an aural equivalent of a Barthesian *punctum,* except that I became engrossed in wondering whether this was indeed an "accident," as Barthes calls it (1993: 25–26), or whether it was part of the design. It caused me temporarily to lose sight of the plot and pursue instead what had made me prick up my ears. How would listeners without recourse to recordings have taken the journey back in hand? Might some of them have been impelled by *ILaM*'s allusive design to trace Job's lineage to one of the earliest radio serials, *Myrt and Marge* (1931–1942, 1946–1947), which regularly featured a "thitthified costume designer" named Clarence Tiffingtuffer ("Give Us Love" 1934: 14)? Clued-in audionarratology may provide both occasions and justifications for our waywardness by allowing that what preoccupies one auditor as onomastics may become onanistic to another. What "The Thing" leaves in doubt at that moment is whether Job is meant to be a "rotten" fruit or whether he is responsible for the rot.

"Did you ever stop to think..." Reggie starts as he vows to give the absentee host a "piece of [his] mind." His words are cut off by the piercing cries of an infant, followed by sounds of a body taking a tumble. The noise subsides. A voice—stern, elderly, and female—demands to know what happened. Before the visitors can utter her name, the woman introduces herself as "Randolph

Martin," then states: "And I need help. I am having granddaughter trouble." Shrilly, the organ signals the conclusion of the second chapter. The inability to deduce even a character's gender from a proper noun upsets the guessing game just set up. And yet, Grandmother Martin, who asserts her matriarchal independence by rejecting the title "Mrs.," is so protective of the "family name" that she is determined to cover up, at almost any price, "the stench of a decaying family tree," as Jack has it, that manifests in the ignominy of her descendants.

A formidable challenge to the name of Martin and the game of onomastics alike is the eponymous "Thing," an offspring to whose parentage none in the household lays claim. As Fay, the self-proclaimed "vulgarian of the family," declares, "There's not a baby in this house. There hasn't been for years." What made itself heard is the "creeping, unhealthy menace" that Jack sensed from the start. In a tremulous whisper, Cherry intimates at the close of chapter 3 that "every time it cries, something horrible happens." As long as the truth of the statement remains in dispute—and the young woman's sanity seems doubtful indeed—the auditor is encouraged to associate the bawling of a newborn with a threat to life, be it homicidal or preternatural.

"The baby, and then something happens"

Aural foretelling is a recurring narrative strategy in *ILaM*. In "The Monster in the Mansion," an unseen killer plays an organ rendition of Brahms's "Lullaby" to announce each murder. In "Bride of the Werewolf," it is a mausoleum bell that tolls death (Harmon 1992: 65). "The baby, and then something happens," Doc keeps muttering in chapter 4 of "The Thing," reminding us of our conditioning. That the chosen herald of doom is an infant—by definition, somebody unable to speak and thus literally a pre-dictor—is a challenge to the belief that the word is the beginning and end of aural play. Martin Esslin, who headed BBC's radio drama division in the 1960s and '70s, expressed this bias when he argued that such "drama" was "pre-eminently a *writer's* medium" since it relied "almost entirely on *words*" (Esslin 1971: 6). It is a bias that Friedrich Knilli (1961) in his critique of the German *Hörspiel* termed "Verwortung," a privileging of the spoken word that reduces audio play ("Schall-Spiel") to verbal art ("Wortkunstwerk") (7–8). Audionarratology can assist in preventing radio plays from falling prey to readerly "Verwortung." Attuned to broadcasting techniques, it can make our readings *audible*—that is, connected with the sense of hearing—which in turn makes it possible for us to make audible even performances no longer extant as recordings (Heuser 2013: 11).

The sound effects of most radio plays are chiefly expository or atmospheric; they add character rather than being permitted to become one. An announcer's scene-setting "This is Illyria," for instance, is augmented or amplified by the sound of waves lapping the shore. Indicial or incidental, sounds in radio plays rarely speak for themselves; they are often explained in dialogue or narration and, having served their purpose, fade (or "go under") so as not to supersede the actor's voice as the principal carrier of meaning. Most overused among the effects to which Esslin refers as "aural clichés" or "acoustic ideograms" are howling wind and crickets (the indices of night), as well as action-accentuating noises of cracking bones, ricocheting bullets, or the "lovely patty-cake of fist hitting flesh," sounds that effected the derision of contemporary reviewers of radio thrillers in the US.[6] Although its budget-conscious revival was comparatively slipshod, *ILaM* set itself apart from conventional radio melodramas that, instead of exploring nonverbal and nonmusical sound narratively, further diminished such potentialities by resorting to extradiegetic mood music or *misterioso* that "The Thing" does without.

In his seminal study of wireless aesthetics, Rudolf Arnheim (1936) contended that the "urge of the listener to imagine with the inner eye is not worth encouraging," especially not if it inspires the supplementation of "missing" visuals (136–37). "The Thing" does encourage imaging but thwarts the process of supplementation. What is visible to the characters is no more confirmatory than the translative sounds we hear. Cherry's stigmata, the only ocular proof that the "Thing" may be real, are dismissed as potentially self-inflicted. In chapter 11, we hear Hope and Cherry struggle for a gun, the weapon used in the murder of their brother Job. The gun goes off and Hope is wounded. When Doc, the only eyewitness, relates the scene in the next installment, he is unable to say who pulled the trigger. And even when it performs a "striptease" right within our ears—as it does in chapter 10, in which a trail of clothing, "feminine, lacy, and perfumed," leads to a bound and gagged Cherry in front of a furnace "going full blast," as Reggie points out with dread—"The Thing" is a strip show that teases by setting scenes that could not have been fleshed out for public display, at least not on Hays-coded celluloid or early network television.[7] To appreciate the shrewdness of Morse's exploitation of the medium, auditors should bear in mind that chapter 10 was scripted for broadcast on Friday, which meant that, the action resuming on Monday, the

---

6. Esslin (1971: 10); Van Horne (1948: 20).

7. Another such "striptease" was performed over two consecutive days; see Stedman (1977: 179).

suggestive image could burn itself into the listener's mind to achieve maximum afterglow.[8]

ILaM's alchemic aurality, which can transmute woman into tiger (as in "Bury Your Dead, Arizona"), confronts us with sounds that do not comport with the form we might try to ascribe to them. Either our mental encyclopedia of the physical world does not yield a ready match or else the explications offered in words do not seem an echo to the sense we struggle to make of things, such as when, in "The Thing," we become aware that an infant's crying may not confirm the presence of a crying infant. "How interesting it would be," Tim Crook (1999) wrote some six decades after Morse's series first aired, if writers and producers of radio plays had the "courage" to "represent alienation, dislocation and the loneliness of the human condition" by using seemingly "confirmatory" sounds that "cast the anchor" only to set the listener "adrift" (70–71). Without any existentialist pretensions, *ILaM* accomplishes this by rendering the homely sounds of the nursery uncanny.

In the experience of listening, the floating signifier that is the sound of doubtful innocence keeps corrupting the air of respectability and taints the very notion of purity either until it exhausts our reason or until reason discharges it as exhaust. Untraced to its origins, the "Thing"—monstrously undemonstrable—remains a motherless other. Uncanny as the echo of a guitar and the "sweet" disembodied voice accompanying it, which, in Radcliffe's (1966) *Mysteries of Udolpho,* are said to "warn people of their death" (68), *ILaM*'s nocturnal ululations turn into character, their interpretation becoming plot. The inability—or pointlessness—to extricate such sounds from the plot draws attention to the demands made on our sense-making selves by the latter, and one anxiety I experience as a transcribing auditor is the unresolved tension between providing access to plot as a foundation of my reading and responding to my reader's insistence that I get on with it.

Despite the uncertainty as to the origins of the disembodied "Thing," its sonance, its existence as sound, is never called into doubt, even as the act of diagnostic auscultation becomes a source of dissonance for the bodied characters. The auditor hears what is audible to anyone physically present in the Martin household. Faced with the challenge of interpreting and tracing the rug rat oracle, the auditor of *ILaM*, although never addressed, is generally in the presence of at least one of the adventurers, with Jack serving as a reliable guide, Reggie as an equal partner, and Doc—who offers the theory that the

---

8. Currently circulating recordings of this chapter contain continuity from another transcribed broadcast, which invites listeners to tune in "tomorrow." The unreliability of unauthorized recordings, also in terms of speed, pitch, and sound quality, must be borne in mind when analyzing the broadcast performances to which they provide only incomplete access.

crying "Thing" must be a "baby ghost"—as a companion who comforts by virtue of his less than sound reasoning. Since the auditor shares in the experience, Morse's narrative does not communicate what Terry Heller (1987) refers to as "distant terror." Heller asserts that in "most works of the Gothic tradition terror is the experience of characters. The implied reader's role is that of sympathetic onlooker" (48). Being exposed to the sounds that Jack, Doc, and Reggie, despite the ostensible benefit of vision, can neither place nor translate, the auditor becomes embroiled in an event whose urgency and immediacy a print narrative of recalled episodes cannot quite approximate. Auditors, unlike lectors, are earwitnesses to a menace in the making of which they participate. Thus, Morse's terror is decidedly close, and it is safe only as long as the auditor's fictional companions remain within earshot.

Apart from the obligatory lead-in narrative, *ILaM* forgoes those storytelling techniques of commercial radio playwrighting that, in order to foreground the sponsor's message, encourage temporary detachment. Retrospective narration, in which the narrator who sets up a story becomes, via analepsis, one of its experiencers, is rejected in favor of dialogue recall, in which a participant in a discussion or an experiencer of an event relates to other characters what the auditor has already overheard or experienced. Whereas chapter 3 granted us access to Jack's conference with Grandmother Martin, Cherry, and Fay, the subsequent installment reunites the adventurers, with Jack relating the details of his discussion to Doc and Reggie. The occasional separation of the main characters and the recapitulation of dialogue it requires have obvious benefits for the broadcaster, as they protract the narrative while simultaneously reducing the number of performers. In doing so, they counter a gradual decline in ratings by permitting infrequent tuners-in and even audiences new to a program to enter the narrative with relative ease. Yet unlike the announcer's synopsis at the beginning of each chapter, dialogue recall transforms recapitulation into a dramatic event.

Giving auditors an opportunity to share in the act of disclosure and to assess to what degree an experiencer-turned-editor refashions the plot by elision or embroidery, Morse expands on a device radio producer-director Erik Barnouw (1939) referred to as "proxy listener"—a narratee whose interjections provide an occasion for the speaker to articulate thought (50). In *ILaM*, proxy listening becomes a participatory event in which the auditor temporarily gains a perceived advantage over a narratee that is not also an experiencer. Assuming the place left vacant by Doc and Reggie, the constant auditor is rewarded for loyalty to the serial by becoming not only a privileged secret sharer but also a judge of the tale and the character of the teller in the very event of sharing. Hearing Jack tell the truth diplomatically—as he conciliates his companions by pointing out that the reason for their exclusion was Grandmother Martin's lack of trust in the virtue of her kin in the presence of eligible bachelors—draws us still closer to our guide and sets us up for the disconcerting moment of withdrawal.

The broadcast audience's sense of intimacy and immediacy is reinforced through the congruity of action and airtime, as—with few exceptions—each chapter of *ILaM* constitutes a seamless scene without cuts and transitions. Inhabiting and navigating the fictional space, Morse's characters, however implausible the context of their actions, appear to do "no more than could actually be done in about a quarter hour" (Harmon 1992: 64–65). The radio listener partakes in whatever occurs, albeit at varying times of day, within a few minutes in the lives of the three friends. Contributing to this sense of a shared experience is the fact that what Jack, Doc, and Reggie "do," for the most part, is listening for and responding to clues provided by none-too-reliable victims, witnesses, and suspects. "There ain't no sense to nothin,'" Doc grumbles in chapter 7, a triple negative reaffirming the positive threat posed by the disembodied presence haunting the house. That Doc's restiveness results in his momentary loss of brio constitutes one of several reading instructions *ILaM*, like many narratives in the gothic tradition, offers its auditors. Patience, too, is one of the seven virtues. After all, the reward for putting uncertainty to rest is often nothing but the disclosure of a piece of waxwork (*The Mysteries of Udolpho*), an incident of cross-dressing (*Villette*), or a mere laundry list (*Northanger Abbey*). To a true sucker for mystery—a word that has its roots in *muein*, "to close the eyes," as well as *mu*, a "slight sound with closed lips"[9]—the real predicament of being assigned the task of putting a stop to nothing may well lie in being reduced to serving as a pacifier or baby's dummy. "Sound exists only when it is going out of existence," Ong (1982) reminds us; there is "no way to stop sound and have sound" (32). It shares this transient quality with the fantastic.

If, in the *Hörspiel*, the sound's the thing—and if even words are, as Ong (1971) has it, "basically and irreformably sounds" (264)—to what extent should such an art form satisfy or stimulate an auditor's desire to embody or reform sound by tracing it to a physical source of origin? For all its playfulness, Morse's mystery curtails the ludic experience of sound by setting the boundaries of a game that does not encourage the reading of the "Thing" as a severe case of tinnitus or else as a Dadaist "Ursonate." If to transmute the "Thing" means to render it mute, all mystery offers is a delay of a death sentence that is noncommutable. An end to the "Thing" means the end of "The Thing." Just what might "The Thing" be telling us about the state of radio mystery?

---

9. "Mystery" 1909.

"... it shouldn'a happened that way"

Chapter 11 opens with Jack and Doc trying to calm Cherry, whom they have carried back to her quarters. It is a room she claims to have "always hated." Cherry describes how, when she was a child, it was wallpapered with Mother Goose images whose characters seemed to spring to life in the darkness. When asked to return to the events of the night, she recounts being abducted and taken to the furnace room by a faceless creature hovering about in a red hood ("red, like when you stick your finger and the blood comes out"), intent on bloodshed that, she insists, has "got to go on and on and on until there isn't any of us left." All this she claims to "know." "Do you, actually? Or is it just your belief?" Jack asks. Cherry declares that "it's the same thing" and reminds Jack that she has not "been wrong about anything" she warned "was going to happen." Should we take Cherry's word for an elusive *it*? Does her retrospective foretelling suggest second sight or revision?

Having encouraged Cherry's outburst, Jack confounds his comrades by asking her a seemingly unrelated question: "Do you know a girl named Pauline West?" Cherry's bewilderment expresses itself in delayed response and intervals of silence. The flush of evocative images is stanched by a proper noun from which no definitive mental picture can yet be derived. Jack explains that he read the name on a casting sheet he found next to Cherry's body, and that Pauline West appears to be a radio actress. Stating that he "never heard of her before," Doc admits to being an avid listener of broadcast melodramas, "in love with all the women on the air," as Jack puts it. A "couple of 'm I'd like to write dialogue for," Doc confesses, adding that the "words" he'd put "into those babies' mouths'd make the radio censors turn over in their graves." In Doc's expressed preference for fictional characters mouthing his words over the flesh of a female body, stripped and speechless at his feet, Morse asserts his power as a creator of mind games.

The reference to the world of broadcasting brings home as well how near the House of Martin stands to the edge of an industry whose scandalmongers and namedroppers were once fed by the family's disloyal and recently liquidated chauffeur. Now the name of Martin is threatened by a Hollywood nobody who, recasting herself as an instrument of torture, exacts retribution for being reduced to hawking her wares in a marketplace so dehumanized in its production-line approach to the performing arts that it is interested solely in her mimicry of bawling infants—a professional baby crier such as the ones employed on daytime serials, including Morse's own *One Man's Family* (1932–1959). Refusing to materialize, the nominal one remains a hovering signifier, becoming as Delphic as the ominous "Thing" that auditors are now invited to associate with "Pauline West"—another one of Morse's richly evocative names, recalling the heroine of the silent film serial *The Perils of Pauline,* Paulina presenting a suspicious king with his wife's baby in Shakespeare's *The Winter's Tale,* as well as the "Pauline Principle" of not doing evil for the sake of good. Whatever our associations, the fact that the name of "West" is called upon to produce such disorientation heightens the self-consciousness of a chapter play initially titled "Hollywood Cherry" for its 1939 West Coast run (Grams 2003: 76).

Jack expresses his conviction that Pauline West is at the heart of the decline and fall of the Martin family. In conversation with his companions, he claims to have untangled the mystery but delays sharing his solution of it with them. Rebuffing Grandmother Martin's attempt to dismiss her retainers, Jack leaves cryptic instructions (such as peeling off the three top layers of the wallpaper in Cherry's room), to be carried out in the case of his demise. After ordering all parties to their rooms, Jack remains behind in the stillness of the deserted library to confront the "Thing." In the proverbial dark for the first time, the auditor is left hanging on Jack's every word, wondering whether our uncommunicative guide is facing a deathly adversary or dead air. Yet his words do not confirm whether his verbal confrontation spells calculated strike or desperate shadow-boxing:

> I don't quite know where you are. You may be right here in the room with me. You may be watching from some panel I don't know about or one of the windows or doors. I don't know. All I know is that you've been listening to everything that's been said in this room. I know you were there. . . . You may be the murderer. I don't know. But whether you are or not, you're a very unhealthy person. You're afraid. You feed on darkness. Your thoughts are lustful and violent. You're the power of evil in this house. . . . It's been fascinating working against you, and in a way it seems a pity that you're at the end of your rope. I don't know when that end will come. That'll depend on you. An hour, day, not much more than that. And I want to tell you that I . . .

At this moment, Jack is interrupted by Doc, who staggers into the room, stammers that he has been hit over the head, and collapses. The "Thing" begins to make itself heard, and Jack cries out for Reggie.

Our inability to determine whether Jack's words constitute a soliloquy or the intelligible portion of a dialogue with an inaudible, stealthy addressee makes this, to my mind, the most unsettling scene of the sequence. In radio plays, silence generally denotes absence. Since many bodily sounds were deemed unsuitable for broadcasting—and permissible ones, like screams, snores, or sneezes, signaled unsound bodies or absent minds—narratees had to respond verbally to remain alive and well in the consciousness of the auditor; otherwise, as Barnouw cautioned writers of broadcast dialogue, they would soon vanish "into a cloud of non-existence." Sending his heroes and his listeners in search of a missing body—now bawling, now lurking—Morse subverts these conventions by way of a technique Barnouw (1939) termed the "vanishing character utilized" (56–57), thereby heightening uncertainty. After all, if the unseen "Thing" has existence in sound as well as silence, how is it to be quelled?

The penultimate chapter is a nocturnal free-for-all during which the air of the Martin mansion is filled with clamor and chloroform (the ethereal adversary's mind-numbing weapon of choice). Even in its fifteenth and final installment, "The Thing" continues to postpone the business of making sense. At the same time, the pace quickens. This is achieved in the only montage of the sequence in which, for the first time, the auditor is separated, albeit briefly, from all three companions. Determined to prevent the disclosure of Pauline West's identity from becoming "something for the newspapers to gloat over," Fay takes matters in her own hands and eludes our guides by locking them up. As they attempt to break free, the cries of a baby are heard once again. The perspective shifts, and without warning (such as a fade or musical bridge), the auditor is at the mercy of Fay as she takes Cherry to the attic and lures her to the ledge of the roof. Fay's soothing voice is faded out, giving way about two minutes later to a frantic exchange between Jack and Reggie and their noisy escape as they crash through the door.

Having witnessed our unwitting guides succeed, we are subjected to their futile search for Fay downstairs, until the trio reunite and catch up with us by spotting the two women through the "glass roof of the sunroom." In a brief scene that rehabilitates a technique radio writer George Wells (1944) dismissed as the "*look-see* system," a "form of allegedly dramatic conversation in which a character carefully describes all visual incidents to a companion, or stooge" (91), the hapless observers pick up on what the auditor already knows, namely that Fay is about to kill Cherry, but by updating us on the situation, the swift exchanges between the observers—their exclamations of "Look" and "Watch out!"—communicate that Cherry is resisting that attempt. The two crashes that follow are a last aural assault on the truism Arnheim (1936) referred to as the "dangerous illusion that seeing is knowledge" (280). Generating suspense like a Hitchcockian episode of informed but impotent spectatorship, the climactic montage does not simply shatter the Martin mansion or silence the "Thing." By rendering permeable what was believed to be solid, it compromises the very architecture of the maze. Far from being granted momentary transparency, the auditor is subjected to a dissolve just moments before the resolution. "No, no, it shouldn'a happened that way," Doc moans, sounding as incredulous and dispirited as radio reporter Herbert Morrison at the sight of the Hindenburg disaster.

"The House of Martin has fallen," Jack concludes as he nimbly lines up the casualties like so many dominos: Fay killed Cherry, who murdered Job, who silenced the chauffeur. The survivors, Hope, Fay, and Grandmother Martin, are hospitalized for a bullet wound, a fractured skull, and a broken leg, respectively. As Jack explains to his baffled companions, "Pauline West" was a pseudonym that Cherry adopted during her stint in broadcasting as a baby crier, her ability to tackle speaking roles having been deemed insubstantial. Realizing that Job had silenced the Martin's hush money-demanding chauffeur, Cherry shot her brother to save him from the law, and—having always been a "nervous, excitable child" whose "mind absorbed the [figures on her wallpaper] to the point where she could never get rid of them"—lapsed into dementia. Thus ends the story of an aging matriarch who, dreading the thought that her charges might supply fodder for Hollywood's yellow journalism, appoints a triumvirate of headline-making adventurers, only to find the papered-over defects of her kin exposed and the illusion of home torn asunder by the encroachment of Tinseltown.

A narrative of a Hollywood career cut short by a failed audition that ends in the spectacular silencing of a radio voice and its bodied double, "The Thing" draws on a familiar if unlikely contrivance of broadcasting: ventriloquism. Two of radio's highest-rated attractions had promoted voice projection to a figure of transgressive empowerment. Vaudeville throwback Charlie McCarthy aside, radio's premier voice-caster was Lamont Cranston, alias The Shadow, a "technocrat magician" whose "telegraphic speech" and metallic voice reverberate, as Jason Loviglio (1999) has pointed out, with the "idiom of electronic communication" (322, 324). And yet, The Shadow was initially conceived by an advertising agency as nothing more than a promoter of pulp fictions—a spokesperson without personhood. In "The Thing," the dark art of casting voices, narrowly or broadly, is exposed as an impersonation in whose nature we can descry the corruption of communication and the unwholesome fragmentations of modern life. Ventriloquism serves as a figure of speech representing the depersonalizing business of commercial broadcasting and its body of tongue-tied artists and scribes who, generally barred from speaking their mind and forced to mind their speech, endured by devising modes of indirection.

Early in his career, Morse (1932) argued the "mystery play" to be "by far the best medium" through which to "train" the "ear" of an audience new to the "drama on the air" (40). Such efforts, more self-serving than a means to an end, would come to naught as the specter of television—anticipated as being just around the corner since the 1930s—militated against training for a medium that Bertolt Brecht, himself a radio playwright, referred to as an "antediluvian invention" (Brecht 1968: 119). It was a rite of passage for radio writers—Arthur Miller, Irwin Shaw, and Herman Wouk among them—to renounce or ridicule the industry (Heuser 2013: 299–323). Yet writers' responses to the medium are readable in their work for that medium as well. Since the earliest experiments in radio playwriting—Richard Hughes's "Comedy of Danger" (1924) and Hans Flesch's "Zauberei auf dem Sender" (1924)—plays for the medium have foregrounded their writers' responses to the medium, encouraging us to appreciate the challenges they faced. Bespeaking a process of uneasy negotiations, many radio plays reflect on their ephemerality and marginality, as well as on the lack of artistic and economic independence. Reflexive and at times subversive, they puzzle over, mystify, or demonize the source of their subsistence.

Morse's chapter play exhibits what Garrett Stewart (1996) observes in late Victorian gothic fictions, which "unload the burden of psychological disturbance from content onto form." Yet whereas the "metatextual gothic of reading" instituted by fin-de-siècle writers arguably had the "recuperative aesthetic mission" of erasing the tarnish of "rank escapism" of earlier Victorian serial writing, radio gothic did not develop such a shielding aesthetics. If it had any armor, it was its awareness that it could *not* be saved. Fulfilling its obligation to remain in the "healthiest possible circulation" (392), "The Thing" displays the evidence of its own pathology. When radio's corpus was gutted for parts, as *ILaM* was in the mid-1960s, it became clear just how accurately Cherry's cries foretold the fate of the medium that begot them. An unsold television pilot produced about a decade and a half after Morse's radio serial had ended its second and final run played back those cries without tracing them to their origins. Erasing all reference to the crier's past in radio—or any other medium—the once essential sound was reduced to an echo without a source, signifying nothing other than a calculated attempt at closing a generational gap by tempering camp with nostalgia.[10]

Listening to old works for radio anew on the web makes it more difficult still for us to hear their workings. Serials like "The Thing" are rendered mute once they are no longer understood as "structure" responding to "medium." Informed audionarratology can help ready our receptiveness to what radio plays had to say in the first place.

---

10. In *The Unknown* (1946), a film that is part of Columbia Picture's *ILaM* series and loosely based on "The Thing," the cries emanate from a baby doll.

The Gothic of Audition

No reading deserves the term "gothic" if it is strictly academic. I have been haunted by "The Thing" ever since I first happened upon it in the mid-1990s, when it was rebroadcast in weekly installments over WBAI, New York. Drawn into its story world, I felt nonetheless estranged from the world that brought it into being, a sphere in which narrators might be frowned-upon announcers and crying like a baby could be a day job. Plays like "The Thing" made me anxiously aware that radio was not yet my thing. The gothic of audition partakes of what H. Porter Abbott (2009) termed the "cognitive sublime"—"an immersion in a state of bafflement" and the realization that "what is baffling" may not "belong to the text but to ourselves" (132). No determination as to what does and does not "belong to a text" can be made without an attentiveness to the medium. Aside from the estrangement that concerns Abbott—who in turn cites Viktor Shklovsky's concept of *ostranyenie,* of "making strange" or "showing the strangeness of" (Abbott 2009: 131–32)—auditing as retroactive tuning-in can also make strange what once was a familiar experience to millions of listeners. "We must try to define better the anxiety that can take hold of the reader," Dorrit Cohn (2012) declares in her response to Genette's *Narrative Discourse.* Cohn is referring to a "troubling state," a "feeling of disarray," brought on by extradiegetic intrusions into a story world (110–11). Acquainting ourselves with the medium and the conventions of broadcasting can prepare us better to account for our anxieties as transcribing auditors by helping us to tell them apart from the tensions experienced by radio writers and their erstwhile listeners.

A sustained engagement with neglected chapter plays like Morse's should make us suspicious of theoretical approaches that may be more formulaic than the texts under discussion. "Far too much criticism . . . is based on too little actual knowledge of the medium and its programs," the writer of an unpublished master's thesis on radio serials declared. After spending weeks "auditing all the radio serials" available to him for listening at the time via network-affiliate stations in his area, the student determined that no "generalizations other than their being broadcast five times a week for something less than fifteen minutes can be made about all radio serials" (Rowe 1949: 3–4). While such an assessment is unlikely to satisfy scientifically minded readers to whom generalization is the only valid conclusion, closer attention to differences in narratives produced for the same medium will better prepare us critically to respond to studies that propose to examine "serial manifestations across the novel, film, television, comics, radio, podcasts, and online platforms such as Twitter and Facebook—the vast spectrum of media and genres that serials have infiltrated across times and contexts" (O'Sullivan 2019: 51). Listing radio without listening to it, many such studies achieve the crossing of media only by crossing at least one of them out.

Audionarratology must begin with listening. Where it ends—what is germane to it—depends on our imagining the ends it may serve. Back in 1990, Mieke Bal's "The Point of Narratology" sought to invigorate narratology both by broadening its applications, including visual studies, and by interfacing it with practices in other disciplines. Bal (1990) rejected the notion that, as a "systematic theory," narratology is "by definition ahistorical." On the contrary, Bal argued, narratological analysis "helps to position the object within history" (750). In readings of radio plays, the "object" in question is a complex system of relationships that insists on making itself heard—"Do you see anything?"—by asking us to negotiate something of a position. As I see it, the potential of audionarratology to broaden narratology rather than being subsumed under it as a rarefied pursuit lies in our openness to networking among the estranged. And instead of disciplining ourselves so we can get listening down to a science, we might take the unfamiliarity of this emerging field as an opportunity to get down with the strangeness of our unscientific, transdisciplinary, and hybrid selves.

Works Cited

Abbott, H. Porter. 2009. "Immersions in the Cognitive Sublime: The Textual Experience of the Extratextual Unknown in García Márquez and Beckett." *Narrative* 17, no. 2: 131–42. https://www.jstor.org/stable/25609359.

Alvin, Joe. 1940. "We All Love a Mystery." *Radio Varieties* (August 1940): 16.

Andersen, Tore Rye, and Sara Tanderup Linkis. 2019. "As We Speak: Concurrent Narration and Participation in the Serial Narratives '@I_Bombadil' and Skam." *Narrative* 27, no. 1: 83–106. https://doi.org/10.1353/nar.2019.0005.

Arnheim, Rudolf. 1936. *Radio*. Translated by Margaret Ludwig and Herbert Read. London: Faber.

Bakhtin, Mikhail. 1990. "Forms of Time and of the Chronotope in the Novel: Notes toward a Historical Poetics." In *The Dialogic Imagination*, edited by Michael Holquist, translated by Caryl Emerson and Michael Holquist, 84–258. Austin: University of Texas Press.

Bal, Mieke. 1990. "The Point of Narratology." *Poetics Today* 11, no. 4: 727–53. https://www.jstor.org/stable/1773075.

Barfield, Ray. 1996. *Listening to Radio, 1920–1950*. Westport, CT: Praeger.

Barnouw, Erik. 1939. *Handbook of Radio Writing*. Boston: Little.

Barthes, Roland. 1993. *Camera Lucida: Reflections on Photography*. Translated by Richard Howard. London: Vintage.

Bayer-Berenbaum, Linda. 1982. *The Gothic Imagination: Expansion in Gothic Literature and Art*. Rutherford, NJ: Fairleigh Dickinson University Press.

Brecht, Bertolt. 1968. "Radiotheorie: 1927 bis 1932." In *Bertolt Brecht: Gesammelte Werke*, vol. 18. Frankfurt: Suhrkamp.

Chatman, Seymour. 1978. *Story and Discourse: Narrative Structure in Fiction and Film*. Ithaca, NY: Cornell University Press.

Cohn, Dorrit. 2012. "Metalepsis and Mise en Abyme." *Narrative* 2, no. 1: 105–14. https://www.jstor.org/stable/41475353.

Conrad, Joseph. 1996. *Heart of Darkness*. First published 1899. In *Joseph Conrad: Heart of Darkness: A Case Study*, edited by Ross C. Murfin, 17–95. London: Macmillan Education.

Crook, Tim. 1999. *Radio Drama: Theory and Practice*. New York: Routledge.

Dunning, John. 1998. *On the Air*. New York: Oxford University Press.

Elleström, Lars. 2019. *Transmedial Narration: Narratives and Stories in Different Media*. London: Palgrave Macmillan.

Esslin, Martin. 1971. "The Mind as a Stage." *Theatre Quarterly* 1, no. 3: 5–11.

Field, Stanley. 1958. *Television and Radio Writing*. Boston: Houghton Mifflin.

"Give Us Love . . . and Come Back Home!" 1934. *Radioland* (December): 14–15.

Grams, Martin Jr. 2003. *The I Love a Mystery Companion*. Churchville, MD: OTR Publishing.

Harmon, Jim. 1992. *Radio Mystery and Adventure and Its Appearance in Film, Television and Other Media*. Jefferson, NC: McFarland.

Heller, Terry. 1987. *The Delights of Terror: An Aesthetic of the Tale of Terror*. Urbana: University of Illinois Press.

Heuser, Harry. 2005. "Listening to 'The Thing That Cries in the Night' (Chapter One): Danger Is a Block-Long Limousine." *broadcastellan*, October 31, https://harryheuser.com/2005/10/31/listening-to-the-thing-that-cries-in-the-night-chapter-one-danger-is-a-block-long-limousine/.

———. 2013. *Immaterial Culture: Literature, Drama and the American Radio Play, 1929–1954*. Bern, Switzerland: Peter Lang.

Knilli, Friedrich. 1961. *Das Hörspiel*. Stuttgart: Kohlhammer.

Landry, Robert J. 1939. "I Love a Mystery." *Variety*, October 4.

Loviglio, Jason. 1999. "The Shadow Meets the Phantom Public." In *Fear Itself: Enemies Real and Imagined in American Culture*, edited by Nancy Lusignan Schultz, 313–30. West Lafayette, IN: Purdue University Press.

Mackey, David R. 1951. *Drama on the Air*. New York: Prentice.

Morse, Carlton E. 1932. "Murder Will Out." *Radio Doings* (January): 29+.

———. 1944. "One Man's Radio Program." In *Off Mike: Radio Writing by the Nation's Top Radio Writers*, edited by Jerome Lawrence, 116–21. New York: Essential-Duell.

———. 1949a. "Bury Your Dead, Arizona." *I Love a Mystery*. 15 chapters. November 21–December 9. MBS. *Internet Archive*, https://archive.org/details/otr_iloveamystery.

———. 1949b. "The Million Dollar Curse." *I Love a Mystery*. 15 chapters. December 12–30. MBS. *Internet Archive*, https://archive.org/details/otr_iloveamystery.

———. 1949c. "The Thing That Cries in the Night." *I Love a Mystery*. 15 chapters. October 31–November 15. MBS. *Internet Archive*, https://archive.org/details/otr_iloveamystery.

"Mystery." 1909. *Etymological Dictionary of the English Language*, rev. ed. Oxford: Clarendon.

Nye, Russell. 1970. *The Unembarrassed Muse*. New York: Dial.

Ong, Walter J. 1971. *Rhetoric, Romance, and Technology*. Ithaca, NY: Cornell University Press.

———. 1982. *Orality and Literacy*. London: Methuen.

O'Sullivan, Sean. 2019. "Six Elements of Serial Narrative." *Narrative* 27, no. 1: 49–64. https://doi.org/10.1353/nar.2019.0003.

Radcliffe, Ann. 1966. *The Mysteries of Udolpho*. First published 1794. New York: Oxford University Press.

Rowe, Stanley Robert. 1949. "The Radio Serial." Master's thesis, Boston University.

Ryan, Marie-Laure, ed. 2004. *Narrative across Media: The Languages of Storytelling*. Lincoln: University of Nebraska Press.

Solomon, Matthew. 1997. "Adapting 'Radio's Perfect Script': 'Sorry, Wrong Number' and *Sorry, Wrong Number*." *Quarterly Review of Film and Video* 16, no. 1: 23–40.

Stedman, Raymond William. 1977. *The Serials: Suspense and Drama by Installment*. 2nd ed. Norman, OK: University of Oklahoma Press.

Stewart, Garrett. 1996. *Dear Reader: The Conscripted Audience in Nineteenth-Century British Fiction*. Baltimore, MD: Johns Hopkins University Press.

Todorov, Tzvetan. 1973. *The Fantastic: A Structural Approach to a Literary Genre*. Translated by Richard Howard. Cleveland, OH: Press of Case Western Reserve University.

Van Horne, Harriet. 1948. "Just Showing How Dull a Thud Can Be." *New York World Telegram*, May 20.

Wells, George. 1944. "Radio's Strangest Bird." In *Off Mike: Radio Writing by the Nation's Top Radio Writers*, edited by Jerome Lawrence, 86–96. New York: Essential-Duell.

7

Auricularization and Narrative-Epistemic Stance in Louis Nowra's *Echo Point*

JARMILA MILDORF

UNRELIABILITY IN FICTION is often said to be a textual phenomenon that rests on discrepancies between what happens and how a narrator interprets and presents those events (Nünning 2008: 38). However, as Ansgar Nünning (2008) convincingly argues, unreliability is best understood as a multifaceted narrative phenomenon that involves both rhetorical strategies and readers' perceptions of what they are presented with. Tamar Yacobi (2005) also foregrounds the importance of interpretation and readers' strategies for sense-making in her theory of "unreliability." She conceptualizes unreliability as a "reading-hypothesis" that is "formed in order to resolve textual problems (from unaccountable detail to self-contradiction) at the expense of some mediating, perceiving or communicating agent—particularly the global speaker—at odds with the author" (110). Henry James's *The Turn of the Screw* is a case in point for such textual problems (albeit not the example that Yacobi analyzes; she focuses on Tolstoy's *Kreutzer Sonata*). Ever since its publication in 1898, *The Turn of the Screw* has created interpretive conundrums, and scholars have debated whether the novella represents a straightforward ghost story or a complex tale about a governess's delusional mind (Felman 1985; Goddard 1957; Heilman 1948; Wilson 1934). Wayne C. Booth (1961: 311–16) uses the novella as one example for discussing the category of the "unreliable narrator," and he points out that "hundreds of modern works present the reader with precisely the same kind of problem" (315), namely an "unintentional ambiguity of effect" (216), that is, one not intended by the author. Numerous scholars have discussed ambiguity in James's works and have traced this ambiguity to stylistic and narrative-rhetorical features, as did, for example, Shlomith Rimmon (1977) in her rigorous study that is informed by linguistics, logic, Russian Formalism, and French structuralism.[1] Rimmon (now Rimmon-Kenan) is mostly concerned with ambiguity that arises because two mutually exclusive *fabulas,* or stories, are present in one *syuzhet,* or discourse. She demonstrates how there is an interplay between prospective and retrospective ambiguities in *The Turn of the Screw* that hinges on conflicting cues offered to readers to fill in textual gaps. Interestingly, her study also alerts us to the fact that ambiguity need not only be tied to the character-narrator's perceived unreliability but can arise from other textual features. Ultimately, however, the question whether James deliberately used those features to mislead his readers remains open. In his recent book *A History of Ambiguity,* Anthony Ossa-Richardson (2019: 14–18) delineates a controversy that ensued between Shlomith Rimmon and J. Hillis Miller, who called Rimmon's concept of ambiguity "a misleadingly logical schematization of the alogical in literature" (Miller 1980: 112). As Ossa-Richardson critically observes, both scholars lost sight of the question of the author's intention—a question that is not trivial and deserves some reflection in a chapter on ambiguity and unreliability in radio drama. I will return to this point in the following.

The same ambiguity that can be found in James's novella is created—albeit intentionally, I argue—in Australian writer Louis Nowra's radio play *Echo Point,* which was directed by Judith Kampfner and first broadcast on BBC Radio 4 in the afternoon program (14:15) on July 31, 2012. The radio play, which is just under forty-five minutes in length, tells the story of a former pianist, Esther Morris, who accompanies her husband to an excavation site somewhere in the Blue Mountains in Australia, an old spa ("Wentworth Spa," 00:38) where women were treated for drug addiction and "madness." Esther begins to hear music and voices, and when she starts to identify with one of the former patients, she is eventually driven to killing her husband and the caretaker of the place. Like Henry James's *The Turn of the Screw,* the radio play creates ambiguity about whether it is a story about ghostly apparitions (or rather, sonic presences) or about someone merely imagining these apparitions. At the same time, however, when listening to the radio play one cannot avail oneself of the impression that Esther experiences some form of mental delusion, which is mainly supported by circumstantial evidence presented in the story world, as I will discuss in more detail shortly.

---

1. For another study on James's ambiguity in the stylistics tradition, see Norrman (1982).

In this chapter, I want to explore questions of narrative unreliability and ambiguity in radio drama. By taking Nowra's radio play as a case study, I argue that even though—similarly to films—radio plays have their own radiophonic means of narrating (see also Frank 1981; Huwiler 2005) and thus also facilitate effects such as ambiguity and unreliability (Chatman 1978: 235–37; Koch 2011), these effects are qualitatively different from similar effects in written narratives, especially when it comes to aspects connected to sound perception. The reason for this, I contend, is that auricularization seems to make distancing more difficult and potentially contributes to a complicated narrative-epistemic stance because radio audiences do not "read about" the sounds characters hear but in fact hear them themselves. I will look at how radiophonic techniques and elements such as blending, reverberation, and music are used in *Echo Point* to constantly mislead listening audiences while the story unfolds. My analysis of selected moments in the radio play addresses issues surrounding the radio play's paratextual and expectational frames, auricularization and listener engagement, story-world-intrinsic explanatory frameworks, and narrative-symbolic dimensions. Before I move on to my analyses, I briefly discuss narrative unreliability and ambiguity.

Narrative and Ambiguity of Effect

In a written narrative, potential interpretive difficulties may arise because there is a problem of "distancing," as Booth (1961, chs. 11 and 12) contends. Texts like Henry James's *Aspern Papers* and James Joyce's *A Portrait of the Artist as a Young Man* make it difficult to decide whether the implied author's worldview or "norms" are close to or distant from those of the characters he presents. Readers therefore have trouble figuring out whether the characters' experiences are to be taken "at face value" or whether they must be read more critically as being refracted through the implied author's ironic or critical lens. This in turn creates distance on the reader's part. More specifically, Booth delineates three reasons for how distance or lack thereof can create difficulties: (1) "Lack of adequate warning that irony is at work" (316) can cause readers to overlook the implied author's clues and thus the narrator's tacit interpretation and evaluation of events and characters. (2) "Extreme complexity, subtlety, or privacy of the norms to be inferred" (320) may make it difficult for readers to decide how close to or distant from their narrators implied authors actually are. (3) "Vivid psychological realism" (322) might keep us close enough to narrators and characters to influence our evaluation of these personae and to make us buy into their flawed narratives or perceptions. In *The Turn of the*

Screw, the problem arises because we can never be sure if we can trust the governess's story, even though the novella's frame narrative supports an image of her as a respectable and trustworthy character. We simply do not know what James's (implied) stance toward his own character-narrator really is. Furthermore, we cannot be sure whether we should accept a story world in which the existence of ghosts is possible or whether we are to discard this possibility. In Tzvetan Todorov's terms, *the fantastic*—that is, a textual genre in which two realities, one natural and one supernatural, clash, leaving the reader in doubt about which of these realities holds true—persists unless we decide to read the governess's tale as either a genuine ghost story, which would then shift it to the genre of *the marvelous*, where the supernatural element is fully accommodated, or as a figment of the governess's mad mind, which would make it an *uncanny* narrative, one in which seemingly supernatural events are explained in rational terms but still leave the reader with a sense of unease, incredulity or even shock (see Todorov 1975: 41–42; for an excellent reworking of Todorov's theory, see Durst 2010). The problem is that the novella offers no conclusive instruction or, as Rimmon has it, misleads us with mutually exclusive clues for how to read the text, so we are left with a level of uncertainty that Todorov considers the defining criterion for the fantastic. In *Echo Point*, we are equally left with a sense of uncertainty even beyond the ending of the radio play, and this is largely connected to the fact that conflicting "messages" are sent out at both the radio play's story and discourse levels, as I will discuss in more detail below.

In contradistinction to Booth, Gregory Currie (1995) uses a slightly altered version of "unreliability" to also accommodate this concept in film narration, and he introduces another term to complement "unreliability": "ambiguous narrative." A narrative is ambiguous "when it raises a question in the viewer's mind which it fails to answer, and where the raising and the nonanswering seem to have been intentional" (24). Currie starts out from the hypothesis that unreliability, rather than being based on a perceptible discrepancy between the implied author's and narrator's norms, is intricately related to the notion of a "*complex intention* on the part of the implied author" (22), which can be deduced by readers/viewers, albeit perhaps only on second reflection. Thus, an implied author may offer us clues that hint at a possible explanation of what happens in the story world while at the same time wanting us to pursue more "hidden" clues so we eventually arrive at the implied author's "real" intention behind the whole fabrication. This process presupposes a complex communicative system not unlike the one presented by James Phelan in his book *Living to Tell about It*. Phelan (2005) addresses the "complex relationships between the functions of the narrator in relation to the narratee and the functions of the implied author in relation to the authorial audience" (5), which he then captures by the terms "narrator functions" and "disclosure functions" (12), respectively. In this theoretical framework, which focuses on what Phelan terms "character narration"—essentially, first-person narratives—there are therefore two channels of communication emanating from the narrator (but that are, of course, orchestrated by the implied author): one that is directed to the narratee and that transports what the narrator wishes to convey, and another one through which the narrator unwittingly divulges to the authorial audience information that may even contradict what he or she tells through the narrator-functional channel. However, what if there is no narrator-persona who tells us about the story world?

One could argue—as Currie (1995) did for film narration—that it is possible to conceive of narratives without narrators but not without implied authors (20). Similarly, Robert Vogt (2009) distinguishes between unreliable narration that is connected to flaws inherent in a narrator persona, and unreliability that emerged from what he calls "irreführenden Diskurs" (51), that is, a narrative discourse (without an actualized narrator-character) that deliberately misleads readers. *Echo Point* would fall into that category since the radio play does not feature voice-over narration and thus never leaves the mode of "showing" or mimetic presentation. Still, as a mimetic-narrative genre, radio drama clearly "tells"—or let's say, generates—a story, albeit in a different manner than written novels do. Elke Huwiler, building on Mieke Bal's (1997) tripartite division of "narrative text," "story," and "fabula" (5), distinguishes among the abstract *level of narrative communication* ("narrative Kommunikationsebene"), at which the narrative act takes place; the *level of story* ("Ebene der Handlung"), which comprises events, characters, space, and logical relationships in the raw, that is, before they are brought into a narrative relationship; and the *aspect of narrative presentation* ("Aspekt der narrativen Darstellung"), whereby story elements are transformed into an actualized or concrete narrative ("Geschichte") (Huwiler 2005: 84–85). The aspect of narrative presentation determines how story elements are presented but also which perspective orients the action. Huwiler thus also foregrounds focalization as an essential element in radio play storytelling. Coming back to Currie's proposal, I do not think that one ought to discard the level of narrative communication in film and radio drama even in the absence of overt narrator-characters/-speakers. As a compromise, one can regard the conglomeration of media-specific techniques employed to achieve narrativization (e.g., event sequencing through cutting, blending, music, and so on or story-world construction through dialogue, voice characteristics, sounds, etc.) as a kind of narrative instance. To determine what the implied author should be in radio drama or film to my mind is also less straightforward than Currie makes it out to be. In the present example, one can of course posit an implied version of the real author, Louis Nowra, as the primary source of whatever intention we suspect behind this radio play. However, this view grossly simplifies and distorts the fact that the actual radio play performance was produced by a whole production team including a director, a musical composer, voice actors, sound technicians, and many more. Whatever this team produced must be considered an interpretation of the radio play as conceived by Nowra—much as a musical score is interpreted by musicians in an actual performance or concert.

Nevertheless, the notion of a *complex intention* as the source of ambiguity in this radio play is an appealing and helpful theoretical construct, but perhaps we want to modify Currie's "implied author" by saying that there is some original intention located with Louis Nowra that the production team helped realize and turn into the radio play's narrative act, which ultimately rests on the team's interpretation of the original playscript. I also concur with Huwiler in arguing that focalization plays a vital role when it comes to understanding a radio play narrative and, even more so, one that creates ambiguity. Currie (1995) criticizes narratologists such as Seymour Chatman who link unreliability to a narrator persona, and usually to a first-person narrator, for that matter (27). However, the fact that Booth also refers to Jane Austen's *Emma* as an example for how distance can become a problem in understanding irony suggests that third-person narratives equally raise questions about reliability or, to use Booth's framework, about the relative proximity of an implied author to his or her narrator. I argue that in such novels a further mismatch is potentially created between events and actions on the story-world level and the ways in which these events and actions are focalized through one character's "eyes" and are subsequently processed, understood, or interpreted. In other words, there is a discrepancy between the narrator's and the presented character's perceptions of the story world, but it may prove difficult to identify where this discrepancy begins and where it ends. Thus, third-person narratives may cause problems of distance when it is not clear whose perspective orients the presented actions and events at any given moment.

Audio drama can also accommodate narrative effects that are based on focalization or, to use a more media-appropriate term, auricularization ("l'auricularisation"; Jost 1987). Events can be heard as if from a particular character's vantage point or from the position of a technical device (e.g., a recording device; Lutostański 2016), and a sense of positioning is created through distance or nearness to the microphone. Such auricularization may foreground some audible aspects of the story world and background or ignore others. The question arises whether radio plays can thus also create unreliability. Chatman (1978) argues that "visuals are no more sacrosanct than words" and can therefore also "lie" (237). However, his example, Alfred Hitchcock's *Stage Fright*, precisely features camera footing that is at the service of the film's narrator-character, who—as it transpires in the end—told an untrue story. I contend that unless the presented story is evidently linked to a more or less overt narrator figure who may or may not make us feel suspicious toward the narrative, we tend to trust the narrative instance in radio plays much as we would trust a traditional extradiegetic-heterodiegetic (omniscient) narrator. In other words, we believe that what we hear gives us an adequate picture of what happens in the story world—until we are encouraged to think otherwise. This is where Nünning's synthetic approach to unreliability is helpful because it allows us to take into consideration listeners' perceptions. Furthermore, I want to use Currie's term "ambiguous narrative" rather than "unreliable narration" because, as I hinted at earlier, Nowra's radio play creates epistemic conundrums as the presented perspective (i.e., Esther's) is not literally told or reported but is "enacted" (or should one say "ensounded"?). The radio play's media-specific interplay between diegesis and mimesis on the level of sound will be shown to raise and *not* fully answer the fundamental question mentioned at the outset of this chapter, namely whether Nowra's play constitutes a ghost story or not.

At this point, I also want to distinguish between the term "ambiguity" and other related terms such as "indeterminacy" or "obscurity," for example. Unlike these latter terms, "ambiguity" implies the existence of alternative readings or interpretations that can be identified but that cannot ultimately be decided upon (see Bode 2007: 68). Both "indeterminacy" and "obscurity," by contrast, suggest the impossibility to know or penetrate all possible layers of meaning. In radio drama, it may, for example, be difficult at times to figure out what exactly it is one hears, for example, whether a sound means that floorboards are squeaking because someone is walking over them or that a door squeaks while it is being opened. This local indeterminacy is different from the question—a question of ambiguity—of whether the sound one hears (and clearly recognizes) is one that actually exists in the story world or whether it is only one imagined by a character. As my analysis will show, Nowra's play is rich both in potential local indeterminacies and ambiguity.

Paratextual Framing and Ghost Story Conventions

One question that is pertinent when analyzing radio plays is how a radio play is framed paratextually. How is the radio play advertised on the radio station's website? How is it introduced by the continuity announcer? Is it given a specific slot in a program that we associate with a particular genre? Interestingly, the announcer introducing *Echo Point* on BBC Radio 4 referred to it as "a dark, haunting story," and the audio download website Soundcloud expressly gives the radio play the label "ghost story."[2] Thus, the story is already presented as belonging to this specific generic category, and the implication for our subsequent listening experience is that Esther's sound perceptions must be real. Another airing of the radio play on BBC Radio 4 on October 3, 2016, was scheduled for midnight—the time slot that, because of its association with the witching hour, is particularly suited to eerie stories. Thus, the radio play is once again framed as a ghost tale, even if more implicitly.

This implicit framing can also be seen in a number of conventions we typically link to ghost or horror stories. Thus, when Esther and Gavin Morris drive to the spa in the Blue Mountains at the beginning of the radio play, their car is enveloped by a thick mist or fog and they nearly have a car accident with what sounds like a fast motorbike that appears unexpectedly without its lights on (01:15). As I will discuss, the fog can also be said to have symbolic implications, especially when it is interpreted in connection with other images evoked in the radio play. At this stage in the radio play, it simply foreshadows further danger. The very setting reminds one of the Gothic tradition: The spa is located in a faraway place in sublime natural surroundings, and, more importantly, it is a place with a past, as we learn from Esther, who reads out a description from a "*Guide to the Health Resorts of Australia*" (01:32) from 1905. Later, Esther comments, "This spa seems to be creepy to me" (16:23). At that point, she has already heard voices and piano music (see the following).

The spa's full historical background is only revealed by the janitor, Mr. Harrison, nearer the end of the radio play (35:00 and following). Thus, while the only information Esther gathers from the guidebook is that "Dr Merrill makes disease peculiar to women his speciality" (01:36), we later learn that the spa was a sanatorium where women were treated for "drug dependency" (35:30) and also that one of the inmates, composer Freda Barrymore, killed her husband and the doctor (35:38). Interestingly, this backstory is juxtaposed with another revelation about Esther's own medical history: Gavin tells the janitor that as a young woman, Esther believed she was "in spiritual communication" with the composers whose works she played, that she had a "severe breakdown" at seventeen, was "put on anti-depressants," and became a heroin addict before she eventually came off it (34:53–35:16). In the following, I will explore further how this kind of information sets up an internal explanatory frame-

---

2. https://soundcloud.com/ judithkampfner/echo-point-by-louis-nowra.

work for the "madness hypothesis." However, the very fact that those revelations take place late in the play and, indeed, that Esther herself comes to learn more about the events that led up to Freda's killing of her husband and Dr. Merrill only piecemeal suggests a plot design that is reminiscent of mystery stories more generally. Additionally, almost clichéd sound features such as a clock that strikes in an eerie metallic sound in the late hours (12:15), a screeching owl (14:05), and the repeated sounds of old creaking doors and floorboards as well as echoes, which characterize the site, sufficiently cue us into the mood of a ghost story. There is apparently an intention that audiences should recognize or at least be stimulated by these sonic markers of "ghostliness."

This kind of stimulation also operates on a subtler level. Thus, the radio play constantly creates short moments of suspense by confusing listeners about what they actually hear. For example, after the owl screeches, the sound tapestry becomes slightly confusing because a number of sounds are mixed: We hear very deep individual piano notes and then fragments of a melody, as if from a distance at first but then increasing in loudness; these musical notes are given an echo-like quality through reverberation. There are footsteps and Gavin obviously snores while Esther tries to alert him to the sounds she hears: "Gavin, [pause] did you hear that?" (14:16–14:19). This is followed by the rustling sound of the bedding Esther apparently pushes aside to get up and then a squeaking sound when a door is being opened. The implication is that Esther leaves the room to explore the sounds and music she hears. The music is discontinued and makes way for an unidentifiable rattling sound that reminds one of metal being pulled along a surface and that gradually increases in loudness. At the same time, a voice can be heard—only faintly at first but then more clearly. Soon, we hear a female voice say at a high pitch, "No! Let me out" (14:33), and then, after she has made some puffing and panting sounds as if from physical exertion, she says in a quite determined manner, "No, it's not doing any good" (14:39–14:42). While the rattling sound quite disturbingly continues in the background, the woman says, "No, I don't want this. No, I'm not here. Please! No. Help? You can't help. I'm cured" (14:42–14:56). The pronunciation of the vowel sound in "please" is drawn out, which makes the woman's voice sound imploring at that point. She also comes across as quite desperate. Strangely, the voice quality changes slightly with the question "Help?"—as if there was another female person present. This would also be substantiated by the subsequent address pronoun "you," which suggests the presence of two interlocutors. However, the two female voice qualities are sufficiently similar to also allow the interpretation that the woman talks to herself in different voices. The radio play in its performed version remains ambiguous in this regard.

Then, we hear again a door opening, which is followed by a dull sound of something heavy dropping into water. The sound is never clarified: Has the woman drowned? This mixture of disparate sounds and the introduction of an as yet unidentified character create a sense of disorientation in the listener. At the same time, suspense is built up precisely because of this uncertainty. As listeners, we are very much in the same position as Esther, who, at the culmination point of this sequence asks loudly and clearly, "Who's there?" (14:47) and then repeats three times a questioning "Hello?," which is quite rhythmically punctuated by the loud and unpleasant sound of something like glass smashing into pieces. At first, the listener—who has already been on edge because of the preceding sequence—might at this point well believe that someone dropped something onto the floor or that a window broke. At any rate, the way this sound is integrated into the entire sequence, we parse it as belonging to that moment in the story. However, the next thing we hear is one of the construction workers who have been hired to systematically demolish the place and to excavate and preserve anything of value that can be found of the old spa hotel. He addresses his coworker ("Oh, c'mon Dale"), and it suddenly becomes clear that the smashing sound we heard a moment earlier really belongs to this subsequent scene, which takes place the next morning. The workers destroyed a wall and found a collection of old bottles—containing drugs and medicines that stem from a pharmacy that had been attached to the old spa, as we then learn from Gavin.

What we see here is how the radio play uses radiophonic means such as blending to connect two spatiotemporally distant scenes while at the same time creating confusion about that very transition point. It is only with hindsight that the indeterminate sound starts to make sense to us. Our heightened sense of suspense is relieved for a moment before we move on to similarly eerie scenes. What happens here in miniature form is the strategy the radio play adopts on a larger scale as well: Fantastic situations that seem to be resolved in the direction of the uncanny ultimately still leave us with a lot of open questions. Thus, in this scene our curiosity is piqued regarding the strange woman and her seemingly desperate situation. Furthermore, we still cannot know what this scene actually presented to us. Is this possibly a first indicator for the sexual abuse the patient suffered at the hands of Dr. Merrill, who—as a later scene makes clear (38:16–38:35)—used the woman's drug addiction to coerce her into sexual activities ("You know what the payment is"; 38:25–38:26). On first listening to the radio play, we may have a hunch that this is what is happening, but it is again only with hindsight (and after listening to the radio play several times) that things begin to make better sense. One question, however, still remains unanswered: Are these ghostly scenes real or does Esther only imagine them? This is where auricularization comes into the picture.

Auricularization and the Problem of Reliability

Echo Point is by no means exclusively focalized through Esther's sense perceptions. In fact, there are a number of scenes when she is not even present, for example, when Gavin interacts with the construction workers or talks to the janitor. However, Esther's point of sound perception seems to be the only "audioposition" (Verma 2012: 35) that also allows us access to the strange soundscapes at the spa. Put differently, we hear what Esther hears, while none of the other characters seem to be able to hear the voices and the music (although the radio play also creates ambiguity in this regard, as I will point out). What is most interesting in this connection is the fact that both the voices and the piano music change their qualities from vague and distant at first to loud and clear later in the radio play. Thus, when Esther hears the piano tune for the first time (10:23), it is barely audible and located at a far distance. The tune blends into the sound of a male voice talking (from 10:35 onward)—again rather muffled and distant and thus not unlike the voice of Dr. Merrill. We hear how Esther opens a door (10:47), and at that moment, the hitherto quiet and distant male voice is foregrounded and becomes very clear. It turns out to be Mr. Harrison, who explains, "Just been talking to myself; I, I can get a better-quality conversation that way" (10:56–10:59). In contrast to the scenes where Esther hears Dr. Merrill, the male voice here is "naturalized" when Esther realizes (just as we do) that the voice has been Mr. Harrison's. Not only does this moment at least temporarily mislead the listener once again, it also marks the janitor as a somewhat "odd" person. More importantly from an audionarratological perspective, the clarity of the voice—once the speaker is identified—suggests that this story moment is located at the story world's "realistic" level: The janitor unmistakably exists. By analogy, the radio play's audiophonic aesthetics suggest the same for Dr. Merrill and Freda Barrymore. When we hear the conversation between the doctor, his patient, and her husband from 37:32 onward, their voices are also foregrounded and very clear—that is, their presentation is no different from how the other characters' voices are presented in the radio play. The fact that these voices are no longer defamiliarized by means of electroacoustic manipulation such as reverb, backgrounding, or decreased volume seemingly brings the characters onto the same story-world-internal ontological plane as the other characters. At least we hear them now as if they "really" existed. The only question is whether they "really" exist as ghosts or if they only do so in Esther's imagination.

As I already indicated, the radio play creates further ambiguities in this regard. About halfway through the radio play, Esther asks Mr. Harrison about whether he ever hears any voices. His answer is quite interesting as it suggests that Esther may not only be imagining things: "You know, when I first started out as caretaker I heard everything: voices, crying, talking, whispering. But I got used to them, and I realized that they weren't voices but the wind, creaking floorboards, grounding water paths, you name it. This dump doesn't stop making noises" (20:36–20:59). The janitor's explanation is very important, and hence perhaps not coincidentally at the center of the radio play, because it seems to corroborate Esther's experiences. Like her, Mr. Harrison also heard "voices," and even though he discounts his own experiences, the specificity of the various voice qualities he mentions ("crying, talking, whispering") makes them very similar to the voices Esther and, by implication, the audience, heard. In other words, there is another "ear witness" of the spa's strange soundscapes, which may make us rule out the "madness hypothesis." However, this character is himself not entirely reliable. It is implied that he enjoys his drink, and he comes across as a rather scurrilous person, not least because he talks to himself and keeps late hours. Later, when he has a lengthy conversation with Gavin, he somewhat deprecatingly says of Esther, "She thinks she's channeling that dead woman" (34:50–34:52)—as if this was something "crazy." He thus seems to be "ganging up" on her with Gavin, much as Dr. Merrill and Mr. Barrymore were ganging up on Freda before she decided to kill them. The radio play at this point enacts the idea that history repeats itself, and it underlines the shadiness and ambiguity of the janitor's role in Esther's story.

Esther increasingly has to justify her actions and the "fact" that she hears music and voices. For example, when she overhears a conversation between Dr. Merrill and Freda (again presented at a distance and lower volume), Gavin surprises her and asks, "What are you listening to?" (23:51–23:52), which gives her a fright. The question suggests to the listener that Esther must have placed her ear on the wall to hear the conversation on the other side better. This is a good example for how the dialogue provides information for listeners and thereby actualizes a concrete scene of the story world in their minds. Esther explains to Gavin that she hears sounds through the wall, but she is also quick to reassure him that she is simply not used to the noises in this strange place and she says, "Don't worry, I'm not going bananas" (24:12). Esther's defensive attitude can be explained by the fact that Gavin, at an earlier moment in the radio play, dismissed her hearing of the piano music as being "in your head" (18:48), thus implicitly stigmatizing her as the "crazy" woman he believes her to be. I will return to this explanatory framework in the following. What these moments also seem to indicate is that Esther is indeed the only person (perhaps apart from the janitor) who can hear things. The audiophonic presentation of the piano music she hears is also very interesting in this connection.

As I already said, the piano music initially remains in the background and is barely audible because Esther only hears it through the wall. However, at 16:38, the piano can be heard loudly and clearly, and a specific melody, which very much reminds one of Erik Satie's *Gymnopédies,* is now foregrounded: At first, the notes a and e of the small octave range alternate and constitute the bass pattern against which a tune in the first octave range then sets in. The music thus oscillates between relatively deep or dark tones and a tune that appears "lighter" because of its higher pitch and greater variation in tone lengths. It is also played in three-four time, which is typical of dance tunes. The key is "a minor," which—despite the melody's buoyancy—does not make it a "happy" tune. It rather sounds "dreamy" and seems to express a sense of longing. The first few notes are played reluctantly and with interruptions; we hear Esther sigh. Apparently, she is trying out the tune that has been "haunting" her, as she says later in the radio play (26:40). What is most striking in this scene is the fact that one tone sounds "tinny" or inharmonious because the string is out of tune. Esther is quite frustrated by this. Strangely, however, when she plays the piano again (25:16), the same tone sounds perfectly all right, as if the piano had been tuned in the meantime. Esther becomes very excited about this and fetches Gavin to play the melody to him, but then the piano is out of tune again. This upsets Esther very much, as one can hear in her voice quality, which expresses her surprise when she says, "That's impossible. [Plays the inharmonious note again.] It was working perfectly before" (26:50–26:58) and assumes a whining quality when Esther continues, somewhat defensively, "I did hear it!" (27:00). What Esther then says agitatedly gives the listener a good impression of Gavin's nonverbal reaction: "This is not possible. Don't look at me that way, don't patronize me. I know what I heard!" (27:03–27:10)—which is followed by a cut before the scene transitions to the next scene. Apart from displaying Gavin's behavior, which stigmatizes Esther as the "mad woman," that moment in the radio play is also significant because it highlights the problem of (un)reliability in connection with auricularization. When Esther exclaims, "I know what I heard!" listeners can perfectly identify with her sentiments because they also know what they heard. The fact that we actually heard Esther play the tune on the piano and that the piano was all right contributes to our sense of Esther's reliability, I would argue, because we are not given any reason to assume that she only imagined all this. Her sense of irritation and despair also strike a chord with us; it is easy to see why she would be frustrated at that moment. If we assume that this moment was "real," then the "ghost theory" becomes more feasible. We may imagine Esther to have been possessed by Freda's ghost. However, the radio play does not use any of the clichéd presentations of possession, such as a change in Esther's voice quality or in her behavior more generally.

So, the fact that we are constantly "ear witnesses" to Esther's experiences potentially makes us side with her. There is only one moment when we cannot hear what she hears: after she has killed Mr. Harrison and Gavin, Esther is found by the proprietor, Mr. Auldred, in the room where the piano is, and she seems to have an experience of ecstasy where she apparently can hear exquisite music. She says to Auldred, "Mr Auldred, would you leave us in peace? Freda and I want to hear the music of the gods" (42:08–42:14). And a bit later she exclaims, in a tone as if she had an orgasm, "Uh, isn't that the most beautiful music you've ever heard?" (42:21–42:26). The audience, by contrast, cannot hear any music. There is only a very dark and dull sound like subcontraoctave piano tones, but they are barely distinguishable. The sound here is extradiegetic and creates an eerie atmosphere. Like Mr. Auldred, who looks at the scene from the outside, we also no longer side with Esther but are invited to perceive her as a psychotic person who now succumbs to her hallucinations.

Mental Illness as an Explanatory Framework

It thus seems as if Esther's mental illness is strengthened as an explanatory framework for what happens in this radio play. Toward the end, many little details contribute to substantiating the "madness hypothesis": For example, just before Esther kills Harrison, we hear how she, humming to herself, whets a knife (from 38:38). She then also speaks in a tone of voice that suggests that now she is possessed by Freda's spirit. She says, "Come to mommy, come to *Mutti!* [pause] I spy. [pause] Ah, there you are!" (38:56–39:06). The German word *Mutti,* which also means *mommy,* links Esther with Freda, who was German. The exclamatory particle "Ah" is extremely drawn out and spoken with a simultaneous exhalation of breath, like a deep sigh. At this very moment, the piano music sets in again, loud and clear. It is quite obvious that this cannot be Esther playing the piano, so it must be either ghostly music or music in her head that now guides her toward killing Mr. Harrison and her husband. All these circumstances seem to build up an image of Esther as the "mad woman" who is now going to go on a bloody rampage. The conventionality of the sound of a knife being whetted is noteworthy in this connection because there is no real reason why Esther should be doing this. However, for listeners used to this sound from horror films, it strongly suggests danger and the coming closer of the terrible culmination point. Here, it also implies a degree of deliberation: Esther prepares herself for the killing. We can see once again how sound cues us into the narrative.

Significantly, this scene occurs straight after the scene where we heard Dr. Merrill coerce Freda Barrymore into complying with his sexual wishes.[3] This also reinforces the parallels between the two women. Both women are musicians, and both have a history of drug addiction. Moreover, Esther played the tune that runs through her head when she was in the first year at the conservatorium. The recollection of this fact happens fairly late in the radio play (at 32:31), but it constitutes an important piece of the puzzle for the listener. If this is a story about "madness," then this memory indicates the ways in which things can bubble to the surface of consciousness from the unconscious—some memories that have been lost or suppressed. If it is a ghost story, it is easy to see why Esther of all people should have been chosen to become a channel for the dead Freda: They already had a connecting point in the past. Looked at from the outside, the situation appears to point to Esther's psychotic state, and it is therefore not surprising that her husband does not validate her experiences. When she admits to him that she keeps hearing "this piece of music" (18:44), he immediately responds, "In your head" (18:47–18:48). Later, she flushes her medication down the toilet, justifying this by saying to herself, "Get rid of them. They're clouding your mind. I have to be clear. Clear as glass" (24:17–24:39). The last phrase, "clear as glass," is echoed twice, and it recurs once more exactly in the same tone at the end (42:44–42:45), when Esther kills herself after she has murdered the two men and dramatically collapses on the piano. This again creates ambiguity: On the one hand, it is easy to interpret Esther's behavior in the light of her mental illness, which—because of lack of sufficient medical intervention—is aggravated and leads to her psychosis. At the same time, because we are mostly given Esther's subjective perspective on the events, we are bound to feel more sympathetic toward her in her situation and perhaps even to condone her actions as an act of rebellion. In this regard, it is also interesting that Gavin is not necessarily presented as a likable person. As Esther says at some point, he "patronizes" her, and by not showing his support when she feels troubled by the sounds and voices she hears, he also does not come across as a loving husband. Furthermore, as I already discussed, his talking to Mr. Harrison about her mental state could be interpreted as a "gang-

---

3. Interestingly enough, the sexual nature of Dr. Merrill's wishes is never expressly verbalized. Still, we fill this gap of surface information by drawing on our cultural knowledge of similar interaction patterns in many other stories and films.

ing up" against her in a situation where she no longer complies with what he deems "normal."

The parallels between Esther and Freda operate on a subtler level as well. Thus, we early on form the impression that Esther's marriage is not a happy one. When Gavin tries to make love to her near the beginning of the radio play, she rejects him, and one senses disappointment in Gavin. Later, when she stays outside drinking all night, Gavin's reproachful attitude in the morning is made clear to the listeners when Esther says to him, tauntingly, "Disapproval suits you" (32:15–32:16). Gavin responds, in a rather dismissive tone, "I can't take you like this" (32:17–32:19). This parallels Mr. Barrymore's outrage when he discovers that Freda has been consuming eau de cologne and tried to break into the pharmacy at the sanatorium (37:30–37:53). Since we are never really given an insight into how Gavin feels about the whole situation, we may well see his resentment in a more negative light. Furthermore, his concern about Esther's mental illness may also be reinterpreted as a power game intended to keep her in a submissive state. The fact that Esther repeatedly speaks up against the way Gavin treats her (for example, when she says defiantly, "Don't Esther me!" [30:01] and "Esther is going sane!" [30:25–30:26]) points to an unhealthy dynamic in their relationship that, at least from her point of view, involves oppression. The question of Esther's "madness" thus also becomes potentially ambivalent.

The Symbolic and Metaphysical Dimensions

There are numerous aspects on the symbolic level of the radio play that underline this ambivalence regarding Esther's mental problems. For example, it is no coincidence that the place in which Esther retrieves her memory of the composer Freda Barrymore is an archaeological-architectural excavation site. Just as the workers gradually discover the original foundations of the sanatorium, Esther seems to move deeper and deeper toward her unconscious mind, where she is finally united with Freda. In this connection, it is interesting to note that Sigmund Freud (1974) himself used the image of the archeology of Rome as a comparison—albeit a problematic one, as he remarked—to the "archeology" of the psyche (201–4). The fog at the beginning of the radio play already signals the place's mysteriousness, and it could also be regarded as an image for secret knowledge that is covered up before the fog is lifted. The echoes that permeate the former spa represent the ways in which Freda's past resonates with Esther—on the levels of both personal experience and emotions. Thus, both women need their "madness" in order to be creative, and both resent the oppression they experience at the hands of men. The process of a (re)awakening of the unconscious is symbolized by the moment when the workers tear down a wall and are suddenly flooded with water from one of the former baths (from 36:50). Moreover, there are plenty of eels in the water. Eels are very mysterious animals that play a symbolic role in numerous cultures. In Oceanic folklore, the eel "served as an intermediary between the people and their god" (Werness 2003: 155), and because of its phallic shape, it is often associated with fertility and seduction (just like the snake in the Christian tradition). In the context of the radio play, one could interpret the eels as representing the creative, but also sexual power in Esther that bursts forth again once she stops taking her medication. Thus, she is able to remember the tune she once played and can actually perform it perfectly on the piano. She also increasingly behaves in a lascivious manner, for example when she dances on the table (from 28:32) while she and Gavin are having a party with the workers—just as one would expect of a clichéd "madwoman" (think of Bertha Rochester in *Jane Eyre* and *Wide Sargasso Sea*).

The religious symbolism is strengthened toward the end of the radio play when Esther experiences the ecstatic moment in which she can finally hear the "music of the gods" (see above). I already pointed out the sexual suggestiveness of that moment because Esther sighs in a way that is reminiscent of sounds produced during sexual intercourse. At the same time, ecstasy is a religious experience, a "coming out of oneself" that brings one closer to God. On this interpretation, Esther's ecstasy at the very moment when she dies implies that she finally reaches fulfilment. Freda can then be regarded as a kind of "messenger" from the realm of the dead whose function it is to lead Esther toward her fulfilment. At that moment, both women also overcome the restrictions imposed on them, not least the social and patriarchal fetters that hampered their creativity.

Conclusion

The latter interpretation of course only suggests itself once one thinks more deeply about the potential symbolic implications of what happens in the radio play. This interpretation competes with other interpretations that hinge on Esther's mental problems. In a Western cultural paradigm, the ghost story interpretation and the madness hypothesis are irreconcilable—hence the ambiguities that the radio play creates by communicating divergent messages. It makes sense to assume that Louis Nowra meant us to pursue the various interpretive tracks the radio play offers (Currie's "intention") and ultimately to be perplexed by the unanswerability of the question whether Freda is "real" or not. As I pointed out throughout my discussion, the radio play's audiophonic means support the diverse interpretive possibilities. The auricularization of piano music and eerie sounds at the spa validates Esther's experience to the extent that we can also clearly hear those sounds. Put differently, there is a certain "realism" about these sounds because they are precisely not defamiliarized through electroacoustic manipulation. We thus experience them as belonging to the actual story world (rather than Esther's fantasy world). Furthermore, many conventional features such as clocks striking, owls screeching, and doors creaking set us in the mood for a ghost story. By contrast, the way other characters talk about Esther and explain her "strange" behavior suggests an alternative view, namely that Esther clearly does have mental problems. However, as I have indicated, those judgments are mitigated by the fact that these other characters (Gavin and Mr. Harrison) do not come across as very reliable or even likable characters either.

What thus emerges in the end is a complex picture that resembles the complexity in written stories marked by unreliable narration. Just like in *The Turn of the Screw*, the radio play's channels of narrative mediation work on our minds, gripping our attention and creating this pleasurable and taunting sense of ambiguity. It may perhaps matter less to a radio audience whether the ambiguities created stem directly from the author. Indeed, as I discussed earlier, the fact that a whole team of radio practitioners is responsible for a play's production in a sense "dilutes" the very notion of authorship. Still, from a theoretical and analytical perspective it makes sense—at least to my mind—to posit that ambiguities are not merely random textual or, in this case, radiophonic effects but rather effects created for a purpose: to draw readers/listeners in and to give them a challenge by posing unanswerable questions. Even with the example of James, I am not convinced that he could have been truly oblivious to the ambiguities he created in and through his writings.

Works Cited

Bal, Mieke. 1997. *Narratology: Introduction to the Theory of Narrative*. 2nd ed. Toronto: University of Toronto Press.

Bode, Christoph. 2007. "Ambiguität." In *Reallexikon der deutschen Literaturwissenschaft*, edited by Klaus Weimar, 67–70. Berlin: De Gruyter.

Booth, Wayne C. 1961. *The Rhetoric of Fiction*. Chicago: The University of Chicago Press.

Chatman, Seymour. 1978. *Story and Discourse: Narrative Structure in Fiction and Film*. Ithaca, NY: Cornell University Press.

Currie, Gregory. 1995. "Unreliability Refigured: Narrative in Literature and Film." *The Journal of Aesthetics and Art Criticism* 53, no. 1: 19–29.

Durst, Uwe. 2010. *Theorie der phantastischen Literatur*. Berlin: LIT.

Echo Point. 2012. Produced and directed by Judith Kampfner, script by Louis Nowra, performed by Brandon Burke, Lucy Bell, and John Gaden. BBC Radio 4.

Felman, Shoshana. 1985. *Writing and Madness: Literature, Philosophy, Psychoanalysis*. Ithaca, NY: Cornell University Press.

Frank, Armin Paul. 1981. *Das englische und amerikanische Hörspiel*. München: Fink.

Freud, Sigmund. 1974. "Das Unbehagen in der Kultur." First published 1930. In *Kulturtheoretische Schriften*, 192–270. Frankfurt a.M.: Fischer.

Goddard, Harold C. 1957. "A Pre-Freudian Reading of *The Turn of the Screw*." *Nineteenth-Century Fiction* 12, no. 1: 1–36.

Heilman, Robert B. 1948. "The Freudian Reading of *The Turn of the Screw*." *Modern Language Notes* 57, no. 7: 433–45.

Huwiler, Elke. 2005. *Erzähl-Ströme im Hörspiel: Zur Narratologie der elektroakustischen Kunst*. Paderborn: Mentis.

James, Henry. 1999. *The Turn of the Screw*. 2nd ed. Edited by Deborah Esch and Jonathan Warren. First published 1898. New York: Norton.

Jost, François. 1987. *L'Œil-caméra: Entre film et roman*. Lyon: Presses universitaires de Lyon.

Koch, Jonas. 2011. "Unreliable and Discordant Film Narration." *Journal of Literary Theory* 5, no. 1: 57–80.

Lutostański, Bartosz. 2016. "A Narratology of Radio Drama: Voice, Perspective, Space." In *Audionarratology: Interfaces of Sounds and Narrative*, edited by Jarmila Mildorf and Till Kinzel, 117–32. Berlin: De Gruyter.

Miller, J. Hillis. 1980. "The Figure in the Carpet." *Poetics Today* 1, no. 3: 107–18.

Norrman, Ralf. 1982. *The Insecure World of Henry James's Fiction: Intensity and Ambiguity*. London: Macmillan.

Nünning, Ansgar. 2008. "Reconceptualizing the Theory, History and Generic Scope of Unreliable Narration: Towards a Synthesis of Cognitive and Rhetorical Approaches." In *Narrative Unreliability in the Twentieth-Century First-Person Novel*, edited by Elke D'hoker and Gunther Martens, 29–76. Berlin: De Gruyter.

Ossa-Richardson, Anthony. 2019. *A History of Ambiguity*. Princeton, NJ: Princeton University Press.

Phelan, James. 2005. *Living to Tell about It: A Rhetoric and Ethics of Character Narration*. Ithaca, NY: Cornell University Press.

Rimmon, Shlomith. 1977. *The Concept of Ambiguity—The Example of James*. Chicago: The University of Chicago Press.

Todorov, Tzvetan. 1975. *The Fantastic: A Structural Approach to a Literary Genre*. Translated by Richard Howard. Ithaca, NY: Cornell University Press. (French original: *Introduction à la littérature fantastique*. Paris: Editions du Seuils, 1970.)

Verma, Neil. 2012. *Theater of the Mind: Imagination, Aesthetics, and American Radio Drama*. Chicago: The University of Chicago Press.

Vogt, Robert. 2009. "Kann ein zuverlässiger Erzähler unzuverlässig erzählen? Zum Begriff der 'Unzuverlässigkeit' in Literatur- und Filmwissenschaft." In *Erzählen im Film: Unzuverlässigkeit—Audiovisualität—Musik*, edited by Susanne Kaul, Jean-Pierre Palmier, and Timo Skrandies, 35–55. Bielefeld: Transcript.

Werness, Hope B. 2003. *The Continuum Encyclopedia of Animal Symbolism in Art*. London: Continuum.

Wilson, Edmund. 1934. "The Ambiguity of Henry James." *Hound & Horn* 7: 385–406.

Yacobi, Tamar. 2005. "Authorial Rhetoric, Narratorial (Un)Reliability, Divergent Readings: Tolstoy's *Kreutzer Sonata*." In *A Companion to Narrative Theory*, edited by James Phelan and Peter J. Rabinowitz, 108–23. Malden, MA: Blackwell.

8

"Arthur Lolled"

Audiophony and Humor in
The Hitchhiker's Guide to the Galaxy

OLIVIER COUDER

COGNITIVE HUMOR THEORY explains humor as a phenomenon owing to the coinciding activation of two or more overlapping but opposite scripts. In literature, this incongruity generally materializes as a discrepancy between the textual information on the one hand and readers' schemata on the other hand. Schemata are structured representations of events, objects, or actions acquired through experience. In the context of the radio play, textual information is supplemented by or translated into auditory information that is also included in readers' schemata. Auditory cues and techniques, then, have considerable impact on the narrative humor as they, for example, add to the characterization, setting, and narration. This chapter focuses on the relationship between these narrative categories and auditory features in Douglas Adams's radio play *The Hitchhiker's Guide to the Galaxy* and how both work together to create humor. First, I provide some additional context on the genesis of the radio play and its characteristic humor as well as cognitive humor theory.

When Adams (1952–2001) wrote and conceived of *The Hitchhiker's Guide to the Galaxy*, he initially envisioned it as a television series, only to end up settling for radio as he felt he was "too junior to do television" at that time (Adams qtd. in Roberts 2014: 92). Adams, however, quickly embraced the opportunities the medium of radio offered. He decided early on that *Hitchhiker* would be "full of ideas, full of detail, experimental" and "unlike anything done on radio before. Epoch-making. A milestone in radio comedy" (Gaiman

2009: 31). But above all else, he "just wanted to do stuff [he] thought was funny" (Adams qtd. in Gaiman 2009: 32). Judging by the global success and immense popularity of everything *Hitchhiker,* Adams's sense of humor was obviously shared and appreciated by many.

Adams had always shown a great interest in and love for comedy. While a student at Cambridge, he was allowed to join the Footlights Dramatic Club, following in the footsteps of one of his greatest comedy heroes, John Cleese. The innovative and absurd comedy style of Monty Python's highly successful *Monty Python's Flying Circus* had a huge impact on Adams (Roberts 2014: 25) and has undoubtedly left its mark on *The Hitchhiker's Guide to the Galaxy*.[1] The 1960s and '70s were also a successful era for science fiction. In the wake of Isaac Asimov's *Foundation* trilogy, science fiction authors such as Ursula K. Le Guin, Philip K. Dick, and Arthur C. Clarke enjoyed both critical and commercial success. Science fiction also made its mark on television, with three seasons of *Star Trek* airing between 1966 and 1969.[2] Closer to home for Adams were the popular television shows *Blake's 7* (which ran between 1978 and 1981) and *Dr. Who,* particularly the seasons with actor Tom Baker as the fourth incarnation of the eponymous doctor. Adams himself briefly worked as a scriptwriter on *Dr. Who,* a show he had enjoyed even though it did not always share the comedic tone Adams preferred (Webb 2006: 105–6). In fact, some of the feedback Adams received from the script editor on *Dr. Who* was that he had made his script too absurd and too much of a comedy show.[3] Luckily Adams could pour his energy and his considerable comedic genius into the first series of *The Hitchhiker's Guide to the Galaxy,* which had recently (1977) been commissioned by the BBC.

The Hitchhiker was conceived of, then, during an era when its audience would have been very much familiar with the conventions of the genre of science fiction. Science fiction comedies, however, were much less prevalent

---

1. Adams really always wanted to be a member of Python. He finally got his wish, to some extent, when he was invited by Graham Chapman to collaborate on a number of sketches, one of which actually made it to air and earned Adams a writing credit on the show and also saw him performing on television alongside his comedy heroes (Roberts 2014: 47–48; Webb 2006: 72).

2. The final words of the show's now immortal introduction ("to boldly go where no man has gone before!") are hilariously spoofed at the beginning of the third episode of *The Hitchhiker's Guide*: "And all dared to brave unknown terrors, to do mighty deeds, to boldly split infinitives that no man has split before and thus was the empire forged" (Adams 2003: 53; "Fit the Third," 01:10–01:20).

3. Adams toned it down somewhat, and two of his episodes made it to the screen to mostly favorable reviews (Gaiman 2009: 48–50).

(Roberts 2014: 90–91).[4] BBC executives were initially unsure as to how the radio play would be received, as were producer Geoffrey Perkins and Adams himself. A radio comedy, a science fiction one at that, which was recorded without the presence of a studio audience and which was the first radio comedy to be broadcast in stereo, presented too many uncertainties to inspire much belief in its success. *Hitchhiker*, however, held nothing back, and the science fiction tropes and conventions of the time, such as the exploration of the universe, the ideal of the selfless and noble protagonist, or the belief in the power of technology, were frequently exposed to ridicule. One need only think of Zaphod Beeblebrox, or the android Marvin.

The first episode of *The Hitchhiker's Guide to the Galaxy* was broadcast on BBC radio 4 on March 8, 1978. The broadcasts were scheduled on Wednesday evenings, when, says Neil Gaiman (2009), "they hoped nobody would be listening, with no pre-publicity, and expected it to uphold Radio 4's reputation for obscurity" (36). It was with some trepidation that Adams arrived at the BBC the following days in search of the reviews, although he had it pointed out to him that radio plays rarely if ever got any reviews at all. Imagine his pleasure when he discovered that *Hitchhiker* had in fact not only garnered some reviews but that these were generally favorable as well (Gaiman 2009: 36). The radio comedy was also a hit with listeners and through word-of-mouth acquired a rapidly growing fan base—a popularity that ultimately provided the impetus for a decade-spanning franchise that included, among others, five radio series, six novels, a television series, a film adaptation, numerous theater productions, a comic book adaptation, and a video game.

The first series of *The Hitchhiker's Guide to the Galaxy* consists of six episodes, broadcast between March 8 and April 12, 1978. This first season was followed by a Christmas special (on December 24, 1978), and a subsequent second season consisting of five episodes aired between January 21 and 25, 1980.[5] *The Hitchhiker's Guide* undoubtedly owes much of its success to its

---

4. One exception was Robert Sheckley's sci-fi comedy *Dimension of Miracles* (1968). Some controversy surrounds Adams's relationship with this novel. There are some striking similarities between Sheckley's work and *Hitchhiker*, which suggests that Adams plagiarized some elements from Sheckley. Adams initially claimed only to have read *Dimension of Miracles* after *Hitchhiker* had been published. As Roberts (2014) shows, however, claims of plagiarism have been greatly exaggerated despite some obvious similarities (76–77). At that time, British comedic powerhouse John Lloyd was also working on his own sci-fi comedy novel, *GiGax*. The novel was never published, but Lloyd did borrow from it when he cowrote the fifth and sixth episodes with Adams (Webb 2006: 119).

5. Three more series were broadcast between 2004 and 2005, but these were adaptations of the last three of Adams's trilogy in five parts: *Life, the Universe and Everything* (1982), *So Long, and Thanks for All the Fish* (1984), and *Mostly Harmless* (1992). Here the radio broadcasts follow the book publications, whereas the two first series actually precede the publication of the

characteristic humor, often described in terms of its absurd and Pythonesque quality, its witty dialogue, and its parodying of science fiction genre conventions. However, despite its immediate success as a radio comedy, critics have only rarely considered how audiophonic effects contribute to or enhance the humorous experience. In this chapter, I will explore how the original radio play, comprising the twelve episodes of the first two series, interweaves humor and narrative structure through the use of audiophonic elements.[6] As Elke Huwiler (2016) has stated: "In a radio piece, there are other sign systems beside language that can also convey meaning to the audience," such as "*voice, music, electro-acoustic manipulation*," or even "*silence*" (101–2). And just as audiophonic tools can convey narrative meaning, so too can they convey narrative humor, whether it be directly or indirectly. These extralinguistic elements, for instance, contribute significantly to the process of characterization. They are equally important in fleshing out the narrative setting and as such help provide the necessary context for listeners to better understand the characters as well as their actions and interactions that generate humor.

"What a Strange Book": Humor and Incongruity

At the forefront of cognitive humor studies today is the incongruity-resolution theory of humor, which posits that humor is caused by a discrepancy between the conceptualization or expectation of certain objects, events, or actions and their actual or concrete realization. The origins of the incongruity theory can be found in philosophy, for example in the works of Kant, Schopenhauer, and Kierkegaard, all of whom believed that the sudden perception of incongruity generates humor. Incongruity theory, however, really gained momentum in the psychological research of the early '70s. Of particular interest was Jerry Suls (1972), who described the humorous experience as a two-stage process. First, a listener's or reader's expectations about a specific text are proven to be inaccurate by that text. In the second stage, the listener or reader must then try to figure out how to resolve that incongruity between text and expectation (84).

---

novels *The Hitchhiker's Guide to the Galaxy* (1979) and *The Restaurant at the End of the Universe* (1980).

    6. Quotes are taken from the twenty-fifth anniversary edition that collects all the original radio scripts (Adams 2003). All the examples used in this chapter were included in the original broadcasts. Time notations refer to the episodes as they were first broadcast.

In a similar vein, linguist Salvatore Attardo (2002) postulated that humor was caused by two or more overlapping but opposite scripts.[7] In other words, they hold that "a joke text (T) is funny if T contains one or more incongruous elements any of which may or may not be fully or in part (playfully or not) resolved by the occurrence of the punch line, which may or may not introduce new incongruities" (27).[8] Attardo et al. (2002) believe that every humorous experience is caused by the incongruity, also referred to as a "script opposition," between an object or a situation as it is described and the default representation of that object or situation stored in our memory. We then have to try to resolve that script opposition by successfully integrating conflicting sets of information. The setup of a joke calls up one script, leading to an interpretation that conflicts with the punch line, thus necessitating a process of reinterpretation in light of additional information.

Consider, for example, Vroomfondel, a representative of the "Amalgamated Union of Philosophers, Sages, Luminaries and Other Professional Thinking Persons," who insists that the supercomputer Deep Thought be taken offline so that it cannot find the answer to Life, the Universe, and Everything. One of the demands he and his colleague Majikthise make is that of "guaranteed rigidly defined areas of doubt and uncertainty" (Adams 2003: 77; "Fit the Fourth," 07:04–07:07). The humor here is created by the inherent semantic incongruity of the presupposition that doubt and uncertainty can be rigidly defined. The incongruity is resolved when we interpret Vroomfondel's nonsensical statement in the broader narrative context. The incongruity serves to highlight his idiocy as well as offer a satirical dig at the supposedly pointless concerns and activities of philosophers in general. This is made abundantly clear when Deep Thought allays the philosophers' worries, pointing out that in the seven and a half million years it will take him to calculate an answer, they can "get on the pundit circuit" and "go on the chat shows and the color supplements and violently disagree with each other about" the answer Deep Thought will eventually come up with (Adams 2003: 77; "Fit the Fourth,"

---

7. A script, here, can best be understood "as some form of knowledge structure stored in the brain or mind of the individual to assist in the interpretation of experience" (Middleton and Brown 2005: 16).

8. Studies on humor generally distinguish three main categories. The first category includes cognitive theories of humor. The second encompasses psychoanalytical theories of humor (as, for example, the release/relief theory of humor), which claim that "laughter provides relief to various tensions and allows repressed desires to be satisfied" (Ermida 2008: 22). The third category consists of sociological theories of humor, particularly superiority theory, which situates the "roots of laughter in triumph over other people (or circumstances) . . . . Elation is engendered when we compare ourselves favorably to others as being less stupid, less ugly, less unfortunate, or less weak" (Keith-Spiegel 1972: 6). For more information on these three groups, see Martin (2007) or Raskin (1985).

07:48–08:37). The incongruity here is created through predominantly linguistic means, but audiophonic elements such as voice (specifically intonation, pitch, and accent), music, and electroacoustic manipulation play an equally important part in creating the incongruous experience that is so characteristic of the humor of *The Hitchhiker's Guide*.

Each episode of *The Hitchhiker's Guide to the Galaxy* is framed by an extradiegetic narrator. The term "extradiegetic narrator," or third-person narrator, is used to describe a narrator who is not part of the story and usually remains unspecified. The extradiegetic narrator occupies the highest hierarchic narrative position—not necessarily in terms of importance; the term simply denotes that there is no higher narrating entity than it. An intradiegetic narrator, in contrast, is situated on a lower tier. His or her account of the events is itself narrated by the extradiegetic narrator (Herman and Vervaeck 2005: 85). In *The Hitchhiker's Guide*, the extradiegetic narrator—given voice by venerated actor Peter Jones—is introduced by the song "Journey of the Sorcerer" by The Eagles. He describes the narrative context and summarizes what has occurred in the previous episode. Similarly, at the end of the broadcast, and to the same tune, the narrator tries to pique the interest of the audience by hinting at what might transpire in the subsequent broadcast.[9] Peter Jones also serves as the voice of the Guide itself when it is consulted by Arthur Dent or Ford Prefect, for instance. Thus, the extradiegetic and intradiegetic levels of narration become intertwined. Mostly, but not always, the intradiegetic narration is preceded by different music. This music plays in the background as specific passages from the Guide, pertaining to the events playing out in the broadcast, are read out loud. The intradiegetic narrator, then, is predominantly used as an expositional device (usually to the benefit of the clueless Arthur as well as the listener), whereas the extradiegetic narrator acts as an omniscient narrator commenting on the characters and the narrative actions as it unfolds. What both narrators have in common, however, is the humor that permeates their interventions, often taking the form of ironic and satirical commentary.

Hitchhiker loosely focuses on the exploits of ordinary earthling Arthur Dent and his friends as they try to find their way in Space, which is really big. At the start of the first episode, Arthur is trying to prevent the destruction of his house in order to make way for a bypass, as you simply have "got to build bypasses" (Adams 2003: 18; "Fit the First," 02:48–02:53). Unfortunately for Arthur, and indeed the entire human race, Earth, too, is scheduled for

---

9. This, of course, owes to the specificities of the medium of radio, where episodes could generally not be revisited immediately. For a discussion of further implications of seriality in radio broadcasting, see Harry Heuser's contribution in this volume.

demolition to allow for "the building of a hyperspace express route" so as to further develop "the Western Spiral arm of the Galaxy." Arthur only manages to escape the destruction of Earth thanks to illegal alien Ford Prefect, who works as a writer for the "*Hitch-Hiker's Guide to the Galaxy,* perhaps the most remarkable, certainly the most successful book ever to come out of the great publishing corporations of Ursa Minor" (Adams 2003: 18; "Fit the First," 00:55–01:05). They manage to hitch a ride with the Vogon Destructor Fleet, which sets them off on a series of crazy adventures across the galaxy.

After narrowly escaping death, they meet up with Zaphod Beeblebrox, a relative of Ford's; Trillian, another survivor of Earth; and Marvin the paranoid android. Zaphod, the two-headed, three-armed former President of the Galaxy, has stolen the Heart of Gold, the most advanced spaceship in the universe. After landing on the planet Magrathea and learning that the Earth was nothing more than an experiment in behavioral psychology conceived of by mice, the crew are forced to run away from the police. Seeking cover from the gunfire, they hide behind a "hyperspatial field generator," which unfortunately explodes. The explosion, rather than handing them a one-way ticket to the afterlife, transports them to Milliways, the Restaurant at the End of the Universe.

"Welcome to the Restaurant at the End of the Universe": Audiophony and Narrative Setting

Literary humor is frequently the result of the interaction between literary characters, between character and narrator, or even between narrator and listener. That interaction takes place in a specific setting that frames the narrative action and consequently has a significant impact on the humorous experience. Humor in turn also influences how we perceive and interpret that setting. "Setting" here is understood as a term denoting the physical space in which the narrative action unfolds at a specific time in the story. Radio drama is ideally suited to make that setting more tangible through its use of audiophonic elements such as electroacoustic manipulations, music, and sound effects. The fifth episode, set in the Restaurant at the End of the Universe, aptly illustrates the interaction between setting, characters, and humor.

The characters' arrival at the restaurant is audibly made evident as they are welcomed by a waiter against the backdrop of casual cabaret music, which firmly roots the restaurant setting in the listener's mind. We then hear the feedback of the microphone as the well-seasoned master of ceremony, Max Quordlepleen, welcomes diners from all over the galaxy to the restaurant. His slick and polished performance indicates that he has done this many times before. When his routine is interrupted by customers asking directions, Max is unperturbed and simply picks up where he left off. There are no breaks, no hesitations, only a smooth transition between answer and monologue.[10] He inserts little cues in his discourse, such as little moments of laughter inviting the audience to join in. Or he generates interest and excitement through means of various interjections or by deliberately stressing specific syllables. All these verbal cues serve the purpose of eliciting positive responses from the audience in the form of applause and laughter. His playful irreverence for the seriousness of the event is clearly conveyed by his tone of voice, as when he advertises the restaurant's "fine selection of Aldebaran liqueurs" (Adams 2003: 95; "Fit the Fifth," 10:43–10:46) or his tongue-in-cheek welcoming of the party from the "church of the second coming of the Great Prophet Zarquon," whom Max makes fun of repeatedly (Adams 2003: 96; "Fit the Fifth," 11:42–12:10). The character of Max as an entertainer only really makes sense in the setting of the restaurant, just as the setting itself demands someone like Max to serve as the host for the visiting guests.

The radio play then reverts back to our foursome while the background music and diners' chatter continue, further anchoring the narrative action. Ford elaborately and, as it turns out, jokingly tries to explain to Arthur how the universe was created, but the punchline seems to fall flat, as evidenced by Trillian's most unenthusiastic and obviously sarcastic response. A whooshing sound then signals the return of Max Quordlepleen, who continues on with his routine, once more injecting (and eliciting) humor through little sounds of laughter and intonation. Sound effects, too, play an important role in generating humor in this passage. When called out by Max, the minor deities from Asgaard exuberantly throw around lightning in the restaurant. Similarly, the members of Zansellquasure Flamarion Bridge Club proudly make their presence heard, which incidentally sounds like a flock of bleating sheep. And let us not forget about the barking Young Conservatives from Sirius B. The presence of alien and seemingly bizarre races is not surprising within the context of the science fiction genre, but because of the deliberate mimicking of the actual sound of bleating sheep or barking dogs, one cannot help but relate these aliens to the animals we know from everyday life, and this again underscores the banality and apparent absurdity of a restaurant that, each night, hosts a panoply of extraterrestrial races and species to watch the end of the universe.[11]

---

10. Interestingly, this was one of the many on-the-spot additions by actor and comedian Roy Hudd, who voiced Max.

11. In the novel, the party of Sirius B is actually described as a group of smartly dressed young dogs (Adams 1995: 230).

Max is then faded out gently as the action once again focuses on Ford, Zaphod, Trillian, and Arthur. He does, however, make another appearance nearer to the end of the fifth radio broadcast, as the universe is about to explode. Accompanied by drum roll, Max gleefully announces that the moment has finally arrived. Suddenly he is interrupted by the Hallelujah chorus of Handel's Messiah oratorio heralding the, unfortunately late, arrival of the prophet Zarquon. The contrast between the epic nature of the chorus and the untimely, and therefore anticlimactic, appearance of Zarquon seems to justify Max Quordlepleen's earlier quip aimed at the prophet. This is not the only reference to an earlier joke made obvious through use of audiophonic means, however. As the universe explodes, the final sound that can be heard is that of water running down a drain, which is actually the reverse of what Ford tried to convince Arthur happened when the universe was created, and seems somewhat of an ignoble end to the universe as it implies that the end of the universe is no more special than removing the plug from the bathtub.

Considering this passage in terms of the earlier mentioned incongruity theory of humor reveals that audiophonic elements are essential in creating the humor that pervades this scene (and also the radio play in its entirety). At the end of the fourth episode, the last thing we hear before the narrator intervenes is the sound of the hyperspatial field generator exploding. This explosion, and the last seconds leading up to it, also feature early in the fifth episode. But this time, the sound effect mimicking the explosion seamlessly fades into cabaret music being played in the Restaurant at the End of the Universe. The tension created by the initial sound effect that suggested our foursome was in grave peril peters out as the music makes abundantly clear that Arthur and his friends are no longer in danger. That the crew's fortunes have changed for the better is also made clear to the listener through the demeanor of Garkbit, their waiter at Milliways. Not perturbed in the slightest by the sudden appearance of Trillian, Arthur, Ford, and Zaphod, Garkbit simply asks if they have a reservation. His cool tone of voice and his sophisticated accent successfully convey a mixture of amused condescension and a blasé attitude, reinforced by his chuckle when Garkbit has to explain where Arthur and the others have ended up. Distinct audiophonic features such as accent and tone of voice are used here to enhance the verbal humor, as evidenced by Garkbit's deadpan delivery of the following punchline:

> ARTHUR: You mean we've travelled in time, but not in space?
> ZAPHOD: Listen you semi-involved simian, go climb a tree won't you?
> ARTHUR: Oh go and bang your heads together four eyes.

GARKBIT: No, no. Your monkey has got it right, sir. (Adams 2003: 97; "Fit the Fifth," 13:20–13:30)

Garkbit never breaks character, not even when cracking a joke at Arthur's expense, talking about the hapless earthling as if he is not even there. The delivery makes the joke all the funnier. The entire scene at Milliways abounds in the clever use of audiophonic elements that serve to highlight the incongruity between a momentous event such as the end of the universe, on the one hand, and the banal and mundane way in which it is described, on the other hand.

The end of the universe is the end of everything, after which there is nothing, and thus it is by definition a finite thing. But at Milliways, this extraordinary phenomenon has just become business as usual, something that can be commercially exploited. The restaurant is safely enclosed in "a vast time bubble," which "has been projected into the future to the precise moment of the End of the Universe. This, is, of course, impossible," as the Guide itself tells us (Adams 2003: 93; "Fit the Fifth," 06:04–06:11). Nevertheless, time is continuously reset, and the restaurant's guests can comfortably enjoy their meal and a night's entertainment as they wait for the end of the universe.

The entire fragment at Milliways, then, is not only funny because of the many jokes and absurd situations it contains, but also because of the way in which these jokes and absurdities are presented to the listener. As Nancy Bell (2017) shows in her study on failed humor, the context in which the humorous interaction takes place is of great importance. And one of the determining parameters for the success of the humorous experience she identifies is "the degree of intimacy between the interlocutors" (366). In *Hitchhiker,* audiophonic strategies are used to great effect to establish that intimacy on two levels. Within the fictional context, for instance, Max Quordlepleen's segments are very similar to a stand-up comedy act as they in many ways highlight the interactional aspect of humor. The comedian and his audience become partners in the night's events. Max knows his audience and how to get them involved. The diners in Milliways, in turn, show their appreciation and understanding through laughter, applause, and participation, effectively establishing a high degree of intimacy between the compere and his audience. This interactional aspect and the intimacy it invites are mirrored in the relationship between radio play and listener as voice and intonation, music, electroacoustic manipulation, and silence (pauses) all work together to help create an immersive story world that draws listeners in. These affordances of the medium of radio (the background music, the relaxed and blithe atmosphere, etc.) also allow for the creation of a richly textured story world. The setting, then, created through audiophonic means, fulfils a crucial role in conveying the incongruity at the heart of the humorous experience to the listener.

"Who . . . Who Are You?": Audiophony and Characterization

Audiophonic elements in *The Hitchhiker's Guide to the Galaxy* play an important role not only in providing detail to the narrative setting or scene but also in terms of characterization. This is especially the case for the more prominently featured AI life forms, a staple of the science fiction genre, such as Eddie the shipboard computer on the Heart of Gold and the robot Marvin. We first meet Eddie at the end of the second episode. The moment Eddie introduces himself, the audience cannot help but notice his chipper comportment, as well as his metallic-sounding voice and obvious American accent. These auditory features contribute to Eddie's indirect characterization as they speak to his frame of mind and to his personality.

His cheerful and generally obsequious disposition, however, is not at all appreciated by the crew members. When asked what their "current trajectory is," Eddie happily obliges: It is a "real pleasure fella. We are currently in orbit at an altitude of . . . three hundred miles . . . around the legendary planet of Magrathea. Golly!" (Adams 2003: 55; "Fit the Third," 03:24–03:33). When he offers to give further assistance, he is swiftly told to just shut up. Eddie is not deterred, not even as the crew ignore his warning and fly straight into a missile barrage, prompting Eddie to start singing "You'll Never Walk Alone," originally from the musical *Carousel* (1945) and made famous by Liverpudlian band Gerry and the Pacemakers. Even as the crew are trying their best to escape certain death, Eddie proudly keeps on singing, only interrupting himself to provide updates on how close the missiles are to impact. Luckily, they are saved by the Infinite Improbability Drive, which turns the missiles into a sperm whale and a bowl of petunias. The Heart of Gold lands safely on Magrathea and the crew gets ready to start exploring the planet when suddenly Eddie switches back on without being prompted. However, Eddie is no longer Eddie.

Instead of the good-natured and helpful Eddie, the ship's computer has assumed, or rather has been given, a new voice. Eddie—although still voiced by actor David Tate—has adopted the voice, accent, and tone of a strict headmistress. The changes in Eddie's demeanor are not restricted to his vocal characteristics but have had a significant impact on his personality as well. Rather than obeying the crew without question, Eddie's new and overbearing persona seeks to impose its will on Arthur and the rest, instructing them to dress warmly before venturing out and warning them not to play "with any naughty bug-eyed monsters" (Adams 2003: 61; "Fit the Third," 15:02–15:06). Not impressed with Eddie's new personality, Zaphod has a crack at him before asking Eddie to open the hatch, which Eddie refuses:

> EDDIE: Not until whoever said that owns up.
> FORD: Oh God.
> EDDIE: Come on.
> ZAPHOD: Computer . . .
> EDDIE: I'm waiting. I can wait all day if necessary.
> ZAPHOD: Computer, if you don't open that exit hatch this moment I shall go straight to your major data banks with a very large axe and give you a reprogramming you'll never forget, is that clear?
> *(Pause)*
> EDDIE: I can see this relationship is something we're all going have to work at. (Adams 2003: 62; "Fit the Third," 15:10–15:32)

Choosing self-preservation over obstinacy, Eddie finally relents and opens the hatch but still cannot resist having the last word. Most listeners have a rather clear idea of what a computer can and cannot do based on their own schematic representations. Initially, Eddie certainly seems to confirm those expectations. His advanced intelligence is not surprising within the context of the science fiction genre. His bubbly nature may be less typical, but he still does what the crew asks of him and shows little or no assertiveness, and certainly gives no indication of any capacity for self-determination. This changes significantly when Eddie assumes, or rather is given by Zaphod, his "emergency back-up personality" (Adams 2003: 61; "Fit the Third," 14:53–14:56). The stark contrast between the original Eddie and his alter ego is surprising and highlights the idiosyncrasy of the latter's domineering and peremptory behavior. But what both iterations have in common is that they subvert the science fiction trope of the highly intelligent and sophisticated computer. As Eder et al. (2010) make clear, genre activates certain "mental schemata" and can best be understood as cognitive "structures of information with slots to be filled by specific instantiations of the general pattern" (43). Considered within the context of the genre, listeners will form expectations about how characters are presented, what situations they are faced with, and how they develop. James Gunn (1986) wrote that science fiction generally centers on some type of technological or scientific advancement and how characters deal with and respond to that change (70–71). In this particular scene, the computer asserts itself, to which Zaphod responds by behaving like a troglodyte and threatening to "reprogram" Eddie by smashing his circuitry with an ax. Reprogramming comes to stand for destruction—a destruction carried out by the most basic of means, serving as a hard counterpoint to intricate and complex technology. Throughout *The Hitchhiker's Guide,* Adams continuously satirizes science fiction (Pawlak and Joll 2012: 239). The use of audiophonic elements, here specifically tone, accent, speech mannerisms, and even silence, is essential in realizing that satire and communicating it to the audience.

Eddie is not the only artificial life form used to satirize the genre of science fiction. Featuring even more prominently in the radio play is Marvin the android. When Arthur and Ford are picked up by the Heart of Gold, near the end of the second episode, it is Marvin who brings them to the bridge to meet Zaphod and Trillian. Marvin is no ordinary robot, however. He is a robot with a brain the size of a planet who is thoroughly depressed. He is, ironically, also a prototype, developed by the Sirius Cybernetics Corporation and fitted with the Genuine People Personality feature, which is

> MARVIN: Ghastly. It all is—absolutely ghastly. Just don't even talk about it. Look at this door. "All the doors in this spacecraft have a cheerful and sunny disposition. It is their pleasure to open for you, and their satisfaction to close again with the knowledge of a job well done."
> MARVIN: Hateful, isn't it? Come on I've been ordered to take you up to the Bridge. Here I am, brain the size of a planet and they tell me to take you up to the Bridge. Call that job satisfaction? 'Cause I don't.
> FORD: Excuse me, which government owns this ship?
> MARVIN: You watch this door. It's about to open again. I can tell by the intolerable air of smugness it suddenly generates.
> MARVIN: Come on.
> MARVIN: Thank you, the Marketing Division of the Sirius Cybernetics Corporation.
> MARVIN: "Let's build robots with Genuine People Personalities" they said. So they tried it out with me. I'm a personality prototype. You can tell, can't you?
> FORD: Er . . .
> MARVIN: I hate that door. I'm not getting you down am I?
> FORD: Which government owns this ship?
> MARVIN: No government owns it. It's been stolen.
> FORD & ARTHUR: Stolen?
> MARVIN: "Stolen"?
> FORD: Who by?
> MARVIN: Zaphod Beeblebrox

FORD: Zaphod Beeblebrox?

MARVIN: Sorry did I say something wrong? Pardon me for breathing—which I never do anyway so I don't know why I bother to say it, oh God I'm so depressed. Here's another of those self-satisfied doors. Life, don't talk to me about life . . . (Adams 2003: 45; "Fit the Second," 17:15–18:58)

Marvin's depressed nature, which seamlessly blends with his sarcastic disposition, is continuously foregrounded through his monotonous voice—brilliantly portrayed by British actor Stephen Moore—which defines him as a character. As such, Marvin defies listeners' expectations and again subverts the artificial intelligence stereotype that is commonplace in science fiction. Marvin is highly intelligent, but woefully underused and only tasked with menial labor. Another trope of science fiction is that of the artificial life form trying to become "more human," trying to experience human emotions. Ironically, Marvin is fitted with a "Genuine People Personality" but only experiences depression, meaning that he could not be farther removed from the traditional science fiction hero who embodies "the triumph of the human spirit . . . over seemingly impossible odds" (Kropf 1988: 62). Marvin's distinctly metallic-sounding voice does conform to the trope of the science fiction robot but allows him to really only convey one emotional state, a state of depression that is reinforced by his dull and monotonous intonation. Marvin's "voice," in the broadest sense of the word, generates humor by playing on listener's intertextual schemata.

In the third episode, "Fit the Third," the crew of the Heart of Gold are ready to explore Magrathea, a planet renowned for designing planets precisely tailored to suit the wishes of their clients. This activity made it the richest planet in the galaxy, but also forced the planet to go into stasis five million years ago as no one was able to pay their exorbitant fees any longer:

ARTHUR: It's fantastic!
FORD: Desolate hole if you ask me.
TRILLIAN: It's bloody cold. It all looks so stark and dreary.
ARTHUR: I think it's absolutely fantastic!
ARTHUR: It's only just getting through to me a whole alien world, millions of light years from home. Pity it's such a dump though.
ZAPHOD: Hey! Just beyond this ridge you can see the remains of an ancient city.
FORD: What does it look like?
ZAPHOD: Bit of a dump. Come on over. Oh and watch out for all the bits of whalemeat.

ARTHUR: Do you realize that robot can hum like Pink Floyd? What else can you do Marvin?
MARVIN: Rock and roll?
TRILLIAN: I wish I knew where my mice were.
ZAPHOD: OK, I've found a way in.
ARTHUR: In? In what?
ZAPHOD: Down to the interior of the planet—that's where we have to go. Where no man has trod these five million years, into the very depths of time itself . . .
ZAPHOD: Can it, Marvin. (Adams 2003: 62–63; "Fit the Third," 15:46–16:50)

The first music we hear as the crew leaves the ship is the intro to Pink Floyd's "Shine on You Crazy Diamond." We soon learn that it is actually Marvin humming the song, prompting Arthur to ask him what other music he can do. Marvin then starts to play a version of "Rock and Roll Music" (originally written and recorded by Chuck Berry, later covered by the Beatles). Only this time the music clearly sounds distorted, so there can be no doubt that it is Marvin singing. The song suddenly stops and we hear the unaltered opening of "Also Sprach Zarathustra" by Richard Strauss. The fact that it is not distorted, as opposed to "Rock and Roll Music," suggests that it is part of the extradiegetic level. This seems plausible as the orchestral and epic piece appears, certainly initially, to be well matched with Zaphod's excited tone in trying to convey the momentous occasion of being the first "man" to go down into the interior of the planet in five million years. Again, however, it is revealed by Zaphod's annoyed response that it was in fact Marvin who was playing the music all along, deliberately undermining Zaphod's portentous rendezvous with history. The humor here is created by the sudden switch between the extradiegetic and the diegetic levels, which underscores Marvin's sardonic and sarcastic personality and exposes his need to take Zaphod down a peg. This fits with Marvin's character as his perpetually depressed state makes it impossible for him to share Zaphod's excitement and find any joy in the current situation. But this example also contains some intertextual humor. "Also Sprach Zarathustra" of course famously features in Stanley Kubrick's *2001: A Space Odyssey* (1968). This movie has its own artificial intelligence in the form of HAL 9000. HAL is the ship's computer who, while initially friendly and helpful, tries to kill the crew—a stark contrast to the depressed and snarky Marvin, who repeatedly ends up saving the lives of the Heart of Gold's crew.

Often audiophonic elements work in concert to reinforce or outright create the humorous experience. Take, for instance, the two mice, Benjy and

Frankie, who are members of a species that has been "more or less running [Earth] for the last ten million years in order to find this wretched thing called the Ultimate Question" (Adams 2003: 83; "Fit the Fourth," 19:45–19:54). Unfortunately, Earth was destroyed by the Vogons before they received the answer (or, rather, the question). The mice's voice is heavily manipulated and very high-pitched. This squeaky sound matches well with their diminutive stature but is seemingly incongruent with their high intelligence and powerful status in the universe. While humans were under the assumption that they were experimenting on rodents, it was in fact these mice who were running the experiment using humans as guinea pigs. The electroacoustic manipulation here contrasts with their distinct upper-class vocabulary and accent. The mental image of casting these tiny mice with their "avaricious giggle" and their high-pitched voice as some of the most powerful creatures in the galaxy is humorous in and of itself. It is made even funnier by their distinctive speech patterns (their intonation, their crisp and exaggerated pronunciation, and how they stress certain syllables).[12] Once more, these audiophonic elements are crucial in communicating the humor to the audience.

I have discussed here some specific examples to illustrate how audiophonic elements are intertwined with the narrative structure of the radio play and how they contribute to the humorous experience. These examples, however, are by no means isolated instances, and many more such examples can be found in *The Hitchhiker's Guide to the Galaxy*. Think only of the Vogon captain who announces the destruction of Earth over the public address system, or when sound and music are contrasted with the spoken word to stress the ridiculousness of the narrative action (e.g., when Arthur and Ford are bullied by the Vogon captain into saying that they like his poetry, Ford's rendering of Beethoven's fifth symphony being broadcast concurrently with the actual fifth symphony, etc.), or when Arthur and Ford are subjected to a ludicrous interrogation by the Golgafrinchian captain while he is sitting in the bath and we can actually hear the water running and him splashing about in the tub. From the start, Douglas Adams indicated that he wanted to take full advantage of the possibilities radio offers in order to push the limits of radio comedy. He certainly succeeded in his ambition.

---

12. Particularly interesting is that the stage directions specify that the voice of the mice should "suggest mouse-likeness," but "shouldn't sound silly" as they are highly sophisticated. That the producers did not quite achieve this ambition is obvious from the fact that they changed the "voice treatment" of the mice after the first broadcast, much to the displeasure of the public, many of whom preferred the original version (Adams 2003: 88).

Conclusion

General cognitive theories of humor hold that humor is caused when we draw on overlapping but opposite scripts. In the context of literature, incongruity is often caused by a comparison of textual information with a reader's schemata, which essentially amount to structured representations of events, objects, or actions gained through experience. But schemata also include auditory information. The radio play *The Hitchhiker's Guide to the Galaxy* takes full advantage of the technical possibilities radio comedy offers as it uses auditory cues to activate scripts only to subsequently subvert or frustrate them. These range from general knowledge scripts, such as the knowledge or experience of visiting a restaurant; scripts specific to the genre of science fiction, such as the metallic-sounding voice of a robot; or even intertextual scripts. Audiophonic elements, then, enable listeners to construct a more detailed narrative setting and evoke a highly detailed and sophistically layered story world in which the action takes place. Similarly, they also contribute significantly to the process of characterization by highlighting the eccentric personality and qualities of both the cast of characters and the world they inhabit. As such, they are integral to the creation of narrative humor in *The Hitchhiker's Guide to the Galaxy*.

Works Cited

Adams, Douglas. 1995. *The Hitch Hiker's Guide to the Galaxy: A Trilogy in Five Parts*. London: William Heinemann.

———. 2003. The Hitchhiker's Guide to the Galaxy: *The Original Radio Scripts*. Edited by Geoffrey Perkins. London: Pan Books.

Attardo, Salvatore, et al. 2002. "Script Oppositions and Logical Mechanisms: Modeling Incongruities and Their Resolutions." *Humor* 15, no. 1 (2002): 3–46.

Bell, Nancy D. 2017. "Failed Humor." In *The Routledge Handbook of Language and Humor*, edited by Salvatore Attardo, 356–70. New York: Routledge.

Eder, Jens, et al. 2010. "Characters in Fictional Worlds: An Introduction." In *Characters in Fictional Worlds: Understanding Imaginary Beings in Literature, Film, and Other Media*, edited by Jens Eder, Fotis Jannidis, and Ralf Schneider, 3–64. New York: De Gruyter.

Ermida, Isabel. 2008. *The Language of Comic Narratives Humor Construction in Short Stories*. Berlin: Mouton de Gruyter.

Gaiman, Neil. 2009. *Don't Panic: Douglas Adams & The Hitchhiker's Guide to the Galaxy*. London: Titan Books.

Gunn, James. 1986. "The Readers of Hard Science Fiction." In *Hard Science Fiction*, edited by George E. Slusser and Erik S. Rabkin, 70–81. Carbondale, IL: Southern Illinois University Press.

Herman, Luc, and Bart Vervaeck. 2005. *Vertelduivels*. Brussel & Nijmegen: VUBPress & Vantilt.

Huwiler, Elke. 2016. "A Narratology of Audio Art: Telling Stories by Sound." In *Audionarratology: Interfaces of Sound and Narrative*, edited by Jarmila Mildorf and Till Kinzel, 99–116. Berlin: De Gruyter.

Keith-Spiegel, Patricia. 1972. "Early Conceptions of Humor: Varieties and Issues." In *The Psychology of Humor: Theoretical Perspectives and Empirical Issues*, edited by Jeffrey H. Goldstein, Paul E. McGhee, and H. J. Eysenck, 3–39. New York: Academic Press.

Kropf, Carl R. 1988. "Douglas Adams's 'Hitchhiker' Novels as Mock Science Fiction." *Science Fiction Studies* 15, no. 1. 61–70.

Martin, Rod. A. 2007. *The Psychology of Humor: An Integrative Approach*. Burlington, MA: Elsevier Academic Press.

Middleton, David, and Steven Brown. 2005. *The Social Psychology of Experience: Studies in Remembering and Forgetting*. London: SAGE.

Pawlak, Alexander, and Nicholas Joll. 2012. "The Funniest of all Improbable Worlds—*Hitchhiker's* as Philosophical Satire." In *Philosophy &* The Hitchhiker's Guide to the Galaxy, edited by Nicholas Joll, 236–68. Basingstoke: Palgrave Macmillan.

Raskin, Victor. 1985. *Semantic Mechanisms of Humor*. Dordrecht: Reidel.

Roberts, Jem. 2014. *The Frood. The Authorised and Very Official History of Douglas Adams & The Hitchhiker's Guide to the Galaxy*. London: Arrow Books.

Suls, Jerry M. 1972. "A Two-Stage Model for the Appreciation of Jokes and Cartoons: An Information-Processing Analysis." In *The Psychology of Humor: Theoretical Perspectives and Empirical Issues*, edited by Jeffrey H. Goldstein, Paul E. McGhee, and H. J. Eysenck, 81–100. New York: Academic Press.

Webb, Nick. 2006. *Wish You Were Here: The Official Biography of Douglas Adams*. London: Del Rey.

9

Gargantuan Adaptations

Narrative and Non-Narrative Soundscapes in English and German Radio Plays and Radio Operas Based on François Rabelais and Johann Fischart

TILL KINZEL

WHEN ONE LOOKS at the history of sound art, radio plays as well as radio operas constitute an important link between the realms of sound and music on the one hand and of literature on the other. It is hardly surprising that the modernist poet Ezra Pound was one of the pioneers of this art form. Pound not only created some of the first radio operas for the BBC (see Fisher 2002) but also showed a keen interest in medieval and Renaissance literature. In this connection, his work on François Villon is a case in point. Pound also penned an imaginary dialogue between François Rabelais and a student, *Anachronism at Chinon,* that employs this particular form of orality for literary critical purposes, giving to Rabelais a voice that speaks across the centuries. Pound, as a student of French literature, would of course have known earlier authors who included Rabelais in their imaginary dialogues, such as Voltaire. However, at least to my knowledge, Pound's Rabelais dialogue has not yet been performed or adapted to radio, or made the topic of detailed analysis, although he did make use of radio performances in various ways (most perniciously, of course, in his World War II radio speeches from fascist Italy addressed to American audiences; see Doob 1978). As a pioneer of sound art himself, Pound appropriately became the inspiration for a largely non-narrative radio piece (*Radiostück*) by one of the most experimental and intriguing German radio artists, Klaus Buhlert, *Meine Lieder singt man nicht. Radiostück mit Texten von Ezra Pound* (NDR 1992), that was directed by Jörg Jannings, one of the most important directors of German literary radio plays in the second half of the twentieth century. This radio piece is not based on any kind of narrative in the first place, but rather creates an impressionistic picture of Pound that is underscored by verbal and sonic repetitions that function as leitmotifs. However, these leitmotifs do not create eventfulness and thus do not contribute anything to the progression of a story. They rather serve to acoustically create a "presence" onto which members of the audience can project their own thoughts. This introduction of elements of circularity is a typical feature of more experimental radio art. The *Radiostück* on Pound thus already foreshadows the various issues connected with the adaptation of Renaissance and modernist literature for radio that can be detected in more recent productions: Narrative is not necessarily a dominant feature of this kind of radio art even where the pre-texts, (that is, the earlier texts serving as the basis for the adaptations) are predominantly narrative on account of their plot structure and a narrating instance. Pound's concern with Renaissance literature, his poetic emphasis on images, and his penchant for experimenting with mixtures of verbal art, music, and medial transformation prefigure more recent adaptations or appropriations of narrative Renaissance literature to radio that will be the main focus of this chapter.

François Rabelais's (1494–1553) famous novel *Gargantua and Pantagruel* (1532/34) has been adapted not only as an audiobook both in English and German (NDR 1994, spoken by Helmut Krauss) but also as a BBC radio play (adapted by "Lavinia Murray," a radio drama writer's pen name).[1] Late in the sixteenth century, the same Gargantuan story as that presented by Rabelais was transposed (rather than translated) into German in a way that exceeded all bounds: Johann Fischart (ca. 1545–1591) produced his *Affentheurlich Naupengeheurliche Geschichtklitterung* (1575/90), which became one of the most famous monsters of a book in literary history. This strange book, which has been aptly called a "confused pattern of a confused world" (Mühlemann 1972), was not a long time ago adapted into a piece of radio art with minimal narrative structure (Deutschlandradio Kultur 2015). In comparing and contrasting these two adaptations, this chapter explores an art form that is rarely investigated but offers a fascinating mixture of tall tales and challenging soundscapes. It focuses particularly on narrative and non-narrative sounds as well as modes of (oral or oralized) storytelling. At the same time, this current audio art also demonstrates the viability of old literature and its lasting appeal while

---

1. Lavinia Murray has also written a dramatization that created a "Cock-and-bull story loosely based on Robert Burton's Jacobean tome," *The Anatomy of Melancholy*. See http://www.bbc.co.uk/programmes/b00738gx.

undergoing a process of medial appropriations and transformations, including the reduction of the narrative dimension due to lack of eventfulness.

First, I will take a look at some key features of the stories, and especially the stylistics, of Rabelais and how they translate into sound. Second, the BBC radio drama of parts of Rabelais's novel will be discussed. Third, Fischart's adaptation of Rabelais as mediated through the radio opera mentioned earlier will be considered in more detail.[2]

Rabelais and Orality in Written Form

In his book on French culture in the light of language development, Karl Vossler stresses a number of stylistic features in Rabelais's use of language that point to the strong oral as well as aural character of *Gargantua and Pantagruel*. Vossler links Rabelais's approach to language to a general outlook on the world that he juxtaposes with that of Calvin, emphasizing "eine unbändige, trunkene, rauschartige, lärmende Freude" (an immense, drunken, feeling-high-like, noisy joy) in Rabelais's worldview. This in turn translates into "tolle, geräuschvolle, donnernde, rauschende, murmelnde, schwatzende, lachende Sprachfreudigkeit" (a crazy, noisy, thundering, swooshing, murmuring, chattering, laughing propensity to talk), as Vossler writes. Rabelais plays around with parts of sentences, with the words themselves, punning, lengthening, shortening, throwing different languages together, and fabricating "immer neue, groteske und possierliche Ungetüme und Wundergebilde von Wörtern" (ever new, grotesque and cute monsters and wonderful creatures made of words). Vossler concludes that Rabelais's work amounts to "ein lexikalischer Karneval" (a lexical carnival) and employs various terms derived from the area of music to sum up the orchestra-like style of Rabelais, which, he argues, culminates in a Dionysian polyphony (Vossler 1921: 260–61). This description is important because it highlights some of the crucial textual and narrative features of *Gargantua and Pantagruel* that would later facilitate audio adaptations. Those features entail not only the many sounds that are inscribed in the polyphonic reality of the novel but also the dialogical presentation of many passages in which the different voices interact and become integral parts of the storytelling. Sound effects already play an important part in Rabelais's

---

2. I will not discuss the structure of Fischart's book as such since this would take the discussion too far away from radio art as my main concern. I will also disregard other versions of Rabelais, such as the eight-hour-long audiobook adaptation of the first two parts of the novel for German radio (Norddeutscher Rundfunk) mentioned earlier.

form of storytelling (see also Cornilliat 2000, 2003), underscoring the often grotesque actions.

Rabelais Spoken and Performed in English

In Lavinia Murray's one-hour adaptation of Rabelais's text dealing with *Gargantua*,[3] the listeners are explicitly addressed as such (not as *readers*, as in the printed book), and they are addressed as if they were part of a company of drinkers: "Bon santé, to life, to carnival, to abundance, yes, a toast to you, my lusty listeners!" Only after this toasting address does the nondiegetic speaker announce the title and author as well as the adapter's name of the radio drama. This is then again followed by the narrator's addressing the listeners as if there was in fact a close *physical* proximity, something that by definition is not the case in broadcast (as opposed to staged) radio drama: "Life is not for the easily offended, and neither are my stories. So, quaff, laugh, cuddle up close." While creating an imaginary narrative space through this announcement, the narrator also offers a *captatio benevolentiae* by suggesting that those who are going to listen to his stories will not be easily offended.

The whole sequence at the beginning also includes a kind of music that adapts Renaissance folk dance music, thereby suggesting that the setting of the story will rather be among simpler folk than at court, and it will be entertaining rather than serious. The music also reminds one of table music, which suggests a conversational setting during a meal, where telling stories is part of the fun (see Hobl-Friedrich 1991: 37). As the narrator then announces that he will tell a story about giants, the grotesque nature of his story becomes immediately clear. The narrator, after some Rabelaisian introductory matter that serves to set the scene, then explicitly marks the beginning of the narrative proper by saying: "My story begins with a giantess . . ." This story is presented in a combined form of narration proper by means of voice-over narration and mimetic representation: While the fictional characters engage in dialogue and interact in various ways during the meal, the narrator adds a further level by commenting on the story that he is required to tell in accordance with what Rabelais had written down. Here, we can see a meta-referential playfulness that is carried further when Rabelais himself is introduced as a speaking character in the very story that was originally penned by him.

---

3. I merely take into account this first part of the radio drama adaptation, ignoring for the present analysis the second part dealing with Pantagruel, of roughly the same length.

This instance of metalepsis continues after the characters' talk turns to issues of tripe-eating as well as the giantess's pregnancy. The narrator invites the listeners to join him when he acoustically moves into the womb of Gargantua's mother, Gargamelle, in order to inspect the fetus, and he even invites them to taste the amniotic fluid. The narrator introduces the "marvelous eleven-month old fetus, the hero of my first tale," but then also verbalizes an objection some listeners may raise about the truthfulness of what he has just said: "The nitpickers among you are saying Gargamelle is eleven months pregnant." He then takes up the role of one listener who specifically calls into question Rabelais's knowledge of women or of pregnancy. Rabelais, now speaking in his own voice, immediately justifies himself by noting that he is a medical doctor who has "dissected a fair few" women, so that he actually knows them inside out. By dialogically integrating Rabelais himself into the story, the radio play adaptation adds another level of joking to the pre-text, partly akin to postmodern devices such as can be found in the radio play version of Alasdair Gray's *Lanark* (1981), in which the literary figure of "the author" is even spoken by Alasdair Gray himself, who thus becomes a kind of character in his own fiction (see Mildorf 2017; see Kinzel 2017 for a different form of including the author's voice in radio drama). Rabelais's presence as a voice in the presentation of his tale also foregrounds the construction of the narrative itself as a (fictional) negotiation between author, narrator, and audience. The extra-diegetic author becomes an intra-diegetic commentator on his own story world who explains his narrative decision. The narrator, who almost seems to merge with Rabelais, then even engages in conversation with the unborn Gargantua, urging him to move out of the womb into the wonderful world outside, because he, the narrator, is, as he says, "making a rather nice story for you." The narrator can therefore be regarded as the actual obstetrician helping to give birth not only to Gargantua but also to the story of Gargantua. The scene then shifts again to the outside world and is aurally focalized through Gargamelle, who is now experiencing ominous movements inside her.

The story of the pregnant giantess Gargamelle is not only narrated as well as presented through dialogue, but constantly accompanied, as it were, by various sounds or noises that can be attributed to the giantess's and other people's bodily functions. These noises, such as burping and farting, underscore the listeners' perception of the grotesque nature of the giants, as the sounds are comparatively loud and therefore appear indecent. These sounds make sure that listeners will not expect the telling of a story that obeys the demands of decorum; instead, the listeners' ears are tickled by transgressively obscene and gross discussions, for example on the best way to wipe one's behind. This particular sequence makes use of narrativity in the form of a list, as Gargantua details his experiments on the best way to wipe his behind by listing everything he employed for this purpose, including food as well as living animals. The bodily noises at the same time complicate the listening experience, as they can have a distracting effect. The story becomes inextricably linked to the diegetic sounds that project the image of actual bodies, which constitutes a contrast to mind reports, in which the body can virtually vanish into thin air. This adaptation presents a very strong in-yer-face storytelling in which the sounds are meant to appear physically close to the listener. The soundscape enhances the grotesque nature of the giants' narrative, even though the sheer force of the accompanying sounds also occasionally distracts the listeners' attention from the story that is narrated and mimetically presented in favor of the way the story is told.

Fischart Spoken and Performed in the German Radio Opera *Affentheurlich Naupengeheurliche Geschichtklitterung* by Reinhold Friedl (2015)

Fischart's *Geschichtklitterung* as a creative reworking of Rabelais's *Gargantua* is sui generis (Fischart 1997: 406); the word used in the title of the book already indicates that the author produced a story that he had written down quickly and hastily, blotting the paper and introducing all kinds of phantastic and strange notions (Fischart 1997: 35). It is difficult to give a brief overview of Fischart's transposition that would not be a distortion. I will therefore simply begin by taking note of a pertinent remark made in a German introductory essay on Fischart that gives a good account of the key features of the text. The *Geschichtklitterung* contains an episode (chapter 8) that is widely known as the "Trunkenlitanei," a so-called litany of the drunkards, the equivalent of Rabelais's chapter 5 in the Gargantua part of his novel (Fischart 1963: 117–45; see Weinberg 1972: 62–66; Weinberg 1986: 55–63). In her essay on Fischart's text, Barbara Könneker (2000) contends that this episode is one of the most famous pieces of German prose,

> das wie in einem modernen Hörspiel den Verlauf eines Zechgelages bis hin zur völligen Betrunkenheit aller Beteiligten durch rein akustische Effekte, Stimmengewirr, Gesprächsfetzen, grölende Gesänge und in wüstes Getümmel ausartendes Geschrei zur Darstellung bringt. (94)

To paraphrase: This piece of prose operates like a modern radio play by presenting a kind of drunken revelry that ends in the complete intoxication of everyone. The way that this drunken party is presented on the level of discourse is through purely acoustic effects, through a medley of voices, fragments of conversation, loud singing, and wild partying. Although she does so only in passing, Könneker highlights a very important feature of Fischart's text, namely its proto-radio-drama-like character and the narrative potential of its aural dimension. In an earlier study, Dieter Seitz (1974) pointed out that in chapter 21 of the *Geschichtklitterung,* Fischart had created a "Hörszene," that is, a scene that can be heard and in which sounds play a crucial role in the narrative presentation more generally (54). In this particular chapter, Seitz noted, Fischart had presented something that is part of the action, namely a speech by Bragmado, not through narration after the fact but through creating the fictive image of an acoustic impression.

If Fischart constructs his text in such a way that not only oral speech is given a certain prominence, but also diverse nonverbal sounds as well as music, this indicates an openness of the text itself toward acoustic presentation.[4] I will turn to a fascinating radio piece that took up Fischart's text to show how much such a radio adaptation can move away from straightforward storytelling.

The radio opera by Reinhold Friedl, first broadcast in 2015 by Deutschlandradio Kultur, properly begins only after a speaker has presented a few sentences from the radio theorist Rudolf Arnheim's famous book *Rundfunk als Hörkunst (Radio: An Art of Sound),* which was first published in English translation in 1936. This introduction as well as further quotations later on offer a kind of theoretical frame for the sound art that is meant to evoke some of the themes and sounds found in Fischart, sometimes by way of contrast, as I will explain in the following. In these short excerpts from Arnheim, one may detect a kind of implicit commentary on what the director of the radio drama wants to achieve here. Arnheim argues, for example, that radio drama tries to depersonalize the speaker by all possible means. His bodily presence in the studio should not become apparent through anything that can be heard, so his body movements have to be controlled and rather subdued. Voice is thus meant to become a kind of abstraction, something that is no longer linked to a particular body but is an uprooted or placeless sound that is also decontex-

---

4. Since Fischart's text is also a very idiosyncratic reworking and rewriting in German of parts of François Rabelais's *Gargantua and Pantagruel,* it would make sense to examine in detail whether the distinctively aural nature of Fischart's text can already be found in some form in Rabelais's pre-text. However, I will refrain from a detailed philological analysis of Fischart's rendering of the text, since that would require me to give too many explanations of words and expressions in a form of early modern German that is not easily communicable, as is evidenced by the comprehensive glossary published with the Nyssen edition of the novel. See also Ernst Sander's (1983) pertinent remark on the linguistic insufferability of Fischart's translation (57).

tualized. If body movements are not supposed to be heard, nonverbal expressions that normally accompany speech must be eliminated. In the case of the Fischart radio opera by Friedl, however, as in the case of the English Rabelais radio drama, this advice is not adopted. Although the studio as studio is not itself made audible, it is thematically relevant to the extent that the sounds of the speaker(s) are accompanied by a mixture of atmospheric music-like sounds as well as by sounds such as belching, indicating drunkenness and satiety.

The text spoken after the quotation from Arnheim's essay is a somewhat vulgar address to the drinkers as listeners or the listeners as drinkers, a text that is spoken by a couple of voices at the same time. This list of address terms and epithets is terminated when a rather unharmonious music becomes more dominant, while only a few moments later another introductory text is spoken by one speaker alone. This text continues the introductory material insofar as it still does not present a form of narrative. Arnheim is quoted as stating that the text in a radio production is treated like a musical score and that one should take account of the way that words overlap to create this kind of music. These remarks are inserted before a passage in which at least two voices utter words (mostly repetitions of the addresses already mentioned earlier) that begin to overlap until it is no longer possible to clearly make out their meaning.

The sections of the radio opera devoted to presenting the original Fischart text offer a somewhat irritating sound scene in which any action to which some kind of eventfulness could be attributed is very much reduced to background noises of people talking and drinking. This feast is an event that takes place, but it cannot be made out what its purpose or narrative context actually are, as one cannot really understand what people are saying. The narrative thus recedes to the background to make space for an extended presentation of a scene and its atmosphere. The speaking voices are further emphasized through the obvious attempt to articulate the words almost as whispers, which creates the impression of clearer pronunciation combined with a hissing sound until the voices fade completely, giving way to a sound that may be described as a form of music. This sound then continues as the speaker again recites Arnheim to the effect that the "rediscovery of musical sound in noise and language, the combination of music, noise and language into a unified sound material is one of the great artistic tasks of radio." At this point, after more than eleven minutes, there still is no narrative structure. Electronically produced musical sounds become dominant, while only occasional whispers can be heard. Then a short sequence of a female voice singing introduces the next sequence, in which not only the musical sounds continue but various voices speak with different degrees of clarity. Hissing sounds as well as sometimes recognizable words do not cohere into anything that could be described as a linear narrative. The only thing that minimally resembles narrative content is the sounds in the background that could be attributed to cutlery and plates being collected after a meal. This narrative is minimal as no further context is provided about what is really going on and no narrative voice presents any clue whatsoever about who participates in the scene and in which relation these characters might stand to each other. Roughly in the middle of the piece, we hear a list of words that play on the word *Löffel*, which means "spoon," that Fischart also uses with gusto in his text, especially as many of these words carry connotations of foolishness and fools (Fischart 1963: 124). The performance of a list of words seemingly referring to different kinds of spoons fits the context of a communal meal that involves drinking and singing. Interestingly, the list of "spoon words" also includes snippets of poeticization in the form of lines that are obviously sung by the revelers: "Sind löffel do, So sind wir fro [sic]" (As long as there are spoons we are happy). In the radio opera, this is turned into actual singing, as is the case with the text further on that is clearly meant to represent singing at the table but also seems to be meant as a parody of actual music (Fischart 1963: 125): "Singt nur mit Schall, ihr Löffel all, hoho Löffel do" (Sing loud and clear, ye spoons all, hoho ye spoons there).

The almost constant parallel sound production of narrative voice and background noises creates a strange soundscape that indicates the precarious nature of the radio opera as a narrative proper. For all sounds seem to possess equal importance and thus significance, which means that there is no privileged position of verbal storytelling to which musical elements only provide a supporting accompaniment. Nor could it be said that the dominant music becomes clearer in its function through verbal interactions, because the latter do not offer much enlightenment about what goes on. This has two effects. First, narrative as a verbally constructed sign system recedes into the background, and second, the sounds themselves show at least a tendency to acquire narrative potential insofar as they indicate a change in the state of affairs. However, this is a mere tendency, indicating perhaps a further decline of the "characters," who remain entirely unspecified, into drunkenness or the general disintegration of coherent perception and thinking. The radio opera thus performs on the level of sounds what Fischart's book explicitly professes to be, namely a confused pattern of a confused world ("ein verwirretes ungestaltes Muster der heut verwirrten ungestalten Welt"; Fischart 1997: 39–40; see Fischart 1963: 8). The somewhat confusing, if not confused, combination of verbal and nonverbal sounds cannot be expected to form a coherent narrative pattern—in fact, the narrative incoherence of Fischart's text, which is already anticipated as a poetological requirement in the author's own introduction to the book, is mirrored in the radio opera in an ingenious way. Fischart's poetics of confusion is hinted at early on in the radio opera when the lines just quoted are spoken by the narrator in a rather hurried way. However, this only becomes clear once the end of the radio opera has been reached and the confused listeners are implicitly asked to move beyond the radio opera in order to really understand what was going on.

The telling of strange stories—exactly those stories that were not really told in the present radio opera—is finally justified by the narrator *after* the radio opera has concluded and the typical references to the participants and the director have been made. After the announcer has concluded in the standard fashion by saying "Produktion: Deutschlandradio Kultur 2015," the radio opera is not over yet. A strange kind of singing that was heard all through the announcer's statements continues and becomes even louder while the voice of either Rabelais or the narrator recites one of the last paragraphs of chapter 34 of Rabelais's book II (*Pantagruel*), in which he confronts the hypothetical criticism that he has presented, as Fischart writes, mere "Flausen und Flunkergeschichten" (Fischart 1997: 382),[5] that is, nonsensical and tall tales or "gay and empty balderdash" (Rabelais 1955: 277; in the original French "balivernes et plaisantes mocquettes"; see Rabelais 1994: 336).

This ending points to a particularly strange feature of the radio opera, namely that the alleged, strange stories of Pantagruel, for example, are absent from the actual recording, so that the listeners either have to fill in fitting stories from their prior knowledge of *Gargantua and Pantagruel* or have to read the stories after listening to the essentially non-narrative radio opera— an opera that does not offer anything in the way of a recognizable operatic action—in order to complete its acoustic suggestions. In the first case, narrative would then be the product of cognitive operations in the listeners' minds *after* listening. In the latter case, the radio opera can hardly be regarded as an adaptation of Gargantuan stories but rather as a trace leading to the absent stories if the listeners decide to follow this trace. In both cases, narration is what happens after the sound of the radio piece has stopped. The paradoxical structure of the radio opera is further emphasized by the speaker's reference to the enjoyment that one has gained from listening to the "Flausen und Flunkergeschichten," an enjoyment that obviously cannot be attributed to the alleged presentation of stories, which did not really take place, but only to the combination of sounds, if anything. The radio opera based on Fischart finishes

---

5. The text spoken derives not from Fischart but from Rabelais, excerpts of which are printed in German translation in Fischart (1997: 381–82).

with a presentation of Rabelais's text, but it does so with a slight, yet significant change that underlines my claim that the actual cognitive reconstruction of narrative begins only at or after the end: Whereas Rabelais's concluding remarks at the end of book II are closed by noting that this is the end of the chronicles of Pantagruel (Rabelais 1955: 278; Rabelais 1994: 337), Fischart includes a pun at the end that problematizes the very notion of an ending (of narrative) itself. For he not only adopts Rabelais's conventional closing formula but adds to the word FINIS another line that reads: "Win uß" (Fischart 1963: 429). This signifies first that the word meaning "end" is not the real end. The real end is expressed by the impure rhyme created through the expression "Win uß," which means: There is no more wine left to drink. The formal ending is thus supervened by the end of the drinking party.

These remarks, however, can only be found in Fischart's book, not in Friedl's radio opera, where the text spoken at the end includes no finality—and this is, I would argue, in accordance with my hypothesis that the radio opera's end only opens up a new beginning for the true story of *Gargantua and Pantagruel* that was never presented here in the first place. *Gargantua and Pantagruel* are then only present as an absence in this strange radio opera that hardly qualifies as an example of the older genre of "Funkoper," in which language was supposed to make the nonverbal element of music more comprehensible and a holistic musical conception is aimed at (Hobl-Friedrich 1991: 61–62). In contrast to the earliest experiments with radio opera undertaken by Ezra Pound (Fisher 2002), the texts spoken in Friedl's radio opera hardly qualify as a libretto (Gier 2000: 33; see Hobl-Friedrich 1991: 61). What links the Fischart radio opera to the earlier forms of "Funkoper" is therefore merely the decidedly experimental approach to storytelling—in this case, however, without a proper fable that could have been made more vivid by a combination of music and storytelling. The listener, in order to bring the non-storytelling of the radio opera to some closure, will have to pick up either Fischart's *Geschichtklitterung* or Rabelais's *Gargantua and Pantagruel* or both. Otherwise the listener might never know what he or she was missing out on. In a sense, the radio opera's "ending" signifies its ultimate self-cancellation. This seems to be precisely the point of Friedl's meta-non-narration.

Concluding Remarks

The works of literature and their audio adaptations that I discussed in this chapter demonstrate the high degree of complexity that inheres in the study of radio drama and especially of radio play adaptations. First, there is a level at which the implicit and explicit sound qualities of the pre-text need to be explored. Even a text that is merely transmitted to us in written form may well have been read aloud and thus been part of some sort of multimodal reception from the beginning. And even written literary texts will invite readers to imagine sounds and voice qualities (see Stewart 1998; Zymner 2006). A further issue that plays a much more pronounced role in audio art than in text-to-text translation is the actual substitution of sound-dominated words or word-like components and word combinations by others in line with the properties of the target language. However, much more important than this seems to be the fact that in both works by Rabelais and Fischart, verbal play can at times become more pronounced than any narrative propulsion. So, for example, the *lengthy* enumeration of linguistic items such as address terms tends to destroy narrativity in favor of a poetics of the list or enumeration (see Eco 2011 as well as Mainberger 2003). The same can be said of the mere sound of talk from which no meaningful narrative evolves because what is actually said can hardly be distinguished. The text of Rabelais's novel is transformed into a modern radio drama narration in which mimetic representations of actions take place at the same time with the act of narration, as if the narrator was only making the story up in the process of telling it. In addition, the narrator gives up his position as a purely nondiegetic narrator and at various points moves metaleptically into the story world and out of it, becoming a character actually interacting with the hero of his own story. No such narrative instance is discernible in the radio opera based on Fischart, except in the paratextual introduction that frames the non-narrative substance of the drunkards' litany. Both works of radio art thus choose very different ways of dealing with the sound potentials written into their respective pre-texts.[6]

---

6. The Rabelaisian (and Fischartian) technique of creating verbal sound has not lost its productive potential; it has been adopted, to give a particularly prominent example, by the American writer Philip Roth in one of his lesser-known novels, *The Great American Novel* (1973), in which alliterative enumeration is a prominent feature. Although there is an audiobook adaptation of the novel, it has not been adapted for radio yet. But the novel would surely merit the attempt and could serve as the basis for another Rabelaisian soundscape in which narrativity itself as well as the connections between sound and narrative are negotiated between non-narrative passages, mimetic dialogues, and more pronounced narratorial interventions. Roth's adaptation of Rabelaisian wordplay and a kind of autonomization of sound to the detriment of precisely defined meaning shows the direction toward which experimental sound art can tend: It can lose almost all meaningful narrativity, as in Friedl's radio opera, and thereby probe into the limits of narrativity—radio drama's "need for narration" (Rodger 1982: 27)—itself.

Works Cited

Affentheurlich Naupengeheurliche Geschichtklitterung. 2015. Directed by Vinzenz Weissenburger, script by Reinhold Friedl based on a text by Johann Fischart. Deutschlandradio Kultur.

Arnheim, Rudolf. 1936. *Radio.* Translated by Margaret Ludwig and Herbert Read. London: Faber & Faber.

Buhlert, Klaus. 1992. *Meine Lieder singt man nicht. Radiostück nach Ezra Pound.* Directed by Jörg Jannings. NDR.

Cornilliat, François. 2000. "On Sound Effects in Rabelais (Part 1)" *Etudes rabelaisiennes* 39: 137–67.

———. 2003. "On Sound Effects in Rabelais (Part 2)" *Etudes rabelaisiennes* 42: 7–55.

Doob, Leonard W., ed. 1978. *"Ezra Pound Speaking": Radio Speeches of WW II.* Westport, CT: Greenwood.

Eco, Umberto. 2011. *Die unendliche Liste.* München: dtv.

Fischart, Johann. 1963. *Geschichtklitterung (Gargantua): Text der Ausgabe letzer Hand von 1590.* Edited by Ute Nyssen. Düsseldorf: Rauch.

———. 1997. *Affentheurlich Naupengeheurliche Geschichtklitterung, Mit einem Auszug aus dem Gargantua des Rabelais.* Frankfurt/M.: Eichborn.

Fisher, Margaret. 2002. *Ezra Pound's Radio Operas: The BBC Experiments, 1931–1933.* Cambridge, MA: MIT Press.

Gier, Albert. 2000. *Das Libretto: Theorie und Geschichte einer musikoliterarischen Gattung.* Frankfurt/M.: Insel.

Gray, Alasdair. 1981. *Lanark: A Life in Four Books.* Edinburgh: Canongate.

Hobl-Friedrich, Mechtild. 1991. "Die dramaturgische Funktion der Musik im Hörspiel: Grundlagen—Analysen." PhD thesis, Erlangen-Nürnberg.

Kinzel, Till. 2017. "Narrativity and Sound in German Radio Play Adaptations of Paul Auster's *The New York Trilogy.*" *Partial Answers* 15, no. 1: 151–65.

Könneker, Barbara. 2000. "Johann Fischart." In *Deutsche Dichter Band 2: Reformation, Renaissance und Barock,* edited by Gunter E. Grimm and Frank Rainer Max, 89–99. Stuttgart: Reclam.

Mainberger, Sabine. 2003. *Die Kunst des Aufzählens. Elemente zu einer Poetik des Enumerativen* (Quellen und Forschungen zur Literatur- und Kulturgeschichte 22). Berlin: De Gruyter.

Mildorf, Jarmila. 2017. "Sounding Postmodernity: Narrative Voices in the Radio Adaptation of Alasdair Gray's *Lanark.*" *Partial Answers* 15, no. 1: 167–88.

Mühlemann, Christoph. 1972. *Fischarts "Geschichtklitterung" als manieristisches Kunstwerk: Verwirrtes Muster einer verwirrten Welt.* Bern/Frankfurt/M.: Lang.

Rabelais, François. 1955. *Gargantua and Pantagruel.* Translated by J. M. Cohen. London: Penguin.

———. 1994. *Œuvres completes.* Edited by Mireille Huchon with François Moreau. Paris: Gallimard.

Rodger, Ian. 1982. *Radio Drama.* London: Macmillan.

Roth, Philip. 2010. *The Great American Novel.* Unabridged audio book read by James Daniels. Brilliance Audio.

Sander, Ernst. 1983. "Vom Übersetzen ins Deutsche." In *Sprachkunst und Übersetzung. Gedenkschrift Ernst Sander,* edited by Hans-Albrecht Koch, 45–71. Bern: Lang.

Seitz, Dieter. 1974. *Johann Fischarts Geschichtklitterung. Zur Prosastruktur und zum grobianischen Motivkomplex*. Frankfurt/M.: Athenäum.

Stewart, Susan. 1998. "Letter on Sound." In *Close Listening: Poetry and the Performed Word*, edited by Charles Bernstein, 29–52. Oxford: Oxford University Press.

Vossler, Karl. 1921. *Frankreichs Kultur im Spiegel seiner Sprachentwicklung. Geschichte der französischen Schriftsprache von den Anfängen bis zur klassischen Neuzeit*. 3rd ed. Heidelberg: Winter.

Weinberg, Florence. 1972. *The Wine and the Will: Rabelais's Bacchic Christianity*. Detroit: Wayne State University Press.

———. 1986. *Gargantua in a Convex Mirror: Fischart's View of Rabelais*. New York: Lang.

Zymner, Rüdiger. 2006. "'Stimme(n)' als Text und Stimme(n) als Ereignis." In *Stimme(n) im Text: Narratologische Positionsbestimmungen*, edited by Andreas Blödorn, Daniela Langer, and Michael Scheffel, 321–47. Berlin: De Gruyter.

10

Music, Voice, and (De)Narrativization in Samuel Beckett's Radio Play *Cascando*

PIM VERHULST

DUE TO ITS CHALLENGING NATURE, Samuel Beckett's work has often been used by narratologists as a testing ground for their concepts and theories. This holds true especially for his prose, but also his theater has received attention, in particular from Brian Richardson (1988), who states that Beckett "almost single-handedly created a theater of narration" (202). Following the lead of Richardson, Tom Vandevelde (2013) has extended this narratological enquiry to Beckett's radio plays, in particular *Cascando,* which he singles out as "a prime example of narrativity in drama" (256). However, Vandevelde's study is confined to the "playscript mode" of radio plays and their "formal combination of stage directions, speech prefixes, and speeches" (256), which, according to Manfred Jahn (2001), are "especially instructive for the purposes of narratological analysis" (673). Although this approach certainly has its merits, it also has important limitations. *Cascando* belongs to the realm of *radio* drama, intended to be broadcast and listened to. In addition to textual elements, it also has acoustic traits that defy some of the key concepts used in classical narratology, including that of the "narrator," and therefore require additional analytic tools that allow for the study of aural narrative elements like voice and music. The emerging field of audio-narratology is much better equipped for this task, as it does not reduce radio plays to their textual manifestation but also takes their audio recordings and broadcasts into account.

In what follows, I would like to expand the methodology even further to include the manuscripts of *Cascando*. By adopting this double focus of genetic (audio)narratology, I follow in the footsteps of Lars Bernaerts and Dirk Van Hulle (2013), who argue that "on the one hand, genetic criticism can provide data to corroborate a narratological analysis," while "on the other hand, narratology can serve as an aid to the genetic examination of the narrative's development across version" (281).[1] Not only do the drafts of *Cascando* elucidate its narratological analysis, they also bear witness to a transmedial process inherent in the genesis of a radio play. As Beckett transposes *Cascando* from a text into a script and eventually into a recording for broadcast, he gradually homes in on the unique potential that radio has to offer as an acoustic medium. In doing so, he combines the textual and the vocal with the musical to create an effect of *denarrativization*, which is different from *denarration* in "unnatural narratology," defined by Richardson (2006) as "a kind of narrative negation in which a narrator denies significant aspects of his or her narrative that had earlier been presented as given" (87). Even though he allows for a broader understanding in which denarration "undermines the world it purports to depict," so that "very little (if anything) is left over after the assaults of textual negation the narrative performs" (91), the phenomenon relies for the most part on contradiction. The effect of *Cascando* is more radical in the sense that it diminishes the narrative predisposition of language, so that it would perhaps be more accurate to speak of denarrativization, that is, a gradual undoing of the characteristics that make us regard a string of words as narrative.

The (Non-)Narrativity of Music

Both narratologists and musicologists have debated whether music is a narrative art form endowed with narrativity.[2] Monika Fludernik broadened these concepts in her *Towards a "Natural" Narratology* (1996) to break with more formalist approaches that held the defining features of narrative to be plot or action. Instead, Fludernik introduced the notion of experientiality, arguing that what characterizes a text as narrative is the degree to which readers

---

1. Genetic criticism, or *critique génétique*, is a branch of literary criticism that originated in France in the 1960s. Unlike textual scholarship, it treats literary manuscripts as an object of study in their own right, not merely as a subservient tool to establish a critical edition. Genetic criticism approaches the literary text as a process, not just a product, and investigates the hermeneutic potential of its variants (deletions, additions, rephrasings, etc.). For excellent English-language introductions to the field, see Deppman, Ferrer, and Groden (2004) and Van Hulle (2014).

2. For a more detailed overview of this debate, see Mildorf (2017).

are able to recognize or relate to a story, which does not have to be a series of events, as Herman and Vervaeck (2005) explain: "It suffices to encounter on any textual level an anthropomorphous agent who has certain experiences" and "displays emotional involvement" to which the reader can relate (172). On the one hand, Fludernik's redefinition of narrative and narrativity is thus more inclusive, because it foregrounds the role of the reader; on the other hand, it has been rightfully criticized by advocates of unnatural narratology, who point out its tendency to naturalize nonhuman narrators and characters, as well as aberrant or illogical depictions of experience and emotionality, even time and space. It is also text-oriented, which makes it problematic for transmedial storytelling or nontextual art forms like music.

In order to allow for the study of music as narrative, Eero Tarasti (2004) posits a "minimal condition of narrativity" that avoids terms like "text" or "reader" and substitutes them with "the transformation of an object or state of affairs into something else through a process that requires a certain amount of time" (283). While this approach is in certain respects more formalist than Fludernik's understanding of narrativity, it is also much broader, so broad perhaps that even, say, cooking might be considered as narrative by these parameters. Even if certain chefs do elevate the rather mundane activity of food preparation to the level of art, to speak of it or even study it in terms of narrativity is another matter. Of course, there are fundamental differences between music and cooking that make us perceive the one as narrative and the other, well, not so much—although recipes, spoken or written, often resort to a number of narrative and rhetorical strategies. Following Tarasti, in order to measure or gauge what kind of change an object or state of affairs undergoes over time, it must have formal building blocks that are affected by structural processes. Consisting of notes that can be arranged and combined in patterns of varying complexity, music certainly meets the minimum conditions of narrativity as formulated by Tarasti. While he "does not claim to be able to show that music is able to *tell* particular stories," its syntactic component enables him to "show which structures in music enable us to *associate* it with stories" (283). Like the reader in Fludernik's conception of narrativity, the listener has a central position in Tarasti's musical redefinition of it. Even though the structural refinement of music is something that only the trained ears of experienced listeners may be able to appreciate and analyze, amateur or casual listeners also relate to music on more conceptual or personal rather than analytical grounds, often determined by the degree to which the music is verbally framed.

In this sense, Tarasti (2004) distinguishes between two types of music that together represent a scale or continuum of increasing abstraction. At the most abstract end, we find the pure or "'absolute' music of the Western erudite tonal art," unmediated by language, in which case "we may think of the meaning that the composition tries to convey as an abstract plot" (283). This vague sense of emplotment, Emma Kafalenos (2004) suggests, allows listeners to "(re)construct a causal sequence of events—events that except for their causal relations remain otherwise unspecified" (278). Applying to music the distinction between "readerly" and "writerly" texts that Roland Barthes introduced in *S/Z*, Kafalenos goes on to argue that "instrumental music, because it is unburdened by the semantic meanings (however polysemous) attached to verbal signifiers, is more writerly than even the most plural constructs made from words" (280). Put differently, the more abstract a piece of music becomes, the more subjective, personal, and associative its meaning will be. From this statement it follows that, within the category of absolute or pure music, a distinction can be made between tonal pieces with recognizable harmonies and atonal or dodecaphonic compositions—including derivatives like serialism—that experiment with varying degrees of dissonance.[3] If we leave such nuances aside, the consensus among narratologists and musicologists seems to be that "when unaccompanied by text or paratext, instrumental music shares narrative features but should probably not be thought of *as* narrative" (Kafalenos 2004: 280).

At the other end of the spectrum, we find music that is in one way or other narrativized by language. As Marie-Laure Ryan (2004) succinctly puts it, being itself "an art made of signifiers without signifieds, music eludes verbal description" (267), but it can be concretized or substantiated with the help of words. Closely related to absolute music is program music, a term usually reserved for classical compositions attempting to convey in music a nonmusical narrative. Typical examples include myths, novels, or fairy tales that are solely expressed through music, sometimes accompanied by a booklet or a program to guide the audience or the private listener. Some of the most heavily narrativized musical forms are the *lied,* a typically German type of song that was famous in the Romantic period and usually set a poem to piano music, and the opera, in which for the most part preexisting stories are acted out and sung under the guidance of an orchestra. Modern incarnations of these classical forms are musicals and pop, which both have a sizeable verbal dimension closely tied to instrumentation, but still we tend to think of them as music

---

3. However, as Caroline Kita (2016) has shown on the basis of Arnold Schönberg's monodrama *Totentanz der Prinzipien* (1926), it is possible for dodecaphonic music to engage in a narrative relationship with language, although in this case the result is a "polyphonic poetics that attempted to mirror the 'abstract polyphony' of his musical language," focusing "not on the semantic meaning of language, but rather its acoustic properties" (38–39).

rather than literature. However, apart from the often "poetic" quality of their language, they can also employ music in "literary" ways that do more than merely set the mood or amplify the emotional gravity of the words. As Peter J. Rabinowitz (2004) has shown, music can provide an ironic counterpoint in opera and musicals, undercutting the action and dialogue performed on the stage, much like a "narrator's commentary" would in a novel or a "voice-over in film" (315). Alan Palmer (2016) and Markus Wierschem (2016) have similarly analyzed more complex interactions of music and lyrics in country, blues, and the "concept album" of progressive rock. One important art form that has somewhat eluded the debate, especially in Anglophone circles, is radio drama.

Unlike the field of film narratology, where the narrative functions of music have long been studied and inventorized, such a systematic approach is yet to be undertaken for radio drama. To a large extent, this is due to the genre's ephemeral nature, broadcast only a handful of times, and the scarcity of (commercially) available recordings, which is the only form in which the role of music can be adequately studied, as scripts provide little more than cues and rarely include scores. Notable exceptions are the studies of Hobl-Friedrich (1991), Shingler and Wieringa (1998), and Huwiler (2005a, 2005b), but these are based on relatively small collections of German- or English-language radio plays and should therefore be regarded as foundational or pioneering rather than definitive—though important nonetheless. As Huwiler (2005a) summarizes the state of the art (60–61), music is generally said to fulfil two primary functions in radio drama, which can be either diegetic or extra-diegetic (i.e., inside/outside of the story world). The first is a structural or syntactical one, bracketing recordings with a prelude and/or a postlude, as well as intermezzos to indicate transitions. The second is a semantic function, which can be further subdivided into a supporting role—intensifying or deepening the content of the words—and a constitutive role. The latter is more independent of the radio play's linguistic component, performing narrative functions like foreshadowing, commentary, contrast, and alienation. Radio plays that are less driven by story, with music almost assuming the role of a character, challenge this traditional process of narrativization. Although Huwiler (2005a) notes that music adopts an "iconic" role in such cases (62), it is difficult to classify them in a typology. Usually associated with the German "Neues Hörspiel" of the 1960s, other literatures, including Dutch, Flemish, French, and English, offer similar examples. In the remainder of this chapter, I will focus on *Cascando*, originally written in French but translated into English, by the Irish author Samuel Beckett, to illustrate the analytical difficulties posed by this divergent type of radio play and how it unsettles the traditional narrativizing relationship between language and music by countering it with one of denarrativization.

Cascando as a "Text-Music Tandem"

In 1961 the French national public broadcasting organization RTF (Radiodiffusion-Télévision Française) commissioned the Franco-Romanian composer Marcel Mihalovici for a project involving words and music. Having previously collaborated with Beckett on an opera version of his stage play *Krapp's Last Tape,* Mihalovici asked him to supply the words for this new radiophonic venture. Beckett agreed and set to work immediately in late 1961, finishing the text in early 1962 and translating it into English in 1963 and 1964. That it was not a typical "radio play" was evident from its first publication in the Brussels-based avant-garde magazine *L'VII* (1963), where it took the subtitle "invention radiophonique pour musique et voix." Although it was later normalized to the standard "pièce radiophonique" for the book publication by Minuit (1966), and "radio play" or "radio piece" for the English editions by Faber (1964) and Grove Press (1968), Beckett never quite liked the term and often referred to *Cascando* as a "text-music tandem" in his letters (see Zilliacus 1976: 114).

The term "tandem" is well chosen, since language and music are made to join forces by a third character who steers the collaboration. As Vandevelde (2013) points out, the framework of *Cascando* "contains several narrative levels" (261). On the highest echelon (level 1), Beckett positions a character called "Opener," who operates a channel for "Voice" and one for "Music" (level 2). In turn, the monologue of Voice consists of two parts as well: a story about a character called Woburn and repetitive phrases in which the Voice prompts itself to finish the story about Woburn (level 3). Sometimes Voice and Music are opened alone; at others they are opened together, complementing each other. According to Vandevelde (2013), Opener can be regarded as a "generative narrator" (260) in Richardson's (1988) terminology for the analysis of dramatic texts, that is, a character "ontologically distinct from the figures who emerge from or are engendered by his discourse" (209). "Such a generative figure," Vandevelde (2013) continues, "narrates what is happening or will happen on stage and functions as a kind of stage director in deciding what will happen next" (258). As I would like to argue in the following paragraphs, the status of Opener is somewhat more complex.

On the first level, he can indeed be said to function like an intradiegetic narrator, as Opener provides the reader-listener with information about himself and his situation. For example, we learn that it is "the month of May" (Beckett 2009: 85), or rather "the close of May" with its "long days" (91), also referred to as "the reawakening" (90). Opener regards the activity he is engaged in as "my life, I live on that" (88) and states "I have lived on it . . . till I'm old. Old enough" (88). On the third level, Voice can similarly be regarded as a genuine narrator, whose monologue consists of two distinct narrative strands. In the first one, it tells the story of a character called Woburn; in the second, it encourages itself to finish the story and be silent at last. However, unable to see Woburn clearly or read his thoughts, Voice is clearly not the traditional omniscient type of narrator. The protagonist hides in shelters during the day, only travels by night, and always shows his back. Whenever he falls, burying his face in the sand, the pebbles, or the water, he rises again and moves on, lowering his head as soon as the voice closes in. This game of cat and mouse between the narrating voice and the narrated protagonist leads to a somewhat paradoxical situation: Woburn exists only because he is narrated by Voice, and yet Voice does not exert control over the character it has narrated into being. In turn, Woburn tries to shake off the narrator, but his attempts are futile, since the course of his journey is plotted out by that voice, thus perpetuating the pattern.

The main problem for any classical approach to *Cascando* is situated on the second level. In addition to being extradiegetic or exclusive to the story told by Voice, Opener does not function like a typical overarching narrator into whose narrative level the story told by Voice is embedded. He does not actually narrate Voice and Music, but merely opens and closes them. Critics have generally dealt with this anomaly by naturalizing the radio play and interpreting it as the depiction of a cognitive, mental, or creative process in which the Opener stands for the author or artist, and Voice and Music represent different aspects of his creative imagination (verbal or rational and nonverbal or emotional). While this approach is certainly helpful and illuminating, it does ignore some of the more resistant or unnatural elements in the radio play. For example, Opener claims that the Voice and the Music he opens do not belong to him. He repeats this claim throughout the radio play to defend himself from "the others" or "They" who believe that "he opens nothing, he has nothing to open, it's in his head" (Beckett 2009: 88). Yet Opener denies this by saying: "There is nothing in my head. . . . I open and close" (88). To further substantiate his claim, he observes that the Voice sounds different from his own: "No resemblance" (90).

It would perhaps be more accurate to regard Opener as a medium itself, through which Voice and Music are transmitted or relayed, thus functioning to some extent like the "audiophonic or multimodal composition device" that Lars Bernaerts introduces elsewhere in this collection, but embedded into the story world. Opener can tune in to the channels of sound, like any listener with a radio set, but he is unable to control what the source says or plays—although he can partially manipulate the output by opening Voice and Music together. He lacks control over the original source of the broadcast, which he receives from elsewhere, not from inside his head—or so he claims. If Beckett is here using the basic principle of radio broadcasting metaphorically to represent an artistic process, it is one in which active creation is reduced to mostly passive acts of listening and recording. By using this constellation of a character who opens and closes two channels of sound while listening in, Beckett is gradually gearing his script more to the acoustic medium of radio, possibly inspired by his many visits to the RTF studios in Paris, where he saw control panels with sliders and other technological equipment used in broadcasting.

Most resistant to any narratological analysis is the role of Music in *Cascando*, which Opener seems to anticipate when asking how he could possibly be the source of Music: "And that . . . is that mine too?" (90–91)—a question that was even more explicit in the manuscript of the radio play: "And that . . . is that my music?" (*BDMP11*, FM1, 04r).[4] In order to answer this question, we must call on the help of genetic and audionarratology.

Music and Denarrativization

In the published version of *Cascando*, Music is merely represented by a dotted line—dashes in the French text and Beckett's typescripts, to avoid confusion with the ellipses in the speech parts—so there is little to work with from a textual point of view. Still, it is worthwhile to focus on the few instances in the script where Voice and Music sound together. In the last stages of the writing process, as Beckett prepared his script for broadcast, he started paying more attention to this aspect, making sure that the parts in which Voice speaks alone contain narrative elements about the story of Woburn, whereas the speech parts that Voice speaks together with Music consist of self-encouraging phrases—labeled the "Self element" in Beckett's drafts. At the top of his second typescript, Beckett noted that Voice and Music sound "5 times together" (*BDMP11*, TS2, 01r). He also numbered these occasions in the left margin of the typescript, thus marking them as important moments.

Several critics have noted that Voice never tells the story of Woburn when Opener "opens" the two channels together, but Clas Zilliacus (1976) is the only

---

4. The manuscripts of *Cascando* can be consulted online in module 11 of the Beckett Digital Manuscript Project (http://www.beckettarchive.org), edited by Pim Verhulst (2022). For example, the abbreviation FM1 refers to the first French manuscript of the radio play (MS-HTC-THR-70-1), which is part of the "Samuel Beckett papers concerning *Cascando*, 1961–1962" held at the Harvard Theatre Collection of Harvard University's Houghton Library. For a finding aid to the collection, see http://oasis.lib.harvard.edu/oasis/deliver/~hou00804. I have translated all passages from the French manuscripts of *Cascando* into English for the sake of convenience. For a more detailed study of *Cascando*'s bilingual genesis, see Verhulst (2022).

one to offer a compelling explanation of this phenomenon. He argues that the "words of Voix in *Cascando* gradually approach the fundamental quality of Musique" as "they rid themselves of their anecdotal content, of the *histoire*" (136). Indeed, whenever the Voice speaks alone, it soon relapses into the story of Woburn, and only when it abstains from storytelling does it meet with Opener's explicit approval: "Good" (Beckett 2009: 90, 92). In this interpretation of the radio play, Opener is not so much trying to finish the story of Woburn as he wants to free or rid language of its traditional storytelling function, by gradually exposing it to music, which in its absolute form is non-narrative by nature.

Beckett's diaries from his trip to Germany in 1936 and 1937 offer further insights into his early thinking about the nature of literature and music, which are still strikingly relevant for *Cascando*, written twenty-five years later. On March 26, 1937, he made a note about the inadequacy of language in relation to music, borrowing concepts from Gotthold Ephraim Lessing's *Laocoon: An Essay on the Limits of Painting and Poetry* (1766) to classify painting as a "simultaneous" art form (in space), and poetry as "sequential" (in time). Even though music is not included in Lessing's aesthetic theory, Beckett adds it to the equation, fascinated by

> the dissonance that has become principle & that the word cannot express, because literature can no more escape from chronologies to simultaneities, from nebeneinander [sequential] to miteinander [simultaneous], tha[n] the human voice can sing chords. (qtd. in Nixon 2011: 167)

Beckett replaces Lessing's original opposition between *nacheinander* (poetry/time) and *nebeneinander* (painting/space) with *nebeneinander* (sequentiality) and *miteinander* (simultaneity), subsuming music under the latter because of its symphonic and contrapuntal arrangement, which likens it to painting and contrasts both with literature. As Mark Nixon (2011) explains, "Beckett was increasingly trying to define literature in terms of techniques derived from the visual arts and from music, in order to escape or circumvent the restrictions imposed by the chronology of language" (167). *Cascando* still thematizes this tension between chronology and dissonance that Beckett sought to overcome as early as the 1930s. The Voice in the radio play, limited as it is to words, always relapses into the linear story of Woburn. It can only detach itself from chronology, and use language in a more dissonant way, when Opener forces Voice, by opening the channel, to engage in a dialogue with Music. To explain this difference and the effect of Music on Voice, it is perhaps useful to compare two brief passages from *Cascando*:

VOICE: —down ... gentle slopes ... boreen ... giant aspens ... wind in the boughs ... faint sea ... Woburn ... same old coat ... he goes on ... stops ... not a soul ... not yet ... night too bright ... say what you like ... he goes on ... hugging the bank ... same old stick ... he goes down ... falls ... on purpose or not ... can't see ... he's down ... that's what counts ... face in the mud ... arms spread ... (Beckett 2009: 86)

VOICE:] [*Together.*] —sleep ... no further ... no more searching ... to find
MUSIC:]. . . . .
him ... in the dark ... to see him ... to say him ... for whom ... that's
. . . .
it ... no matter ... never him ... never right ... start again ... in the
. . . .
dark ... done with that ... this time ... it's the right one ... we're there
. . . .
... nearly ... finish—
. . . .
(89)

In the first passage, the voice speaks alone and the words are used to develop the story of Woburn. Every phrase adds new details to the narrative, which unfurls chronologically as we follow the sequential journey of the character. When music joins in, the words shed their storytelling function. The discourse becomes more dissonant, a limited set of stock phrases being constantly reiterated in a different order, following a pattern that is not random but musical rather than chronological. By thus exposing language to music, the words behave more like notes or, as Kevin Branigan (2008) puts it: "No longer obliged to hold referential meaning, they may chime as musical units" (33). However, language remains essentially and irreconcilably different from music. When dissonance replaces linearity as the structuring principle for discourse, words are still semantic units, even if their meaning does not pattern in the chronological framework of a story. This is apparent from the ending of *Cascando*, which concludes with a chain of nonchronological or dissonant elements, in a prolonged counterpoint of Voice and Music. Just before the last "[*Silence.*]" and the final "END," a narrative element from the Woburn story creeps in again:

VOICE:] —this time ... it's the right one ... finish ... no more stories ...
MUSIC:] . . . .
sleep ... we're there ... nearly ... just a few more ... don't let go ...

> ....
> Woburn . . . he clings on . . . come on . . . come on—
> ....

(Beckett 2009: 92–93)

The phrase "he clings on" had previously only occurred in passages where the Voice speaks alone, unaccompanied by Music, so it is a marker of the Woburn story. The conclusion thus seems to be that no matter how long or extensively language is exposed to the denarrativizing effect of music, words cannot help but tell stories and always slip back into narrative mode.

In Fludernik's definition of narrativity, the repetitive "Self element" in *Cascando* still qualifies as narrative, because it has an experiential agent that reader-listeners can relate to emotionally. Beckett's own working definition of narrativity is thus more formalist, governed first and foremost by chronology or linearity, which diminishes under the influence of musical dissonance—at least in theory.

Absolute Music Made Programmatic

Up until now, I have deliberately concentrated on the nominal presence of music in the script, represented by a dotted line or a series of dashes, and its effect on the linguistic component of the radio play. This is also how Beckett approached it while writing *Cascando*, working from an abstract concept of music that would have to be given concrete shape by a composer, in this case Marcel Mihalovici. The score was not finished until December 30, 1962, almost a year after the text had been completed. When Beckett finally heard the edited production during rehearsal and recording sessions at the RTF studios, he called it "disastrous," writing to the American critic Lawrence Harvey on July 2, 1963: "Mihalovici's music is fine, but the result most disappointing. Not rehearsed, not prepared, realized 'Comme ça te pousse' [as you go along]" (qtd. in Knowlson 1997: 507). Beckett repeated his disappointment in a letter to American director Alan Schneider on July 20, 1963, explaining the nature of the problem in more detail: "The result very unsatisfactory. M's music is fine in itself, but doesn't work with the text" (qtd. in Beckett 1998: 138).

At thirty-eight pages, Mihalovici's score was rather lengthy for Beckett's short script, forcing the production team to make selections, as the composer could not be present for the sessions due to other obligations. The manuscript and corrected proofs for the sheet music offer valuable insight into the composition process.[5] Numbering the instances for which music had to be composed from I to XV, Mihalovici wrote out the musical notation for each of the instruments: flute, two standard clarinets, basset clarinet, piano, celesta, harp, first and second violin, viola, cello, and a range of percussion instruments (cymbal, tam-tam, gong, woodblock, drum, triangle, three temple blocks, xylophone, and marimba). Underneath the number for each musical part, Mihalovici also added the first words of the line that triggers it in the script of *Cascando*, but the notes are never keyed to the actual text, not even on those occasions when Music and Voice sound together. This practice was markedly different from the aforementioned opera adaptation of *Krapp's Last Tape*, for which author and composer sat down at the piano, pairing the syllables of the text to the music while making changes to both (see Van Hulle 2015: 126–27). In the case of *Cascando*, Mihalovici only loosely based his score on the script, not exactly grafting the notes onto the words but providing a musical interpretation of them, which led to all kinds of editing problems.

Leaving practical matters aside, Beckett's disappointment at the result may also imply that Mihalovici's music was simply not what he expected or needed for *Cascando* to work. Seeing as I am not a musicologist, I cannot engage in a full-on technical analysis of the score, so my approach will have to remain impressionistic or intuitive, but Mihalovici's ensemble of instruments makes for an orchestration that is overly lush or sumptuous at times, bordering on the Romantic—a trait that Beckett also disliked about the score for *Krapp's Last Tape* (see Knowlson 1997: 467–68). As an undesired result, the text of *Cascando* is often imbued with emotion or sentiment under the influence of music, which in turn is narrativized by the text—the kind of standard effect that Beckett sought to avoid. As a trained neoclassicist, married to the French concert pianist Monique Haas, Mihalovici was perhaps not the best choice for an avant-garde radio play—yet he was the one originally commissioned by the RTF. In this respect, it is telling that Beckett named Humphrey Searle when scholar Katharine Worth asked him if he would recommend a composer for a new production of *Cascando* by the University of London's Audio-Visual Centre in the late 1970s. A serialist who had studied under Anton Webern and championed the twelve-tone technique in Britain, Searle was a better example of the experimental kind of backing that *Cascando* required. As we have seen, Beckett was interested in the literary potential of dissonance as early as

---

5. These documents are also preserved at the Harvard Theatre Collection (MS Thr 70.1), and Mihalovici's score has been published separately by Les Éditions Heugel in Paris as Op. 86.

the 1930s and, according to the French-Israeli painter Avigdor Arikha, they listened to "quite a bit of dodecaphonic music—Schoenberg, Berg, Webern" in the late 1950s (qtd. in Knowlson 1997: 496)—the period leading up to *Cascando*. Yet Searle faced the same problems as Mihalovici, having to work from a script that gave very little direction about how the music should relate to the words. Should it try to mimic the chronological narrativity of the Woburn story, without giving it concrete shape, or was it to be dissonant throughout and uphold this quality as an example for the nonlinear self-encouragements of Voice? Beckett never quite resolved these dilemmas.

As Worth (1998) explains, Searle would draw out directions for tone and mood from Voice's narrative: "The two versions of the story would flow together, Music always entering at the point reached by Voice, though free to look forward and backward and to emphasize key themes, in ways the internal structures of the music might suggest" (17). To create this effect, instrumental motifs were established for recurring verbal elements such as "Woburn," the "island" and the "journey" (17–18), using a "small orchestra" of "strings, woodwinds, and percussion" (18). What made the production particularly interesting was its combination of "dissonances" and "variations"—for the more "haunting, obsessive themes"—with "piercing harmonies," to establish a musical equivalent for the tension between linear and nonlinear narration in the script (18). In Worth's view, "a playful note sounded through some of the discordancies among the strings and woodwinds, inviting the listener to recognize an element of comic battle going on between breathless Voice and would-be olympian Opener" (18–19). As such, the production sounded closer in kind to what Beckett envisioned, no doubt helped by the fact that Searle established a provisional timing from read-throughs with actors, later pointing his score with "meticulous exactitude" (18). In turn, the much closer involvement of the composer in the production process led to a greater narrativization of the music, which Beckett may have sought to avoid exactly by keeping Mihalovici aloof.

Apart from providing too little directions for a production to be successful, Beckett also underestimated the narrative potential, or indeed power, of music. His script was based on an abstract concept of absolute music that has a unidirectional effect of denarrativization on language, but music's exposure to the words almost inevitably bestows it with narrativity owing to its malleable nature, so that the effect is also reversed. When exposed to language, however minimally, music always becomes programmatic to a certain extent. This, I believe, is the central dilemma of *Cascando* as a "text-music tandem," one that is very hard to bypass but poses interesting questions about the interrelation of music and language.

The Narrative Functions of Voice

A final, but no less important acoustic element for the analysis of *Cascando* is voice. As Theo van Leeuwen (1999, 2009) has shown, vocal characteristics such as pitch range, loudness, tone, articulation, and resonance or timbre are often used in combination to create meaning in spoken messages and have become associated with certain stereotypes. Most of the examples discussed by van Leeuwen derive from film and music, and María Ángeles Martínez (2016) has also illustrated how different vocal renditions of the same song can lead to different interpretations, but radio plays are another example of an art form in which voice figures as an important semantic component. Apart from the verbal, Huwiler (2005a) distinguishes between paraverbal codes that modify the words of a speaker, like dialect, pronunciation, or intonation, and nonverbal codes such as sighing, laughing, groaning, and so on (59). As the following examples show, *Cascando* uses a broad range of vocal features and modulations to blur the borders between the verbal, the paraverbal, and the nonverbal, gradually making voice and music converge.

While the published texts of *Cascando* do not stipulate anything about the pace of delivery, the manuscripts do reveal that speed was of major concern to Beckett in the later stages of the genesis, when he started turning his mind to the practical matters of recording and broadcasting. On both FM2 and FT3, he noted that Voice should recite its lines at a "(rapid pace, panting)" (*BDMP11*, 01r). This out-of-breath quality was retained on FT6, but the note on speed was replaced with the "(low, panting)" (*BDMP11*, FT6, 01r) that also appears in the published version (2009: 85). That Beckett was still interested to hear Voice speak rapidly is suggested by the detailed annotations he made on this same typescript, which have never been included in any edition of the radio play but were implemented for the RTF recording. Next to every speech part of Voice on FT6, he noted the precise durations he had in mind. The shortest is "10 sec" (04r), and the longest "1 minute" (01r), with intermediate timings of "15" seconds (07r), "20 sec," and "30 sec" (03r). Added together, the speech parts of Voice should be recited in just under five minutes, a total roughly matching the more detailed calculation that Beckett made at the bottom of the last page of his typescript:

Voice	}	from 5 to 6 min.	
alone	}		
Music	5 _____		
Opener	3 _____	(*BDMP11*, FT6, 08r)	

According to Clas Zilliacus (1976), "it would require an almost superhuman effort to obey these instructions" (128), but the actor Jean Martin strictly adheres to the stipulated time frames, often managing an even faster delivery than what is projected by the author.[6]

As a result, Voice audibly struggles to keep up with Woburn, who makes himself scarce again the second he senses his narrator draw near. It is not until Voice abandons linear storytelling under the dissonant guidance of music that it recovers its breath and calms down. In this respect, it is important to keep in mind that the original title of the radio play was *Calando*, a musical term denoting a gradual decrease of tempo and loudness that is similar to "diminuendo" or "decrescendo." Beckett replaced it with *Cascando* after RTF officials told him that it sounded the same as "calendos," a popular term for Camembert cheese (Federman and Fletcher 1970: 70). Apart from the title, there is no indication in the text of the radio play, not even in the manuscripts, that the tempo or the volume of Voice's speech should ever diminish. In the French recording, however, Beckett did implement this effect. Whenever Voice and Music draw together, especially toward the end of the radio play, Jean Martin speaks more slowly and softly, which contrasts sharply with the fast pace and loud volume he maintains at the start of the broadcast, when Voice is still in hot pursuit of Woburn. This acoustic evolution, which has Voice and Music merge in the silence, is lost in the BBC production of *Cascando* (Beckett 2006).

Patrick Magee, the actor playing Voice, generally speaks much more slowly than Martin and keeps a steady volume throughout, which makes it easier to understand his words and follow the story. Beckett was not present at the rehearsal sessions, but he did listen to a recording of *Cascando* by the German Süddeutscher Rundfunk (SDR) in the presence of BBC staff before their own production, when passing through London to help with rehearsals of *Play* at the Royal Court Theatre (Pilling 2006: 164). His troubled experience in Paris had taught him how imperative his presence would be to get the speed and the timing of delivery right, but he did not want to play such an active role in the British production, and gave the BBC directorial carte blanche. Their rendition of the script, as well as their choice of actors, reflects an institutional approach to articulation and voice that is notably different from the French context in which *Cascando* was originally conceived. Beckett explicitly requested Jack MacGowran and Patrick Magee for the roles of Opener and Voice, but MacGowran was unavailable and so Denys Hawthorne replaced him. While Beckett preferred the creaky and cracked, high-pitched tenor

---

6. Long thought lost, the French recording of *Cascando* can now be consulted through the Institut national de l'audiovisuel (INA).

voices of the two Irish actors, they sound so alike that listeners would have struggled to keep them apart, which in turn supports the identity between Voice and Opener and undermines the latter's claim about the voice not being his. The script clearly distinguishes the tones of the two voices, "[*Cold.*]" for Opener and "[*Low, panting.*]" for Voice (Beckett 2009: 85), but it allows for similar timbres, the one more vocalized and the other more aspirated, so it seems that Beckett attempted to experiment with different vocal aspects in each production.

The BBC, however, opted for maximal contrast by casting Denys Hawthorne as the Opener, whose baritone-like voice is clearly lower than Magee's. Although he was born in Northern Ireland, Hawthorne speaks in the RP accent he adopted as a stage actor in London, thus creating another point of contrast with the subtle Irish inflexions of Magee.[7] Hawthorne represents the typical "BBC voice," which Dylan Thomas and John Gielgud epitomized for broadcast poetry and drama. Beckett disliked both, dismissing in particular the "pulpit voice and hyperarticulation and sibilation" of Thomas "reading his fat poems and being witty on poetry, poets and himself," whereas Magee and MacGowran came closer to the "Beaujolais Gauloise pantgasp" that he heard in his head while writing (Beckett 2014: 184). The BBC's decision to reduce Magee's pace was probably motivated by similar audience concerns over audibility.[8] The RTF made no such pragmatic concessions, but French radio was congenial to voco-musical experiments like Pierre Schaeffer's *musique concrète* or Henri Chopin's *poésie sonore*, so the fast pace of *Cascando* did not stand out as an oddity. Such cultural differences inevitably affected or even shaped national broadcasting policies and how they were enforced on the level of individual productions.

Still, it would also be misguided to align Beckett all too readily with figures such as Schaeffer and Chopin, or even the Dada poets who preceded them and who were similarly interested in exploiting the sonority of language and celebrating sound over reason by making words behave like notes. As Beckett precariously navigates the liminal but still discursive space between nonsense and narrative in *Cascando*, under the denarrativizing influence of music, he represents something of a cultural hybrid, wedged between a French and an English broadcasting context or tradition, but never completely conforming to either.

---

7. RP, or "received pronunciation": "the standard, most regionally neutral form of spoken British English, traditionally based on educated speech in southern England" (*OED*).

8. We are not always aware of these historical circumstances when listening to relatively pristine recordings of radio broadcasts, but in the 1960s they were still frequently subject to atmospheric disturbance and static interference, seriously hindering reception in unfavorable weather conditions.

Conclusion

Using Samuel Beckett's *Cascando* as a case study, this chapter has attempted to illustrate that manuscripts can be helpful for the narratological study of literary texts, while at the same time arguing that traditional concepts of classical narratology—including those designed for the analysis of dramatic texts—are insufficient for the study of radio plays, especially when voice and music play a central role. To properly analyze these acoustic features, recordings need to be taken into account, as radio scripts merely offer a protocol for broadcast, not the transmission itself. Because these protocols need to be transposed or transmediated from the page to the air, by authors and producers alike, time and again as technology evolves, it is useful to compare multiple recorded broadcasts of the same radio play, in particular when the author was involved in them. As I hope to have shown in this chapter, it is more fruitful to recognize the dual status of radio drama as text or script, on the one hand, and performance, on the other hand, than to reduce the genre to its acoustic dimension and claim it as an art form of pure sound. Like stage plays, radio plays are mediated by a textual or scripted form. Unlike theater, however, broadcast productions were often recorded on media such as tape reels and disks, especially after World War II, which actually makes them less ephemeral and more accessible to study than fleeting stage performances. It is therefore high time that we start preserving and digitizing these precious materials, lest a nearly forgotten but important art form be entirely lost to literary history.

Works Cited

Ángeles Martínez, María. 2016. "Staging the Ghost Blend in Two Versions of the Ballad 'Big Joe and Phantom 309.'" In *Audionarratology: Interfaces of Sound and Narrative*, edited by Jarmila Mildorf and Till Kinzel, 47–63. Berlin: De Gruyter.

Beckett, Samuel. 1998. *No Author Better Served: The Correspondence of Samuel Beckett and Alan Schneider*. Edited by Maurice Harmon. Cambridge, MA: Harvard University Press.

———. 2006. *Works for Radio: The Original Broadcasts*. London: BBC and The British Library.

———. 2009. *All That Fall and Other Plays for Radio and Screen*, edited by Everett Frost. London: Faber and Faber.

———. 2014. *The Letters of Samuel Beckett, Vol. III: 1957–1965*. Edited by Lois More Overbeck, Martha Dow Fehsenfeld, Dan Gunn, and George Craig. Cambridge: Cambridge University Press.

Bernaerts, Lars, and Dirk Van Hulle. 2013. "Narrative across Versions: Narratology Meets Genetic Criticism." *Poetics Today* 34, no. 3: 281–326.

Branigan, Kevin. 2008. *Radio Beckett: Musicality in the Radio Plays of Samuel Beckett*. Bern: Peter Lang.

Deppman, Jed, Daniel Ferrer, and Michael Groden, eds. 2004. *Genetic Criticism: Texts and Avant-textes*. Philadelphia: University of Pennsylvania Press.

Federman, Raymond, and John Fletcher. 1970. *Samuel Beckett: His Works and His Critics. An Essay in Bibliography*. Berkeley: University of California Press.

Fludernik, Monika. 1996. *Towards a "Natural" Narratology*. London: Routledge.

Herman, Luc, and Bart Vervaeck. 2005. *Handbook of Narrative Analysis*. Lincoln: University of Nebraska Press.

Hobl-Friedrich, Mechtild. 1991. *Die dramaturgische Funktion der Musik im Hörspiel. Grundlagen—Analysen*. Dissertation. Erlangen-Nürnberg.

Huwiler, Elke. 2005a. *Erzähl-Ströme im Hörspiel: zur Narratologie der elektroakustischen Kunst*. Paderborn: Mentis.

———. 2005b. "Storytelling by Sound: A Theoretical Frame for Radio Drama Analysis." *The Radio Journal: International Studies in Broadcast and Audio Media* 3, no. 1: 45–59.

Jahn, Manfred. 2001. "Narrative Voice and Agency in Drama: Aspects of a Narratology of Drama." *New Literary History* 32: 659–79.

Kafalenos, Emma. 2004. "Overview of the Music and Narrative Field." In *Narrative across Media: The Languages of Storytelling*, edited by Marie-Laure Ryan, 275–82. Lincoln: University of Nebraska Press.

Kita, Caroline. 2016. "Between Instinct and the Law: Dionysian Dissonance and Polyphonic Poetics in Arnold Schönberg's *Totentanz der Prinzipien*." *Journal of the Arnold Schönberg Center* 13: 35–48.

Knowlson, James. 1997. *Damned to Fame: The Life of Samuel Beckett*. London: Bloomsbury.

Mildorf, Jarmila. 2017. "Musik." In *Handbuch Erzählen*, edited by Matías Martínez, 87–91. Stuttgart: Metzler.

Nixon, Mark. 2011. *Samuel Beckett's German Diaries 1936–1937*. London: Continuum.

Palmer, Alan. 2016. "'Put the Heart into It!': Narrative in Country Music and the Blues." In *Audionarratology: Interfaces of Sound and Narrative*, edited by Jarmila Mildorf and Till Kinzel, 65–78. Berlin: De Gruyter.

Pilling, John. 2006. *A Samuel Beckett Chronology*. Basingstoke: Palgrave Macmillan.

Rabinowitz, Peter J. 2004. "Music, Genre, and Narrative Theory." In *Narrative across Media: The Languages of Storytelling*, edited by Marie-Laure Ryan, 305–28. Lincoln: University of Nebraska Press.

Richardson, Brian. 1988. "Point of View in Drama: Diegetic Monologue, Unreliable Narrators, and the Author's Voice on Stage." *Comparative Drama* 22: 193–214.

———. 2006. *Unnatural Voices: Extreme Narration in Modern and Contemporary Fiction*. Columbus: The Ohio State University Press.

Ryan, Marie-Laure. 2004. "Music." In *Narrative across Media: The Languages of Storytelling*, edited by Marie-Laure Ryan, 267–73. Lincoln: University of Nebraska Press.

Shingler, Martin, and Cindy Wieringa. 1998. *On Air: Methods and Meanings of Radio*. London: Arnold.

Tarasti, Eero. 2004. "Music as a Narrative Art." In *Narrative across Media: The Languages of Storytelling*, edited by Marie-Laure Ryan, 283–304. Lincoln: University of Nebraska Press.

Vandevelde, Tom. 2013. "Narration in Samuel Beckett's *Cascando*." *Samuel Beckett Today / Aujourd'hui* 25: 253–65.

Van Hulle, Dirk. 2014. *Modern Manuscripts: The Extended Mind and Creative Undoing from Darwin to Beckett and Beyond*. London: Bloomsbury.

———. 2015. *The Making of Samuel Beckett's "Krapp's Last Tape" / "La Dernière Bande."* Brussels and London: University Press Antwerp and Bloomsbury.

van Leeuwen, Theo. 1999. *Speech, Music, Sound.* Houndmills: Macmillan.

———. 2009. "Parametric Systems: The Case of Voice Quality." In *The Routledge Handbook of Multimodal Analysis*, edited by Carey Jewitt, 68–77. London: Routledge.

Verhulst, Pim. 2022. *The Making of Samuel Beckett's Radio Plays.* Brussels and London: University Press Antwerp and Bloomsbury.

Wierschem, Markus. 2016. "Animae Partus: Conceptual Mythopoeisis, Progressive Rock, and the Many Voices of Pain in Salvation's *BE*." In *Audionarratology: Interfaces of Sound and Narrative*, edited by Jarmila Mildorf and Till Kinzel, 79–96. Berlin: De Gruyter.

Worth, Katharine. 1998. "Words for Music Perhaps." In *Samuel Beckett and Music*, edited by Mary Bryden, 9–20. Oxford: Clarendon Press.

Zilliacus, Clas. 1976. *Beckett and Broadcasting: A Study of the Works of Samuel Beckett for and in Radio and Television.* Åbo: Åbo Akademi.

CODA

Radio Drama between Mimetic and Diegetic Presentation

MARIE-LAURE RYAN

IF WE INTERPRET its label literally, the narrative form of radio drama is defined by both a medium and a genre. The medium, radio, contrasts with written text, theater, film, television, and computer games. The genre, drama, contrasts within the medium of radio (or more broadly within the medium of audio telecommunication, which also includes internet podcasts) with news, sports broadcasts, talk shows, and audio books, and within narrative genres, with novels, journalism, and historiography. From its medium, radio drama inherits an exclusively aural nature, an aurality that goes beyond that of oral storytelling, since it excludes such signifying elements as the storyteller's gestures and facial expressions. From its genre, it inherits a predominantly mimetic mode of narration, a mode in which the fabula is directly presented to the audience through the dialogue of characters, the sounds of the story world, and occasional extra-diegetic music, rather than mediated through the discourse of a narrator. If one combines these medial and generic features, one obtains a form of narration that may seem severely impoverished: Radio drama lacks the visual information of stage or film drama, and in many cases it lacks the benefits of a narrator who facilitates the audience's cognitive activity by attributing dialogue to specific characters, describing settings, or signaling movements. In the purely mimetic mode, every detail in the fabula must be suggested through what could be captured mechanically by an audio-recording device, except for the extradiegetic music, which does not originate in the story world. Characters are distinguished from each other not through their appearance but through the sound of their voice, which some hearers may be unable to differentiate. Moreover, as a dynamic medium, radio drama unfolds at its own pace and does not let users control the flow of information (or did not until YouTube), as they do in written narrative, by speeding up or slowing down their reading, rereading passages, and moving back a few pages to check details they may have missed. These limitations explain why the popularity of radio drama has been in steep decline since the advent of television, that other great provider of home entertainment. While television drama is a hot medium, in McLuhan's sense of the term, radio drama is among the coldest of narrative media. Everything that is not sound is left to the imagination; as for sound, it must be interpreted as to what causes it, where it originates in the space of the story world, and how it relates to the narrative action. No sound effect is self-explanatory.

It would be wrong, however, to regard radio drama as limited to the mimetic mode. This is for two reasons. First, radio drama is not a simulacrum, or pseudo audio recording of stage drama; it is far more diversified than its name suggests, and the label is misleading. And second, just as diegetic elements can make their way into stage drama through a commentator in epic theater or through the chorus in Greek tragedy, and into film through voice-over narration, they can also infiltrate radio drama through narrated parts. Conversely, the dialogue of diegetic narration can be seen as mimetic moments, though the attributing formulae ("he said," "she said") signal the presence of a quoting narrator. Most of the examples discussed in this book alternate between narration and enactment, a strategy that enables radio drama to compensate for its visual deficiency with respect to filmic and stage drama through the greater explanatory power of diegetic narration. But diegetic narration cannot completely displace mimetic presentation, otherwise radio drama would become indistinguishable from audio books. The examples discussed in this book demonstrate that its expressive resources are significantly different, and arguably richer, than those of audio books. Neither the well-developed narratology of literature, nor the narratology of film or theater can fully describe radio drama: What we need is a model that accounts, on one hand, for how an efficient mimetic presentation can develop in the absence of visual cues, and on the other, for how diegetic narration can complement the mimetic mode and overcome its limitations.

In this coda, I propose to address radio drama in terms of the interplay between mimetic and diegetic narration, and more particularly in terms of how narratology can deal with the mimetic component. Rather than discussing all the contributions, I will focus on the chapters that are the most relevant to my particular purpose. My choice should by no means be interpreted as reflecting on the quality of the chapters I do not comment upon.

The interplay of diegetic and mimetic narration in radio drama is demonstrated by Orson Welles's *War of the Worlds*, the broadcast about the invasion of the US by Martians that supposedly caused a panic among the audience. (Nowadays the panic is suspected of being fake news, or at least of having been greatly exaggerated by the written press, in order to discredit radio, its rival in the news business.[1]) The broadcast is presented as part of a series of radio drama, which makes it hard to believe that some people could have taken it as true, but the possibility remains that some listeners may have joined late after switching from another channel. *War of the Worlds* begins with a diegetic narration in which Orson Welles, speaking in his own name, announces that planet Earth has been under surveillance by extraterrestrials since the beginning of the twentieth century and that this led to the dramatic events of October 30, 1939 (not coincidentally the day on which the broadcast actually took place, a clue to its fictional status). Orson Welles is not telling lies, since the broadcast is framed as drama, but rather making use of the possibility, inherent to fiction, of impersonating a counterpart of oneself in an alternate world. This diegetic introduction is followed by a mimetic simulation of a radio broadcast in which a music program is repeatedly interrupted by "breaking news" announcing the arrival of the spaceships in New Jersey, the landing of the Martians, the killing of witnesses, the defeat of the military forces sent to fight the invaders, their march toward New York City, and the flight of citizens. The fake broadcast is actually full of acts of narration by journalists sent to the scene of the landing, but because these reports describe events happening here and now, in a simulation of real-time action, they must be regarded as mimetic presentation. At 39:00 in the broadcast, its status as radio drama is reiterated, so that if it had generated a mass panic, the gullible audiences would have received the message in a narrow time window, and they would have been ignorant of temporal impossibilities: How could a journalist sent by the studio from New York to Grover's Mill, New Jersey, to cover the event reach his goal within a few minutes? How could New York residents have fled for the past two hours, when the supposedly real-time broadcast has lasted less than thirty minutes when this information is given? How could the US army have launched an attack in such a short time? After the admission of fictionality, the production ends with a diegetic, retrospective narrative by a radio journalist who believes to be the sole human survivor of the disaster, until he meets another survivor.

---

1. See https://www.npr.org/sections/thetwo-way/2013/10/30/241797346/75-years-ago-war-of-the-worlds-started-a-panic-or-did-it.

These multiple narrative layers raise the problem of narrative mediation. The simulated broadcast is controlled by the fictional Orson Welles, and within the broadcast, the reports of journalists in the field are controlled by the announcers in the studio. When the recording studio is destroyed (at the fateful minute 39) and replaced by the retrospective narration of the survivor, the frame of the live broadcast is broken, and the story comes to an end. But mediation takes place not only between the narrative layers of the story world, it also connects the story as a whole to the real-world listener. If mediation, as Lars Bernaerts defines it, "stands for the way stories are presented to an audience," or more precisely, for "the ascription of agency to the narrative arrangement of signifiers," how can the concept of mediation distinguish diegetic from mimetic presentation?

Narratology has long been reluctant to accept mimetic presentation as a form of narration. Even though some of the founding fathers of narratology (Barthes and Bremond in particular) regarded narrative as a phenomenon that transcends media and genres, the influence of the pioneering work of Genette led to a focus of narratology on written literary forms, and to a more or less tacit exclusion of dramatic and lyric texts. The reason behind this exclusion lies in the controversial claim that a narrative needs a narrator, since somebody must be responsible for the act of storytelling. But none is present in the vast majority of dramatic texts, and they cannot consequently be regarded as narratives. The postclassical expansion of narratology can be credited with the recognition that if "narrativity" lies in a text's ability to evoke a story in the mind of the recipient (however one defines "story"), this ability can be found in both narrated and performed texts. But the expansion of narratology to the mimetic mode, which enabled it to claim other media than written and oral language, created the problem that forms the focus of Bernaerts's contribution: the problem of defining narrative mediation. Whereas narrators interpose themselves between the receiver and the narrated events, which are regarded by the receiver as asserted by the narrator[2] (though it is the author who configures the narration), mimetic presentation creates an "illusion of immediacy" (to quote Bernaerts's term) by inviting audiences to imagine that they are directly witnessing the unfolding of the narrative action. Yet audiences remain aware that they are not watching life itself but a representation, which means that the narrative information does not occur spontaneously, but is the product of a deliberate act of narrative communication. How can this act be defined? One possibility would be to restore symmetry between diegetic

---

2. Or, in a non-narrator model of impersonal narration, as presented unasserted by the author.

and mimetic narration by postulating a narratorial figure in the mimetic case; though never seen on the stage, on the screen, or in the imaginary setting of radio drama, this ghostlike figure would be the mediator who brings the text to the audience and who is responsible for its narrative form. Adapting the model of diegetic narration, which relies on an act of verbal communication between a sender (the narrator) and a receiver, scholars have proposed a variety of narrating instances for the mimetic mode: filmic narrator (Chatman) and grand image maker (Jost) for film, monstrator and graphiator (Groensteen) for comics, intrigant (Aarseth) for video games, and nonpersonalized narrating instance (Huwiler) for radio drama.[3] Bernaerts rejects the attribution of radio drama, and by extension of the mimetic mode to a narratorial figure, yet he insists on the importance of acknowledging that "information relevant to the narrative progression is presented to us" in non-narratorial presentation. He defines mediating instance as "a structure, an agency that regulates the flow of narrative information, which can be, but does not have to be, embodied by a distinct entity (either human or nonhuman)." This position is echoed by Siebe Bluijs, who comes up with the term "audiophonic composition device" for audio drama. At first sight, Bernaerts's definition elegantly solves the problem of distinguishing diegetic from mimetic presentation, since the agency may or may not be embodied in a narratorial instance, but it raises the problem of where this agency is located: inside or outside the story world? Standard extradiegetic narrators are logically situated within the story world, since they tell the story as true fact. (It is only when narrators place their own claims under erasure by denying their truth that they dissociate themselves from the story world, since in this case the story world is presented as invention.) If the agency responsible for the presentation of narrative information is located in the real world, it is indistinguishable from the author or authorial team (or, for those who endorse the concept, from the implied author). On the other hand, if it is located within the story world, but is not an embodied narrator, it becomes a ghostlike presence and plays an undefinable role in the act of communication. The litmus test for postulating a mediating instance that is neither the author nor a narrator is whether such an instance is a necessary part of the audience's act of imagination. I believe that it is not, and this is why mimetic narration, though obviously controlled by the author, creates what Bernaerts so aptly calls an "illusion of immediacy."[4]

---

3. See Thon (2016: 138–52) for a discussion of all these proposals.

4. The same reasoning could be applied to deny the existence of a narrator in language-based third-person impersonal narration: Readers do not imagine the narrator, as they do in first-person narration. Or do they?

Whether or not we conceive the narrative source as different from the author, radio drama presents an additional layer of mediation when compared to written narrative. This layer, which it shares with stage drama and film, is the script. Authors produce textual scripts that function as directions to the production team; these scripts are interpreted and turned into performances, which in turn are interpreted by the audience. From a narratological, or more precisely fiction-theoretical point of view, scripts are ambiguous. They are often read as narratives, that is to say, as representations of a fictional world, the didascalia fulfilling the role of descriptions, and the dialogue parts standing for the narrative action. But if we view them as direction for performance, they are not fictional, since they consist of instructions addressed to a real-world director. In her contribution, Janine Hauthal emphasizes this instructional nature by comparing scripts to their possible performances. She describes two interesting types of relations: (1) The script is ambiguous, but the performance resolves the ambiguity by selecting one of the possible interpretations; (2) the script is unequivocal, but its implementation in a purely aural medium cannot avoid ambiguity. Case 1 is illustrated by Beckett's *Cascando*: The script leaves it open whether the characters Opener and Voice are one or two persons. If one, Voice is a voice within Opener's head; if two, Voice is the recording of a stream of words controlled by Opener. But in performance, the ambiguity is resolved by using either one or two actors. Case 2, illustrated by Harold Pinter's *A Slight Ache,* involves a character who does not speak. The script clearly presents this character as an existent. In a theater production, the character would be shown on the stage, but how does one suggest the presence of a mute character through purely aural means? This case illustrates one of the great limitations of radio drama (unless it uses diegetic narration): getting the audience to know who exists objectively, and who is present in the current scene. *Loquor ergo sum*: It is only through speech that characters come into being.

Complementing Hauthal's contribution, Pim Verhulst offers another reading of Beckett's *Cascando* in terms of the duality of script and performance. In addition to the aforementioned characters, Voice and Opener, the play involves a character named Music who is represented in the script by dots. But in the play, Music is real music, specially commissioned to fill the role. Beckett did not like the original music, and the play was later released with a different score, an example of a one-to-many relation between script and performance, though this is rather rare in the case of radio drama: It tends to be recorded only once, like film. (Remakes of films use a different script than the original.) Both Music and Voice are controlled by Opener, who solemnly announces their opening and their closing. Opener is therefore situated on a different narrative level than Music and Voice, as are extradiegetic narrators compared to the intradiegetic characters they quote. But Verhulst rightly observes that Opener's activity cannot be described by the concept of narrator. Is this a failure of narratology? Only if we try to impose the literary model on which classical narratology is based to dramatic media. Since *Cascando* is a mimetic text, and since Opener is a character, there is no reason to expect a diegetic structure based on a narrator-narratee relation. A better way to conceive Opener's role, Verhulst convincingly suggests, is "as a medium itself, through which Voice and Music are transmitted"—the medium of purely aural broadcast. By turning Voice and Music from semiotic resources into characters, *Cascando* offers a meditation on their respective nature, with Voice doomed to narrate but unable to capture the tale, and aspiring to the abstract, non-narrative, nonverbal but emotionally powerful mode of signification of music. That the music originally commissioned for the play failed to satisfy Beckett's idealized conception of music suggests, however, the ineffable nature of musical meaning.

A thread that runs through several of the chapters is whether the concept of focalization, so important to the narratology of literary texts, is applicable to radio drama. Classical narratology has come up with various taxonomies of focalization for diegetic narration, for instance Genette's four kinds (internal, external, zero, and non-focalization), but in the narrratorless mimetic mode, there are only two basic kinds: external and internal. In the external case, the world is represented from an unspecified source of perception, or as recorded by an imaginary (or, in the case of film, very real) technological device such as a camera or a microphone, while in the internal case, the world is represented as perceived by a character. Film has developed various techniques to suggest that the screen image captures the field of vision or subjective perception of a character, from shifts between shot and countershot in the representation of conversation, to technological manipulations such as blurring or color changes to suggest hallucinations or dreams (see Thon 2016: chapter 6). How could such effects be implemented in a nonvisual medium? Siebe Bluijs defines internal focalization in radio drama as the presentation of a sound as it is "filtered through a character's attention" rather than as recorded objectively by a mechanical device. He proposes the "cocktail party effect" as an example of variation in focalization: A radio drama called *Vernissage* simulates the way people move through the crowd at a cocktail party, overhearing different bits of conversation depending on their position. But unless the characters who hear the various conversations are clearly identified, this technique is a matter of varying the point of audition, that is to say, of moving around the imaginary recording device through the setting, rather than of switching between internal and external focalization. It would take a technological distortion of voices to suggest that they are being heard by a character, rather than objectively represented. Bluijs discusses several other potential examples of internal focalization, but he admits that in most cases it is impossible to decide whether focalization is internal or external. The most convincing example of internal focalization is proposed by Mildorf: In the radio drama *Echo Point* (which, incidentally, relies entirely on mimetic enactment), the heroine plays the piano and notices that a key is out of tune. Then she plays again, and the key is in tune. But when she tries to play the piece for her husband, the key is out of tune again: This suggests that when she heard the note in tune, it was a hallucination. Later in the play, the heroine hears music and describes it, in a hysterical voice, as "the music of the gods." But no music is heard, in contrast to previous episodes: Here it is silence that suggests the shift to internal focalization. These examples demonstrate that a purely aural mimetic medium possesses a modest ability to shift the point of view (or rather, the point of hearing, as Mildorf and Bernaerts suggest to avoid visual bias) from objective to subjective, but its toolbox offers nothing as powerful as the free indirect discourse, or narratorial omniscience of diegetic narration to suggest character perception.

Such technical, medium-imposed limitations should not be mistaken for artistic inferiority: From the complex verse forms of the Middle Ages to Oulipo's program, language arts have always been fascinated by self-imposed constraints, because these constraints differentiate them from ordinary language and signal them as art. The rivalry of television has robbed radio drama of its popular audience (though audio narratives survive thanks to the fact that one can listen to them while doing something else, such as driving a car). But, rather than capitulating, radio drama has responded with literary experiments by prominent authors such as Beckett, Handke, and Pinter, who saw in the limitations of the medium the challenge of "less is more." The distinctive language of radio drama consists of the same elements as the aural repertory of film and theater, namely voice, noises, music, and silence, but because in radio drama sound is the sole support of narrative information, it commands greater attention and requires more complex interpretive operations than in other media. While the discourse of radio drama is limited to sound, its story worlds are not: Like the worlds of text-based narratives (a medium even more deprived of intrinsic sensory dimensions), they inspire mental imagery that includes many senses. This is why Tim Crook (chapter 1) has argued that radio drama is not a blind medium, even though it is a medium particularly well suited for blind people. For the hearer who makes the effort to imagine its world (and this is not easy to do, as we are so spoiled by hot media), radio drama performs the miracle of allowing the blind to see. Spanning the variety of radio drama from its golden age to its post-television experimental manifestations, the essays gathered in this book not only reveal how multisensory story worlds can emerge from purely aural data, they rescue the whole genre and medium from obscurity.

Works Cited

Thon, Jan-Noël. 2016. *Transmedial Narratology and Contemporary Media Culture*. Lincoln: University of Nebraska Press.

APPENDIX

List of Radio Plays

The following radio plays and texts are discussed as case studies in this book.

Adams, Douglas. 1995. *The Hitchhiker's Guide to the Galaxy: A Trilogy in Five Parts*. London: William Heinemann.

———. 2003. *The Hitchhiker's Guide to the Galaxy: The Original Radio Scripts*. Edited by Geoffrey Perkins. London: Pan Books.

Böll, Heinrich. 1961. "Klopfzeichen." In *Hörspiele*, 156–65. Frankfurt am Main: Fischer.

Beckett, Samuel. 1968. "Cascando." In *Cascando and Other Short Dramatic Pieces*, 7–19. New York: Grove.

———. 1970. "Embers." In *Krapp's Last Tape and Embers*, 21–39. First published 1959. London: Faber & Faber.

———. 2006. *Works for Radio: The Original Broadcasts*. London: BBC and The British Library.

———. 2009. *All That Fall and Other Plays for Radio and Screen*. Edited by Everett Frost. London: Faber and Faber.

Buhlert, Klaus. 1992. *Meine Lieder singt man nicht. Radiostück nach Ezra Pound*. Directed by Jörg Jannings. NDR.

Cascando. 1964. Directed by Donald McWhinnie, script by Samuel Beckett. Aired October 6, 1964, on BBC Third Programme.

Embers. 1959. Directed by Donald McWhinnie, script by Samuel Beckett. Aired June 24, 1959, on BBC Third Programme.

Echo Point. 2012. Produced and directed by Judith Kampfner, script by Louis Nowra, performed by Brandon Burke, Lucy Bell, and John Gaden. BBC Radio 4.

Grenzgänger. 1960. Directed by Ludwig Cremer, script by Jan Rys, performed by Willi Tenk-Trebitsch, Ernst Stankovski, and Wilhelm Walter. NDR Hamburg.

Handke, Peter. 1970. "Hörspiel." In *Wind und Meer. Vier Hörspiele,* 85–128. Frankfurt am Main: Suhrkamp Verlag.

———. 1991. "Radio Play" (No. 1). Translated by Robert Goss. In *German Radio Plays,* edited by Everett Frost and Margaret Herzfeld-Sander, 195–218. New York: Continuum.

Hoste, Pol. 1987. "Tel." *Dietsche Warande & Belfort* 132, no. 8: 2–7.

I Love a Mystery. 1939–1944 and 1949–1952. Directed by Carlton E. Morse. NBC and CBS.

Klopfzeichen. 1962. Directed by Fritz Schroeder-Jahn, script by Heinrich Böll, performed by Wolfgang Wahl, Jo Wegener, Albert Johannes, Günter Briner, and Konrad Mayerhoff. NDR/SWR.

Krechel, Ursula. 2012. "Wenn man ein gleichschenkliges Dreieck auf den Kopf stellt." Unpublished manuscript. Frankfurt: Verlag der Autoren.

Max Havelaar. 2010. Directed by Marlies Cordia, script by Melissa Prins based on the novel by Multatuli. Hoorspelfabriek.

Partituur in decibels. 1982. Directed by Michel De Sutter, script by Christine Kraft. Aired May 2, 1982, on BRT 1.

Pinter, Harold. 1991. "A Slight Ache." In *A Slight Ache and Other Plays,* 7–40. London: Methuen.

Rys, Jan. 1960. *Grenzgänger.* Hamburg: Verlag Hans Bredow-Institute.

A Slight Ache. 2000. Directed by Ned Chaillet, script by Harold Pinter. Aired October 13, 2000, on BBC 4.

Stoppard, Tom. 1975. *Travesties.* London: Faber & Faber.

Tel. 2002. Directed by Martine Ketelbuters, script by Pol Hoste. Aired April 23, 2002, on VRT.

Vernissage. 1977. Directed by Jos Joos, script by Mark Insingel. Aired March 8, 1977, on BRT 1.

The War of the Worlds. 1938. Directed by Orson Welles, script by Howard E. Koch based on the novel by H. G. Wells. CBS Radio.

Wenn man ein gleichschenkliges Dreieck auf den Kopf stellt. 2013. Directed by Hans Gerd Krogmann, script by Ursula Krechel. Aired May 23, 2013, on SWR 2.

Zonder onderschriften. 1970. Directed by Jos Joos, script by Jeroen Brouwers. Aired April 26, 1970, on BRT 3.

CONTRIBUTORS

LARS BERNAERTS is an associate professor of Dutch literature at Ghent University (Belgium). His research, teaching, and publications focus on narratology, experimental fiction, modern Dutch literature, and the literary radio play. Recent publications include *Confrontational Readings: Literary Neo-Avant-Gardes in Dutch and German* (coedited with Inge Arteel and Olivier Couder) and *Luisterrijk der letteren. Hoorspel en literatuur in Nederland en Vlaanderen* (coedited with Siebe Bluijs).

SIEBE BLUIJS is a postdoctoral researcher at Tilburg University (the Netherlands). He holds a PhD in Dutch Literature from Ghent University (Belgium). His PhD research concerned the postwar literary radio play in the Low Countries (Flanders and the Netherlands) in the period 1960 to 2000, and particularly focuses on innovations in narrative composition. Together with Lars Bernaerts, he coedited a volume on the Dutch and Flemish radio play, titled *Luisterrijk der letteren. Hoorspel en literatuur in Nederland en Vlaanderen*. Together with Inge Arteel, Lars Bernaerts, and Pim Verhulst, he coedited the volume *Tuning in to the Neo-Avant-Garde: Experimental Radio Plays in the Post-War Period*.

OLIVIER COUDER studied Dutch and English literature at the Vrije Universiteit Brussel. He obtained a PhD fellowship from the Research Foundation—Flanders. His dissertation focused on the narrative function of absurdist humor in absurdist literature. Adopting a cognitive perspective, his research centers on the interpretation of humor, absurdist humor in particular, in absurdist novels such as Heller's *Catch-22* (1961) or Adams's *Hitchhiker's Guide* (1979). He has published on the close relationship between absurdist humor and absurdist literature in journals such as *Language and Literature* and the *Journal of Literary Semantics*.

PROFESSOR TIM CROOK, PhD, is an academic, playwright, and author who has been teaching the practice and theory of audio drama at Goldsmiths, University of London since 1990. He has won numerous awards for writing, directing, and sound design as well as mentoring new writing. He is the author of *Radio Drama: Theory & Practice* (1999), the forthcoming *Writing Audio Drama*, and *Audio Drama and Modernism: The Missing Link between Descriptive Phonograph Sketches and Microphone Plays on the Radio* (2020).

JANINE HAUTHAL is an associate professor of intermedial studies at Vrije Universiteit Brussel (tenure track). Her research focusses on contemporary British drama and narrative, transgeneric and transmedial narratology, "fictions of Europe," metadrama/theater, genre theory, postdramatic theater (texts) and performance, and postcolonial literatures. Her work has been published in *English Text Construction, Journal of Contemporary Drama in English, Journal of Postcolonial Writing,* and *Modern Drama* as well as with Brill, De Gruyter, Rodopi, and Routledge. Her current research project is concerned with Europe in the contemporary British and Anglophone settler imagination.

HARRY HEUSER is a writer, curator, and educator. His doctoral study, *Etherized Victorians* (2004), examined canonically marginalized scripts of US American plays broadcast on network radio in the 1930s, '40s, and early '50s. The dissertation formed the basis for his book *Immaterial Culture: Literature, Drama and the American Radio Play, 1929–1954* (2013). As lecturer in art history at Aberystwyth University, Wales, he applies interdisciplinary approaches to visual/material culture to explore its intersections with literature and performance as well as its endurance and mutability in regenerative acts of adaptation. As a curator, he has staged exhibitions engaging with cinema and radio-related ephemera.

TILL KINZEL received his Dr. phil. (2002) and Habilitation (2005) from the Technical University of Berlin. He has published books on Allan Bloom (*Platonische Kulturkritik in Amerika*; 2002), Nicolás Gómez Dávila (4th ed. 2015), Philip Roth (*Die Tragödie und Komödie des amerikanischen Lebens*; 2006), and Michael Oakeshott (2007). He has coedited volumes on imaginary dialogues in English and American literature and philosophy (2012, 2014) and audionarratology (2016), as well as books on Edward Gibbon in Germany (2015) and a number of important representatives of the Enlightenment in Germany. His most recent book is *Johann Georg Hamann. Zu Leben und Werk* (2019).

CAROLINE A. KITA is an associate professor of German and comparative literature at Washington University in St. Louis. She specializes in German and Austrian culture from the nineteenth century to the present, focusing on music and literature, theater, radio drama, and performance. Her book, *Jewish Difference and the Arts in Vienna: Composing Compassion in Music and Biblical Theater* (Indiana University Press, 2019), examines musical and dramatic works by Jewish artists in Vienna around 1900. Her current research investigates the soundscapes of radio drama in post-1945 Germany and Austria, tracing how this acoustic-narrative genre functioned as a mode of cultural critique in the aftermath of the Second World War.

JARMILA MILDORF teaches English language and literature at the University of Paderborn (Germany). Her research interests are in audionarratology, socionarratology and conversational storytelling, dialogue, and literature and medicine/medical humanities. She is the author of *Storying Domestic Violence: Constructions and Stereotypes of Abuse in the Discourse of General Practitioners* (2007) and coeditor of numerous collections, such as *Aural World-Making: Audionarratological Approaches to Sound and Narrative* (in *CounterText* 5.3, 2019), *Dialogue across Media* (with Bronwen Thomas; 2017), *Narrating Sounds* (with Till Kinzel; in *Partial Answers* 15.1, 2017), *Audionarratology: Interfaces of Sound and Narrative* (with Till Kinzel; 2016), and *Radio Art and Music: Culture, Aesthetics, Politics* (with Pim Verhulst; 2020).

MARIE-LAURE RYAN is an independent scholar based in Colorado. She has published on narrative theory, narrative across media, and digital culture and given numerous invited lectures. She is the author of *Possible Worlds, Artificial Intelligence and Narrative Theory* (1991), *Narrative as Virtual Reality: Immersion and Interactivity in Literature and Electronic Media* (2001), and *Avatars of Story* (2006). Recent publications include coedited volumes such as *The Johns Hopkins Guide to Digital Media* (2014), *Narrating Space / Spatializing Narrative: Where Narrative Theory and Geography Meet*, and *Possible Worlds Theory and Contemporary Narratology* (2019).

PIM VERHULST is a postdoctoral researcher and teaching assistant at the University of Antwerp. He has published on Samuel Beckett, James Joyce, Dylan Thomas, Harold Pinter, Tom Stoppard, and Caryl Churchill in a variety of journals and essay collections. He is the coeditor of *Beckett and Modernism* (with Olga Beloborodova and Dirk Van Hulle; Palgrave, 2018) and *Radio Art and Music: Culture, Aesthetics, Politics* (with Jarmila Mildorf; Lexington, 2020) and coauthor of three volumes in the Beckett Digital Manuscript Project (http://www.beckettarchive.org), which received an MLA Prize in 2018. His monograph *The Making of Samuel Beckett's Radio Plays* is forthcoming with Bloomsbury and University Press Antwerp.

INDEX

2001: A Space Odyssey (Kubrick), 178

Abbott, H. Porter, 140
Achebe, Chinuah, 37
Adams, Douglas, 39, 164–81
adaptation, 4, 5, 36, 37, 64, 67, 69, 76, 122, 166, 182–93, 207
Affairs of Anatol, The (Schnitzler), 64
Affentheurlich Naupengeheurliche Geschichtklitterung (Fischart), 183–84, 187–93
Alber, Jan, 73
Albert's Bridge (Stoppard), 39
Allen, Mary Hope, 34
Also Sprach Zarathustra (Strauss), 178
ambiguity, 9, 43, 47–48, 51, 53–60, 88–89, 91, 94–95, 98, 102, 104, 108, 112, 144–50, 152–56, 158, 160–61, 220
Amos'n Andy (Correll and Gosden), 34
Anatomy of an Ordinance (Durham), 35
Andersen, Tore Rye, 126
Anthills of the Savannah (Achebe), 37
Antoine, Frédéric, 4–5
Arikha, Avigdor, 207–8

Armstrong, Louis, 36
Arnheim, Rudolf, 82–83, 84, 91, 131, 137, 188–89
Ash, William, 17–19, 36–37
Aspern Papers (James), 146
Attardo, Salvatore, 168
Attempts on Her Life (Crimp), 47
audience, 4, 5, 7, 8, 18, 19, 20, 22, 27, 29, 38, 46, 63–67, 70–72, 77–78, 102, 105, 125, 127, 133–34, 146, 148, 152, 155, 157, 161, 165–67, 169, 171, 173–74, 176, 179, 182–83, 186, 199, 211, 215, 217–20, 222. *See also* listener
audionarratology, 3, 9, 11, 42, 69n5, 70, 83, 123, 127, 129, 130, 139, 141, 154, 196, 209
audiophonic composition device (ACD), 74–75, 78, 88–91, 202, 219
audiophony, 1–3, 4–6, 8–9, 42, 65, 70, 71, 98, 154, 156, 161, 164, 167, 169, 170, 172–74, 176, 178–79, 180
audiopositioning, 9, 102, 110, 113, 115, 154. *See also* sound perception
audiotopia, 102, 104
auricularization, 12, 86, 98, 144, 146, 149, 154, 156, 161

232 · INDEX

Baker, Tom, 165
Bakhtin, Mikhail, 17, 38, 128
Bal, Mieke, 17, 36, 83, 86–89, 95, 141, 148
Barnouw, Erik, 34, 133, 137
Baron, David. *See* Pinter, Harold
Barthes, Roland, 17, 129, 199, 218
Battle of the Marne, The (Hunting), 24
Battle of the Warsaw Ghetto, The (Wishengrad), 34
Bayer-Berenbaum, Linda, 124
Beckett, Samuel, 8, 9, 31, 37, 43, 48, 53–56, 59–60, 196–97, 200–212, 220–22
Bell, Nancy, 173
Belton, John, 84
Berkeley, Reginald, 18, 28
Bernaerts, Lars, 8–9, 42, 88, 197, 202, 218–19, 222
blending, 146, 148, 153, 154
"blind" medium, 32, 84, 86, 91, 95, 102, 222–23
Bliss, Arthur, 31
Bloom, Ursula, 33
Bluijs, Siebe, 6, 8, 9, 42n2, 74, 106n3, 219, 221, 222
Böll, Heinrich, 9, 102, 106–10, 112, 115–16
Bolter, Jay, 66, 75
Booker T. Washington in Atlanta (Hughes), 34
Booth, Wayne C., 144, 146, 147, 149
Bordwell, David, 84–85, 92
Bortolussi, Marisa, 74, 78
Brahms, Johannes, 130
Branigan, Edward, 84
Branigan, Kevin, 205
Brecht, Bertolt, 76, 139
Bremond, Claude, 17, 218
Bridson, D. G., 34–35
Brouwers, Jeroen, 94–95
Brown, Oscar, Jr., 36
Bruguière, Francis, 28
Buggins Family, The (Constanduros), 33
Buhlert, Klaus, 182
Bunche, Ralph, 35
Burnham, Barbara, 34
Burton, Robert, 183n1

Cahn, Victor L., 57
Calanchi, Alessandra, 86n4
Cameron, Audrey, 34
Caracciolo, Marco, 77
Carey, Alderman Archibald, 35
Carlson, Marvin, 43n3
Cascando (Beckett), 8, 9, 43, 53–56, 60n30, 196–97, 200–212, 220–22
Chaillet, Ned, 58
Chapman, Graham, 165n1
character, 1, 2, 25, 31, 32, 33, 46, 47, 48, 50–51, 54, 56–59, 64, 65, 68, 71, 75, 88–90, 93, 95, 103, 107, 113, 126, 129, 131–32, 137, 145, 147–48, 150, 153, 155, 170, 171, 173, 177, 178, 185, 186, 193, 200, 201–3, 205, 220–22
characterization, 6, 9, 11, 18, 20, 22, 35–36, 49, 127, 152, 164, 167, 174, 180
Chatman, Seymour, 72–74, 84, 121–22, 146, 149–50, 219
Cheatle, John, 30
Cherry, Colin, 90
Chion, Michael, 83n2, 84
Chopin, Henri, 211
Cigarettes and Chocolate (Minghella), 39
Clarke, Arthur C., 165
classical narratology, 69, 73, 196, 212, 221
Cleese, John, 165
cocktail party effect, 90, 221
cognitive aspects in radio drama reception, 64, 74, 75, 77, 78, 86, 98, 175, 191, 192, 202, 215
cognitive humor theory/studies, 164, 167, 168n8
cognitive narratology, 5, 7, 8, 9, 19, 69n5, 76, 77–78
cognitive sublime, the, 140
Cohn, Dorrit, 140
comedy, 8, 25, 164–67, 173, 179, 180
Comedy of Danger, A (Hughes), 4n2, 25, 95, 139
Conrad, Joseph, 121, 123
consciousness of the listener, 18, 19, 29, 30, 137; representation in radio drama, 21–22, 28, 36, 77, 108, 158. *See also* self-consciousness

Constanduros, Mabel, 33
Cooper, Giles, 31–32
Correll, Charles, 34
Corwin, Norman, 34, 122n1
Couder, Olivier, 7–9
Count of Monte Cristo, The (Dumas), 64
Country Mouse goes to Town, The (Kemp), 30
Cranston, Lamont, 138
Crayton, George, 29
Cremer, Ludwig, 110
Crimp, Martin, 47–48
Crisell, Andrew, 5
Croker, Charles, 29
Crook, Tim, 4, 7, 10, 64, 84, 86, 132, 222
Currie, Gregory, 147–49
cutting, 75, 84, 85, 92, 111, 134, 148, 156

Dann, Lance, 6
Dark Tower, The (MacNeice), 95n9
Davies, Betty, 34
defamiliarization/making strange, 97, 140, 154, 161
denarrativization, 9, 197, 200, 203, 206, 208, 211
Departure of a Troopship, The (Hunting), 24
Deppman, Jed, 197n1
Destination Freedom (Durham), 35
dialogue, 1, 7, 21, 23, 33, 35, 36, 38, 43n4, 46–47, 50, 52, 54, 72, 75, 94, 107–9, 111–13, 124–25, 127, 128, 129, 131, 133, 135, 136–37, 148, 155, 167, 182, 184, 185, 186, 193n6, 200, 204, 215–16, 220
Dick, Philip K., 165
diegetic/diegesis, 10, 19, 65, 66, 70, 72, 73, 106, 150, 178, 186, 187, 200, 215–22. *See also* mimetic/mimesis
Dimension of Miracles (Sheckley), 166n4
Dixon, Peter, 74, 78
Doležel, Lubomír, 71
Dracula (Stoker), 64
Dryden, John, 30
Dumas, Alexandre, 64
Dunn, Anne, 5
Durham, Richard, 35–36

Echo Point (Nowra), 7, 9, 144–46, 149–61, 222
Eder, Jens, 175
Elsgood, Roger, 30
Embers (Beckett), 59–60
emplotment, 6, 199. *See also* plot; sequentiality
Esslin, Martin, 56n25, 57, 130–31
experientiality, 33, 77, 116, 179

Fall of the City, The (MacLeish), 34
fantastic, the, 124, 134, 147, 153. *See also* marvelous, the; uncanny, the
Farabet, René, 103
Felton, Felix, 17–19, 29–31, 36
Fielding, Henry, 44–46
Fischart, Johann, 183–84, 187–93
Five Birds in a Cage (Jennings), 24
Flesch, Hans, 139
Fletcher, Lucille, 34
Flowers Are Not For You to Pick (Guthrie), 25
Fludernik, Monika, 73, 77, 197–98, 206
focalization, 5, 6, 8, 9, 11, 19, 36, 41, 42nn1–2, 47, 58–59, 68n3, 70, 72, 73n6, 74–75, 77, 82, 85–98, 148, 149, 154, 186, 221–22. *See also* perspective
Foucault, Michel, 103–4
framing, narrative, 41, 52, 65, 76, 89, 105, 169, 188, 198, 201, 218; generic, 150–51, 156, 157, 193, 217
Friedemann, Käte, 73
Friedl, Reinhold, 187–89, 192, 193n6

Gaiman, Neil, 164–66
Gargantua and Pantagruel (Rabelais), 182–87, 188n4, 189, 191–93
Gee, Shirley, 37
genetic criticism, 8, 9, 19, 197, 203
Genette, Gérard, 6, 8, 17, 66, 68, 72, 73, 87, 140, 218, 221
genre, 76, 78, 83, 84, 86, 124, 140, 147, 148, 151, 165, 167, 171, 174–76, 180, 192, 200, 202, 215, 218
ghost story, 7, 59, 133, 144, 147, 150–52, 158, 160–61
Gielgud, John, 211

Gielgud, Val, 17–19, 25–28, 30
GiGax (Lloyd), 166n4
Gosden, Freeman, 34
gothic, 7–8, 121, 123–24, 127, 128, 133, 134, 139–40, 151
Gray, Alasdair, 186
Great American Novel, The (Roth), 193n6
Greater Power, The (Mott), 29
Greer, Bonnie, 39
Grenzgänger (Rys), 9, 102, 106, 110–16
Grethlein, Jonas, 70
Grice, H. P., 74
Grove, Claire, 38
Grusin, Richard, 66, 75
Gunn, James, 175
Gupta, Tanika, 39
Guralnick, Elissa, 37–38, 57n26
Guthrie, Tyrone, 17–19, 25–28
Gymnopédies (Satie), 156

Haas, Monique, 207
Hall, Lee, 39
Halliday, Sam, 89–90
Handke, Peter, 1–3, 10–11, 222
Harding, E. A., 34
Harvey, Lawrence, 206
Hauthal, Janine, 5, 8, 43n3, 69n4, 220
Hawthorne, Denys, 55, 210–11
Heart of Darkness (Conrad), 121, 123
Heart of George Cotton, The (Durham), 35
Heartbreak House (Shaw), 46
Heller, Terry, 133
Henry, Lenny, 39
Herman, Luc, 74, 198
heterotopia, 102, 103–4
Heuser, Harry, 7, 122n2, 169n9
Hitchhiker (Fletcher), 34
Hitchhiker's Guide to the Galaxy, The (Adams), 8, 9, 39, 164–81
Hobl-Friedrich, Mechtild, 185, 192, 200
Höfele, Andreas, 42n1
Hörspiel (Handke), 1–4, 10–11, 130, 134
Hoste, Pol, 92–93

Houston, Gaie, 37
Hudd, Roy, 171n10
Hughes, Langston, 34, 35
Hughes, Richard, 4n2, 25, 95, 139
humor, 6, 8, 9, 33, 164–65, 167–74, 177–80
Hunting, Russell, 24
Huvenne, Martine, 97
Huwiler, Elke, 2, 4, 75, 84–87, 93, 113n12, 148–49, 167, 200, 209, 219
hypermediacy, 66

I Love a Mystery (Morse), 7, 122–26, 128, 130–34, 139
ideology, 43n4, 86
Imhof, Rüdiger, 57n26
immediacy, 65–66, 72, 104, 105, 133, 134, 218, 219. *See also* mediation
incongruity, 164, 167–69, 172–73, 174, 180
incongruity-resolution theory, 167
Insingel, Mark, 90–92
intercutting, 105, 107, 111
intermediality, 42–43, 46, 47–48, 50, 53, 59, 60, 72
intertextuality, 31, 57n25, 177, 178, 180
Issacharoff, Michael, 43n4, 46, 50

Jahn, Manfred, 43n3, 74, 76, 87–88, 196
James, Henry, 82n1, 144–47, 161
Jannings, Jörg, 182
Jeffrey, R. E. *See* Crayton, George; Croker, Charles; Mott, Francis J.
Jennings, Gertrude E., 24–25
Johnson, Jill, 58
Jones, Peter, 169
Jost, François, 6, 149, 219
Joyce, James, 146

Kafalenos, Emma, 199
Kemp, Robert, 30
Kinzel, Till, 3, 7–9, 42n2, 50n14, 70, 83, 86, 101, 186
Kita, Caroline, 9, 53n20, 199n3
Klopfzeichen (Böll), 102, 106–10, 112, 115–16

INDEX • 235

Knight, Paula, 38
Knilli, Friedrich, 130
Koch, Howard, 39
Könneker, Barbara, 187–88
Kraft, Christine, 95–97
Krechel, Ursula, 8, 43, 48–53
Kristeva, Julia, 17
Kubrick, Stanley, 178
Kun, Josh, 101, 104
Kwei-Armah, Kwame, 39

Lanark (Gray), 186
Lang, Fritz, 28
Le Guin, Ursula K., 165
Lea, Gordon, 28, 36–37
Lessing, Gotthold Ephraim, 204
Linkis, Sara Tanderup, 126
listener, 1, 2, 6, 8, 18, 19, 21, 22, 23, 24, 25, 29–33, 36, 37, 38, 51n16, 63, 65, 66, 68, 72, 67, 82, 90–93, 94, 95, 96, 97, 101–4, 105, 106–13, 115–16, 121–22, 123, 124, 131, 132, 133–34, 135, 146, 153, 154, 155, 156, 158, 167, 169, 170, 172, 173–74, 186, 187, 192, 198, 199, 201, 202, 208, 218. *See also* audience
Littlewood, Joan, 34
Lloyd, John, 166n4
Loviglio, Jason, 138
Lullaby (Brahms), 130
Lutostański, Bartosz, 6, 86, 91–92, 149

MacDonald, J. Fred, 35
MacGowran, Jack, 210–11
Machines (Berkeley), 28
MacLeish, Archibald, 34, 122n1
MacNeice, Louis, 95n9
Magee, Patrick, 55n22, 210–11
Man Who Went to War, The (Hughes and Bridson), 34
Marlow, Charlie, 126
Martin, Jean, 55n22, 210
Martínez, María Ángeles, 209
marvelous, the, 124, 147. *See also* fantastic, the; uncanny, the
Matrimonial News (Guthrie), 25

Max Havelaar (Multatuli), 9, 66, 68, 71, 72, 75, 76
McCarthy, Charlie, 138
McLuhan, Marshall, 103, 216
McWhinnie, Donald, 17, 19, 29, 31–33, 36, 55n22, 56, 60n29, 87
media convergence, 4
media studies, 4. *See also* transmedial narratology
mediation, 2, 5, 8, 9, 41, 42n2, 53, 63–78, 144, 161, 199, 212, 215, 218–20. *See also* immediacy; remediation
medium, 1n1, 4, 6, 10, 18–19, 20, 22, 24, 25, 26–27, 29, 31–33, 36, 37–39, 41–43, 48, 50, 56, 59, 69, 73–74, 77, 82, 84, 85–86, 87, 89, 93, 98, 102, 116, 121–23, 127, 130, 131, 138–40, 164, 169n9, 173, 197, 202–3, 215–16, 220–23. *See also* "blind" medium
Meine Lieder singt man nicht (Buhlert), 182
Meister, Jan Christoph, 68
metafiction, meta-referentiality, 76, 185
metalepsis, 51n15, 186
metaphor, 6, 7, 18, 20, 30, 38, 49, 70, 91, 93, 95n9, 102, 203
Metropolis (Lang), 28
microphone, 6, 17, 27, 28, 29–31, 92, 94, 105, 113, 149, 170, 221
microphone play, 19, 25, 27, 28
Mihalovici, Marcel, 201, 206–8
Mildorf, Jarmila, 3, 6–7, 9, 42n2, 50n14, 55n23, 60, 70, 83, 86, 101, 186, 197n2, 222
Miller, Arthur, 139
Miller, J. Hillis, 145
Miller, Mary Jane, 57n26
mimetic/mimesis, 5, 10, 65, 72, 73, 77, 78, 87, 94–95, 98, 103, 148, 150, 185, 187, 193, 215–19, 221–22. *See also* diegetic/diegesis
Minghella, Anthony, 39
mixing, 26, 75, 83, 85, 92, 94, 96, 98, 152–53, 189
Modisani, Bloke, 37
montage, 24, 75, 84, 137
Morse, Carlton E., 122
Mott, Francis J., 29
multimodality, 63, 70, 74–78, 193, 202
Murray, Lavinia, 183

236 · INDEX

music, 2, 3, 5, 6, 8, 9, 11, 18, 22, 26, 27, 31, 32, 36, 42, 49, 53–56, 65, 68–69, 70, 71, 75, 85, 96–98, 101, 124, 131, 145, 146, 148, 151, 152, 154, 155–58, 160, 161, 167, 169, 170, 171, 172, 173, 178, 179, 182, 183, 184, 185, 188, 189–90, 192, 196–212, 215–16, 217, 220–22
Mysteries of Udolpho (Radcliffe), 126, 128, 132
mystery, 122, 123–24, 128, 134, 136, 138, 152

narrative discourse, 2, 68n3, 140, 148
narrativity, 2, 4, 5, 9, 10, 11, 36, 77, 83, 186, 193, 196, 197–98, 206, 208, 218. *See also* non-narrativity
Nelles, William, 86, 105
New Radio Play (Neues Hörspiel), 10, 200
Nielsen, Henrik Skov, 87
Nixon, Mark, 204
non-narrativity, 78, 182, 183, 191, 193, 197–98, 204, 221. *See also* narrativity
Nowra, Louis, 7, 9, 144–46, 149–61
Nünning, Ansgar, 76, 144, 150
Nye, Russell, 123

On Active Service (Rees), 24
Ong, Walter J., 122
Ossa-Richardson, Anthony, 145

Paige, Satchell, 36
Paine, Nester, 34
Palmer, Alan, 200
paratext, 58, 76, 146, 150, 193, 199
Partituur in decibels (Kraft), 95–97
Pavlik, John V., 5
performance, 8, 10, 19, 21–22, 24, 25, 28, 30, 33–34, 36, 37, 38, 41–43, 46–48, 50, 56, 64, 70, 77, 91n8, 122, 130, 131n7, 132n8, 149, 152, 171, 182, 190, 200, 212, 218, 220
Perkins, Geoffrey, 166
perspective, 5, 6, 7, 19, 20, 21, 49, 51, 63, 70, 72, 75, 82, 83, 86, 87, 91–93, 97, 102, 137, 148, 149, 150, 158. *See also* focalization
Pfister, Manfred, 42n1
Phelan, James, 2, 65, 69, 70, 103n1, 147–48
Philips, Jennifer, 37
Pinnock, Winsome, 39

Pinter, Harold, 8–9, 37, 43, 56–60, 95n9, 220, 222
plot, 3, 6, 32, 77, 101, 102, 124, 126, 127, 128, 129, 132, 133, 152, 183, 197, 199, 202
Portrait of the Artist as a Young Man, A (Joyce), 146
Poschmann, Gerda, 47, 48
postclassical narratology, 6–9, 10, 64, 69, 85, 218
Pound, Ezra, 183–84, 192
Propp, Vladimir, 17

Quarter Million Boys, The (Modisani), 37
Quest of Elisabeth, The (Berkeley), 28

Rabelais, François, 8–9, 182–87, 188n4, 189, 191–93
Rabinowitz, Peter J., 200
Radcliffe, Ann, 126, 128, 132
Rajewsky, Irina, 42, 76
Raquello, Ramón, 65
Raskin, Victor, 168n8
Rattigan, Dermot, 37
Rees, A. E., 24
remediation, 2, 66, 75. *See also* mediation
reverberation, 75, 95–96, 108, 113, 114, 138, 146, 152, 154
rhetorical narratology, 5, 7, 8, 9, 19, 65, 69–70
Richardson, Brian, 2, 56n24, 64, 71–72, 76, 196–97, 201
Ricœur, Paul, 36
Rimmon-Kenan, Shlomith, 82, 86, 89, 145, 147
Rite of Spring, The (Stravinsky), 178
Rodger, Ian, 4, 7, 193n6
Roth, Philip, 193n6
Ryan, Marie-Laure, 3, 10, 69, 83, 105–6, 108, 113, 115, 122, 199
Rys, Jan, 9, 102, 106, 110–16

Sander, Ernst, 188n4
Satie, Erik, 156
scene, 6, 21, 22, 30, 36, 46, 52, 57–58, 66, 67, 71, 82, 97, 109, 113–14, 115, 125, 127, 131, 134,

136, 137, 153, 155, 156, 158, 172–73, 174, 175, 185–86, 188, 189–90, 220

scenery, 23, 46. *See also* setting

Schaeffer, Pierre, 211

Schafer, R. Murray, 83n2

schemata, 77, 164, 175, 177, 180

Schenk-Haupt, Stephan, 43n3

Schmedes, Götz, 4, 75, 85

Schmid, Wolf, 5, 73, 87

Schneider, Alan, 206

Schnitzler, Arthur, 64

Schönberg, Arnold, 199n3

Schönert, Jörg, 68, 87

science fiction, 27–29, 122, 165–66, 167, 171, 174, 175–77, 180

Scott, Harry, 34

script (playscript), 2, 8, 10, 18, 24, 25, 26, 29, 31, 34, 35, 36, 41–60, 69n4, 88, 90, 107, 125, 126n5, 131, 149, 165, 167n6, 196, 197, 200, 203, 206–8, 209, 210–11, 212, 220; (cognitive script), 164, 168, 180

script opposition, 168

Searle, Humphrey, 207–8

Seitz, Dieter, 188

self-consciousness/radio consciousness, 1, 29, 121, 122–23, 136

semiotic elements, 9, 10, 11, 68, 70, 71, 74–75, 76, 77, 85, 86, 87, 92, 94, 98, 221

sequentiality, 199, 204, 205

setting, 1, 3, 9, 11, 21, 22, 23, 59, 68, 72, 101, 102, 131, 151, 164, 167, 170–71, 173, 174, 180, 185, 215, 219, 221. *See also* scenery

Shakespeare, William, 24, 35

Shapley, Olive, 34

Shaw, George Bernard, 46

Shaw, Irwin, 139

Sheckley, Robert, 166n4

Shingler, Martin, 200

Shirazi, Farokh, 38

Shklovsky, Viktor, 140

showing, 5, 20, 23, 31, 70, 74, 88, 102, 148, 220. *See also* mimetic/mimesis; telling

Sieveking, Lance, 17–19, 26–28, 36

Siisiäinen, Lauri, 104n2

simultaneity, 52, 53n20, 58, 72, 82, 83, 84, 85–86, 88–89, 96–97, 98, 101–16, 204

Slight Ache, A (Pinter), 8–9, 37, 43, 56–60, 95n9, 220

Solomon, Matthew, 122n2

Sorry, Wrong Number (Fletcher) 34, 122

sound, effect, 26, 75, 83n2, 84, 92, 94, 97, 103, 108, 172, 173, 187, 208, 210, 216; event, 84, 89, 90, 97, 98; perception, 50n14, 55n23, 97, 146, 151; quality, 5, 59–60, 64, 103, 107n4, 108, 132n8, 134, 152, 193; source, 58, 60, 90, 134, 139, 203. *See also* audiopositioning

sound studies, 3, 70, 85

soundscape, 9, 11, 18, 60, 68, 90, 94, 95, 97, 101–10, 113, 115–16, 154, 155, 182–83, 187, 190, 193n6

space, 5, 6, 19, 41, 48n6, 75, 78, 83–84, 91, 97, 101–14, 106, 108, 110, 115–16, 134, 148, 170, 185, 198, 204, 216, 217

Speed (Croker), 29

Spoonface Steinberg (Hall), 39

Squirrel's Cage (Guthrie), 25, 26

stacking, 102, 105–6, 108–9, 110, 112, 113, 115–16

stage directions, 2, 41–60, 69n4, 179n12, 196, 208, 220

Stanzel, Franz Karl, 17, 72–73, 77

stereophony, 6, 19, 75, 83, 85, 90–91, 94, 98

Stevens, Wallace, 38

Stevenson, Randall, 57n26

Stewart, Garrett, 139

Stoker, Bram, 64

Stokes, Albert, 58

Stoppard, Tom, 37, 39, 46

story world, 2, 6, 65, 68, 75, 95, 103, 105, 108, 115, 140, 145, 146, 147–48, 149, 150, 154, 155, 161, 173, 180, 186, 193, 200, 202, 215–16, 218, 219, 222–23

Strauss, Richard, 178

Stravinsky, Igor, 95–97

Stulberg, Jacob, 57n25–26, 59

Suls, Jerry, 167

suspense, 2, 33, 57n25, 137, 152, 153

Tarasti, Eero, 198

Tel (Hoste), 92–93

telling, 5, 20, 23, 31, 41, 68n3, 69–70, 71, 74, 77, 87, 88, 116, 148, 185, 186, 191, 193, 198, 206, 219. *See also* diegetic/diegesis; showing

text aurality, 48, 50, 53

theatre of the mind, 29

Things Fall Apart (Achebe), 37

Thomas, Dylan, 39, 95n9, 211

Thompson, Emily, 103

Thon, Jan-Noël, 3, 4, 60, 76, 78, 219n3, 221

time/temporal frameworks, 6, 9, 36, 41, 65, 68n3, 70, 73n6, 84, 102–10, 112, 115, 116, 126, 128, 130, 151, 154, 170, 172–73, 189, 193, 198, 204–6, 210, 217

Todorov, Tzvetan, 17, 124, 147

Totentanz der Prinzipien (Schönberg), 199n3

tragedy, 216

Tragedy of Tragedies, The (Fielding), 44–46

transgeneric narratology, 5, 8, 9, 19, 41, 43, 60

transmedial narratology, 3, 4, 5, 6, 8, 9, 19, 41, 42, 60, 69, 70, 72, 73, 76–77, 78, 98

Travesties (Stoppard), 46–47

Tremaine, Rose, 37

Truth about Father Christmas, The (Twigg), 24

Truth, Sojourner, 35

Turn of the Screw, The (James), 144–47, 161

Twigg, Phyliss M., 24

uncanny, the, 124, 132, 147, 153

Under Milk Wood (Thomas), 39, 95n9

unnatural narratology, 2, 69n5, 197, 198

unreliability, 6, 9, 46, 47, 55, 68, 144–50, 161

Van Horne, Harriet, 131n6

Van Hulle, Dirk, 8, 197, 207

Van Leeuwen, Theo, 209

Vandevelde, Tom, 56n24, 89, 196, 201

ventriloquism, 34, 138

Verhulst, Pim, 203n4

Vernissage (Insingel), 87, 90–92, 221

Verstraten, Peter, 84, 88–89

Vervaeck, Bart, 74, 198

Vesey, Denmark, 35

Villon, François, 182

visual aspects/visuals, 3, 11, 25, 36, 38, 66, 83n2, 84, 86, 88, 92, 95, 96, 98, 102, 104, 105, 131, 137, 150, 204, 215, 216, 221, 222; metaphor, 6, 38, 42n1, 70, 82–83, 86–87, 98, 101

Vogt, Robert, 148

Vogt, Willem, 4n2

voice quality, 3, 5, 6, 9, 11, 30, 52, 85, 102, 113, 152, 155, 156, 193, 209

Von Kleist, Heinrich, 48

Vossler, Karl, 184

War of the Worlds, The (Koch), 39

War of the Worlds, The (Welles), 39, 64–69, 122, 217–18

War of the Worlds, The (Wells), 39, 64, 122

Weidle, Roland, 42n1, 43n3, 46, 47

Weis, Elisabeth, 84

Welles, Orson, 39, 64–69, 122, 217–18

Wells, H. G., 39, 64, 122

Wells, Ida B., 35

Wenn man ein gleichschenkliges Dreieck auf den Kopf stellt (Krechel), 8, 43, 48–53

Whaley, Eddie, 34

Wheldon, Fay, 37

White Chateau, The (Berkeley), 18, 28

White, Hayden, 36

Whitehead, Gregory, 103

Wieringa, Cindy, 200

Wierschem, Markus, 200

Williams, Roy, 39

Wishengrad, Morton, 34

Without the Grail (Cooper), 32

Worth, Katharine, 207–8

Wouk, Herman, 139

Wyatt, Stephen, 38

X (Crayton), 29

Yacobi, Tamar, 144

Zauberei auf dem Sender (Flesch), 139

Zephaniah, Benjamin, 39

Zilliacus, Clas, 201

Zonder onderschriften (Brouwers), 94–95

THEORY AND INTERPRETATION OF NARRATIVE
JAMES PHELAN, KATRA BYRAM, AND FAYE HALPERN, SERIES EDITORS
ROBYN WARHOL AND PETER RABINOWITZ, FOUNDING EDITORS EMERITI

Because the series editors believe that the most significant work in narrative studies today contributes both to our knowledge of specific narratives and to our understanding of narrative in general, studies in the series typically offer interpretations of individual narratives and address significant theoretical issues underlying those interpretations. The series does not privilege one critical perspective but is open to work from any strong theoretical position.

Audionarratology: Lessons from Radio Drama edited by Lars Bernaerts and Jarmila Mildorf

Digital Fiction and the Unnatural: Transmedial Narrative Theory, Method, and Analysis by Astrid Ensslin and Alice Bell

Narrative Bonds: Multiple Narrators in the Victorian Novel by Alexandra Valint

Contemporary French and Francophone Narratology edited by John Pier

We-Narratives: Collective Storytelling in Contemporary Fiction by Natalya Bekhta

Debating Rhetorical Narratology: On the Synthetic, Mimetic, and Thematic Aspects of Narrative by Matthew Clark and James Phelan

Environment and Narrative: New Directions in Econarratology edited by Erin James and Eric Morel

Unnatural Narratology: Extensions, Revisions, and Challenges edited by Jan Alber and Brian Richardson

A Poetics of Plot for the Twenty-First Century: Theorizing Unruly Narratives by Brian Richardson

Playing at Narratology: Digital Media as Narrative Theory by Daniel Punday

Making Conversation in Modernist Fiction by Elizabeth Alsop

Narratology and Ideology: Negotiating Context, Form, and Theory in Postcolonial Narratives edited by Divya Dwivedi, Henrik Skov Nielsen, and Richard Walsh

Novelization: From Film to Novel by Jan Baetens

Reading Conrad by J. Hillis Miller, Edited by John G. Peters and Jakob Lothe

Narrative, Race, and Ethnicity in the United States edited by James J. Donahue, Jennifer Ann Ho, and Shaun Morgan

Somebody Telling Somebody Else: A Rhetorical Poetics of Narrative by James Phelan

Media of Serial Narrative edited by Frank Kelleter

Suture and Narrative: Deep Intersubjectivity in Fiction and Film by George Butte

The Writer in the Well: On Misreading and Rewriting Literature by Gary Weissman

Narrating Space / Spatializing Narrative: Where Narrative Theory and Geography Meet by Marie-Laure Ryan, Kenneth Foote, and Maoz Azaryahu

Narrative Sequence in Contemporary Narratology edited by Raphaël Baroni and Françoise Revaz

The Submerged Plot and the Mother's Pleasure from Jane Austen to Arundhati Roy by Kelly A. Marsh

Narrative Theory Unbound: Queer and Feminist Interventions edited by Robyn Warhol and Susan S. Lanser

Unnatural Narrative: Theory, History, and Practice by Brian Richardson

Ethics and the Dynamic Observer Narrator: Reckoning with Past and Present in German Literature by Katra A. Byram

Narrative Paths: African Travel in Modern Fiction and Nonfiction by Kai Mikkonen

The Reader as Peeping Tom: Nonreciprocal Gazing in Narrative Fiction and Film by Jeremy Hawthorn

Thomas Hardy's Brains: Psychology, Neurology, and Hardy's Imagination by Suzanne Keen

The Return of the Omniscient Narrator: Authorship and Authority in Twenty-First Century Fiction by Paul Dawson

Feminist Narrative Ethics: Tacit Persuasion in Modernist Form by Katherine Saunders Nash

Real Mysteries: Narrative and the Unknowable by H. Porter Abbott

A Poetics of Unnatural Narrative edited by Jan Alber, Henrik Skov Nielsen, and Brian Richardson

Narrative Discourse: Authors and Narrators in Literature, Film, and Art by Patrick Colm Hogan

An Aesthetics of Narrative Performance: Transnational Theater, Literature, and Film in Contemporary Germany by Claudia Breger

Literary Identification from Charlotte Brontë to Tsitsi Dangarembga by Laura Green

Narrative Theory: Core Concepts and Critical Debates by David Herman, James Phelan and Peter J. Rabinowitz, Brian Richardson, and Robyn Warhol

After Testimony: The Ethics and Aesthetics of Holocaust Narrative for the Future edited by Jakob Lothe, Susan Rubin Suleiman, and James Phelan

The Vitality of Allegory: Figural Narrative in Modern and Contemporary Fiction by Gary Johnson

Narrative Middles: Navigating the Nineteenth-Century British Novel edited by Caroline Levine and Mario Ortiz-Robles

Fact, Fiction, and Form: Selected Essays by Ralph W. Rader edited by James Phelan and David H. Richter

The Real, the True, and the Told: Postmodern Historical Narrative and the Ethics of Representation by Eric L. Berlatsky

Franz Kafka: Narration, Rhetoric, and Reading edited by Jakob Lothe, Beatrice Sandberg, and Ronald Speirs

Social Minds in the Novel by Alan Palmer

Narrative Structures and the Language of the Self by Matthew Clark

Imagining Minds: The Neuro-Aesthetics of Austen, Eliot, and Hardy by Kay Young

Postclassical Narratology: Approaches and Analyses edited by Jan Alber and Monika Fludernik

Techniques for Living: Fiction and Theory in the Work of Christine Brooke-Rose by Karen R. Lawrence

Towards the Ethics of Form in Fiction: Narratives of Cultural Remission by Leona Toker

Tabloid, Inc.: Crimes, Newspapers, Narratives by V. Penelope Pelizzon and Nancy M. West

Narrative Means, Lyric Ends: Temporality in the Nineteenth-Century British Long Poem by Monique R. Morgan

Understanding Nationalism: On Narrative, Cognitive Science, and Identity by Patrick Colm Hogan

Joseph Conrad: Voice, Sequence, History, Genre edited by Jakob Lothe, Jeremy Hawthorn, James Phelan

The Rhetoric of Fictionality: Narrative Theory and the Idea of Fiction by Richard Walsh

Experiencing Fiction: Judgments, Progressions, and the Rhetorical Theory of Narrative by James Phelan

Unnatural Voices: Extreme Narration in Modern and Contemporary Fiction by Brian Richardson

Narrative Causalities by Emma Kafalenos

Why We Read Fiction: Theory of Mind and the Novel by Lisa Zunshine

I Know That You Know That I Know: Narrating Subjects from Moll Flanders *to* Marnie by George Butte

Bloodscripts: Writing the Violent Subject by Elana Gomel

Surprised by Shame: Dostoevsky's Liars and Narrative Exposure by Deborah A. Martinsen

Having a Good Cry: Effeminate Feelings and Pop-Culture Forms by Robyn R. Warhol

Politics, Persuasion, and Pragmatism: A Rhetoric of Feminist Utopian Fiction by Ellen Peel

Telling Tales: Gender and Narrative Form in Victorian Literature and Culture by Elizabeth Langland

Narrative Dynamics: Essays on Time, Plot, Closure, and Frames edited by Brian Richardson

Breaking the Frame: Metalepsis and the Construction of the Subject by Debra Malina

Invisible Author: Last Essays by Christine Brooke-Rose

Ordinary Pleasures: Couples, Conversation, and Comedy by Kay Young

Narratologies: New Perspectives on Narrative Analysis edited by David Herman

Before Reading: Narrative Conventions and the Politics of Interpretation by Peter J. Rabinowitz

Matters of Fact: Reading Nonfiction over the Edge by Daniel W. Lehman

The Progress of Romance: Literary Historiography and the Gothic Novel by David H. Richter

A Glance Beyond Doubt: Narration, Representation, Subjectivity by Shlomith Rimmon-Kenan

Narrative as Rhetoric: Technique, Audiences, Ethics, Ideology by James Phelan

Misreading Jane Eyre: *A Postformalist Paradigm* by Jerome Beaty

Psychological Politics of the American Dream: The Commodification of Subjectivity in Twentieth-Century American Literature by Lois Tyson

Understanding Narrative edited by James Phelan and Peter J. Rabinowitz

Framing Anna Karenina: Tolstoy, the Woman Question, and the Victorian Novel by Amy Mandelker

Gendered Interventions: Narrative Discourse in the Victorian Novel by Robyn R. Warhol

Reading People, Reading Plots: Character, Progression, and the Interpretation of Narrative by James Phelan

www.ingramcontent.com/pod-product-compliance
Lightning Source LLC
Chambersburg PA
CBHW020123240426
43673CB00038B/572